The Politics of Economic Decline in East Germany, 1945–1989

The Politics of

Economic
Decline
in East
Germany,
1945–1989

Jeffrey Kopstein

The University of North Carolina Press   Chapel Hill and London

The paper in this book meets the guidelines for
permanence and durability of the Committee on
Production Guidelines for Book Longevity of the
Council on Library Resources.

Library of Congress Cataloging-in-Publication Data
Kopstein, Jeffrey. The politics of economic decline in
East Germany, 1945–1989 / by Jeffrey Kopstein.
p. cm.   Includes bibliographical references and
index. ISBN 0-8078-2303-1 (cloth : alk. paper)
1. Germany (East)—Economic policy. 2. Germany
(East)—Economic conditions—1945–1990. I. Title.
HC290.78.K66   1997   96-11614
338.9431'00945—dc20   CIP

01 00 99 98 97   5 4 3 2 1

To my parents,
Joel and Marlene Kopstein

Contents

Acknowledgments

Having put this book to bed, I can now express my gratitude to Andrew Janos. As a mentor and friend at the University of California, Berkeley, he spent many hours with me discussing this project. His lucid thinking on the rise and demise of authoritarian politics in the twentieth century has influenced my own in so many ways that I am no longer certain where his thoughts end and mine begin. He was the first to suggest to me the potential value of a detailed study of East Germany, of what seemed to me at the time a strange little country. Even in my darkest hours of self-doubt, he always had confidence that I would write something worthwhile. For that, and much more, I thank him.

George Breslauer read portions of the manuscript in its very early stages. He may not see much of what he first read, but many of the improvements are due to his insights. Jim McAdams and Peter Rutland deserve a special thanks; they read the entire manuscript in its penultimate form with great care and made a number of important substantive and stylistic comments. Less tangibly, but no less significantly, I benefited from discussions with colleagues at various universities, especially Leslie Anderson, Frank Beer, Steve Chan, Russ Faeges, Hal Hansen, Padraic Kenney, Gail Lapidus, Mark Lichbach, and Sven Steinmo. I would also like to thank several German colleagues and friends, some of whom read parts of the manuscript, others who simply pointed me in the right direction and gave generously of their time in conversation: Gert-Joachim Glaeßner, Jürgen Joneleit, Rolf Kuhnert, Gero Neugebauer, Karl-Otto Richter, André Steiner, Klaus Steinitz, Herbert Wolf, and the late Hartmut Zimmermann. Several former East German officials, who did not wish to be identified, spent many hours leading me through the intricacies of their work and lives. The pages that follow rely heavily on those conversations, far more than is reflected in the footnotes. Having had so much help, it seems rather odd to say that any shortcomings of this study are my own. But knowing, as I do, that many of those who have assisted me along the way will not agree with what I have written, I hereby absolve them of any responsibility.

When I began the project, I initially conceived of it primarily as a study of the final two decades of Communist rule in East Germany. As I immersed myself in the research, the questions I originally asked seemed less important and others began to emerge. Living in East Germany in mid-1989 before the revolution, most people believed that something was going to happen, but no one was sure what. Almost everyone thought that the SED—the Socialist Unity Party—would try to do something to stave off ultimate collapse. As we now know, it did very little. Why? That question, posed in a way that social scientists could appreciate, became the guiding one of my research. How can political continuity be explained amid such obvious signs of economic and social decay? In confronting economic problems, why did the political elite return time and again to the same solutions that did not work? Once I began writing, it became increasingly difficult to answer these questions without delving into the past. The opening of the Communist Party and state archives after 1989 made such a detour into history not only possible but endlessly fascinating. The helpful staff of the SED archives in Berlin and Dresden, and the federal archives in Potsdam cheerfully entertained the naive inquiries of a political scientist and opened up a world that I never would have thought possible a decade ago.

In helping to bring this book to fruition, a number of institutions have been very generous. Foremost among them are the American Council of Learned Societies and the Berlin Program of the Social Science Research Council. Both provided me with the freedom and resources to do the primary research. The Council on Research and Creative Writing at the University of Colorado at Boulder awarded me a junior faculty fellowship to take one last research trip to Berlin in the summer of 1994. The Center for European Studies at Harvard University, where I put the final touches on the manuscript, generously awarded me a James Bryant Conant Fellowship for 1995–96.

I also owe a great deal to the editorial staff of the University of North Carolina Press, especially Lewis Bateman for his professionalism, confidence, and good judgment.

Of course, the greatest debts I have accumulated are emotional ones. My parents, to whom I dedicate this book, have supported me in every way possible from beginning to end. They are my biggest fans and an emotional well that I have dipped into more times than I can possibly count. Finally, I want to thank my wife, Simone Chambers. She read the entire manuscript, many times, and what little eloquence there is to be found in it is largely due to her. More importantly, several years ago she decided to spend her life with me, knowing that I was a first-time author. Such courage can only be marveled at. Without her love and her confidence in me and this project, I could not have finished it.

The Politics of Economic Decline in East Germany, 1945–1989

One month before the opening of the Berlin Wall, most East Germans were busy getting on with their lives. In the industrial provinces, what little protest that did occur was largely nonpolitical, directed against the inconveniences of purchasing the staples of everyday life under socialism. On October 6, 1989, for example, a party first secretary from Altenburg sent off a panicky, encoded telegram to his superior in Dresden, Hans Modrow: the situation was "tense," the miners were protesting with a work-to-rule campaign, what should he do? The miners objected to the poor quality of consumer goods in their district—this was not what was "expected after forty years of socialism." Furthermore, they wanted to be able to shop for "citrus fruit, jams, various types of flour and bread" across the border in Czechoslovakia, which had been closed to them since the summer. On the brink of the greatest political crisis in the history of the German Democratic Republic (GDR), the workers at Altenburg were thinking about fruit, jam, and bread. They wanted a better life and they blamed socialism and the Communist Party for the fact that they could not get it. It was humiliating enough to have to visit a foreign country to buy what they needed; when even this was prohibited, the miners fundamental sense of justice had been violated.[1]

The crisis at Altenburg is a graphic illustration of the larger crisis—the regime's failure to satisfy the rising material expectations of the population. At every level of the political hierarchy, the normal problems of the command economy occupied an inordinate amount of time and energy. Even the most casual reading of the party press, published documents, or internal communications reveals how obsessed the leadership of the SED—Sozialistische Einheitspartei Deutschlands (Socialist Unity Party of Germany)—was with improving economic performance and how focused it was on comparisons with production and consumption levels in the West. At the top of the hierarchy, in the Politburo, several members understood quite well the dimensions and causes of their economy's decline but could only speculate on the long-term political consequences.[2]

If the political leadership understood the causes and extent of the country's economic decline, if the SED worried about the political consequences of continued substandard economic performance, why did it not try to change course or alter the country's economic structure?[3] How can we explain political continuity amid economic decay? As Barrington Moore reminds us in his *Social Origins*, continuity requires as much explanation as change.[4] I believe the answer to this puzzle in the GDR's case is to be found in the orientations and interests of the political elites: the policy makers at the top of the hierarchy, the policy implementers at the middle levels of power, and the interactions between these two groups and the working class.

This book tells a story of political responses to economic decline. It does not offer a new explanation for what ailed the East German or other Soviet-type economies. The work of Kornai, Winiecki, and Rutland in this area remains quite convincing.[5] It does, however, account for the pattern of political response to successive economic crises over a forty-five-year period by examining the behavior and orientations of policy makers, policy implementers, and those whom the policies affected. The argument I develop is straightforward. Despite being initially endowed with a relatively well developed industrial infrastructure and a highly trained work force, the SED could not respond effectively to the economic challenges it faced because of the political environment in which it operated. The pattern of responses reveals a regime hemmed in by three confining conditions: its political and economic dependence on the Soviet Union, the logic and interests (material and ideal) of its bureaucracy, and, perhaps most ironically, the "veto power" of its own working class.

East Germany's two rulers, Walter Ulbricht (1945–70) and Erich Honecker (1971–89), each in his turn, struggled with the contradictions of Soviet-style economics, attempting to reconcile state accumulation with economistic legitimation.[6] The main tools in their policy repertoire, however, were remnants of the Soviet economic culture developed decades earlier, in a different location, for a different purpose. Such tools could not begin to alter the fundamental relationships at work in the economy at large.

By the time Honecker displaced Ulbricht in 1971, political stability could only be bought at the price of economic decay. Consider, for example, the state of the capital stock of the East German economy in 1988 (figure I-1),[7] the relative changes in national income use between 1970 and 1988 (figure I-2), and the yearly decline in accumulation (table I-1). What the figures collectively illustrate is an economy whose infrastructure was in an advanced state of disrepair, an economy that had been devouring its own muscle for quite some time. The paradox here is that despite its capacity to infiltrate and atomize society, to prevent the formation of political opposition, to arrest or even shoot as many people as it wanted, the SED could alter neither the behavior of its economic bureaucracy, the pattern of its trade,

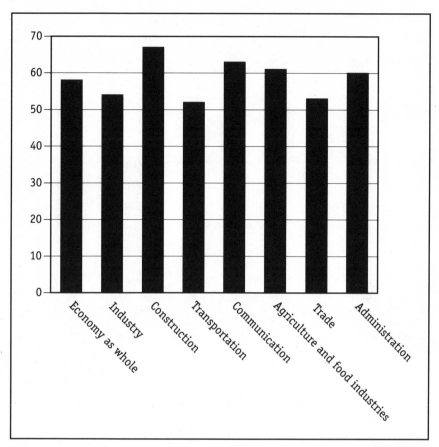

Figure I-1. Decay of Industrial Infrastructure in East Germany, 1988 (100 percent = fully worn out). Source: Günter Kusch et al., *Schlußbilanz—DDR: Fazit einer verfehlten Wirtschafts- und Sozialpolitik* (Berlin: Duncker & Humblot, 1991), 55.

nor its industrial relations in a beneficial direction. From the standpoint of political economy, despite being the most "totalitarian" state in the Soviet bloc, East Germany was in a more important way a weak state.

Economistic Legitimation

Is it really fair to use the word "decline" when speaking of the East German economy? Compared with the economies of the other regimes in the area, many respected scholars contended that the GDR's economy was beyond any doubt the brightest star in the region—the brightest star, to be sure, in an otherwise dim socialist economic universe.[8] Did not the GDR possess

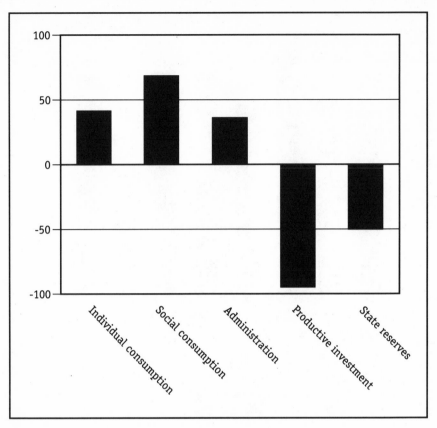

Figure I-2. National Income Use in East Germany, 1970–1988 (in billions of DDR marks). Source: Kusch et al., *Schlußbilanz*, 23.

relatively advanced computer, optics, and machine-building industries? And what kind of declining economy produces refugees who leave their country *in cars*, as so many East Germans did in the summer of 1989? Apart from the questionable statistics on which most sanguine analyses were made, certainly the decline was only relative to that of the GDR's main economic referent, West Germany. But this fact did not make it any less painful or politically significant.[9] East Germans prided themselves very little on living better than Bulgarians, Poles, or Hungarians.

A second potential objection to my focus on the economy is that it trivializes the political background to the revolution of 1989: the desire for political freedom. Although the extent of political alienation in the East German population should not be ignored, I believe during the 1980s the appeal of Western political institutions and social freedoms among East Europeans was indistinguishable from perceptions of Western material abundance. To-

Table I-1. Capital Accumulation as Percentage of National Income in East Germany, 1970–1988

Year	Investment Rate
1970	29%
1971–75	27.5%
1976–80	26.5%
1981–85	22.2%
1986–88	21.5%

Source: Kusch et al., *Schlußbilanz–DDR*, 22.

gether they formed a syndrome—an irreducible and irresistible image of a life-style that consisted both of political and economic elements. This conflation of political liberalism and capitalist development in the collective conscience has since been remedied by the hardships of post-1989 economic changes. But in Eastern Europe in 1989, the connection between relative deprivation and political legitimacy was unmistakable. The vice-president of the Czech Student Union provided a vivid illustration of this complex relationship between scarcity and freedom in his comment on the revolutionary events of 1989 in Prague: "when people went into the streets, they thought communism would fall and they would have cars."[10]

The connection between economic welfare and regime legitimacy seems to be especially intimate in the case of Germans. Studies of political attitudes have noted their special sensitivity to economic performance. For example, in their pioneering work on political culture, Almond and Verba found that in response to the question of what they were proud of regarding their country, West Germans in 1959 picked "economic system" far more frequently (33 percent) than their governmental system (7 percent), in compelling contrast to British and American citizens.[11] As we know, West German attitudes gradually converged with those other Western countries.[12] In East Germany, however, where power was never democratically legitimated and where little effort was made to cultivate a "civic culture," the basis of political stability remained clearly material. It is only logical, then, that popular perceptions of the SED's inability to raise living standards would contribute to the fragility of the regime. The pages that follow discuss the relationship of the SED to the economy, for in this relationship lie the clues to the politics of economic decline.

Party and Economy: Conceptual Orientations

Making sense of the pattern of political responses to economic dysfunctions inevitably involves characterizing the role of the party in the economy. In this task, the student of Communist political economy will find no shortage of competing models. Despite—or, perhaps more accurately, because of—the difficulties in access to reliable data, the field of Communist studies devoted the better part of its energy for thirty-five years to theorizing and modeling the role of Communist parties in various spheres of social life. It is not the purpose of this study to adjudicate between these competing models. Understanding the implications of the following chapters, however, will be aided by placing this study within the broader theoretical issues that have concerned students of East German politics.

The key issue for Western sovietology (and GDR studies) for the past generation was the relationship between economic development and the structure of authority.[13] While scholars recognized the continued relevance of the classical totalitarian model, an approach that emphasized the differences between Communist and non-Communist political systems, most also felt that the desire to industrialize would bring about a change in the way the Communist parties exercised power. Most academics posited a contradiction between the crude mobilization techniques of early Stalinism and the functional necessities of industrial society. Communist parties might never advocate liberal democracy and capitalism but they could and would become more orderly, businesslike, and less "ideological" in working out and implementing economic policy.

Whether influenced by Parsonian modernization theory or Weberian theories of bureaucratization, research on the development of Communist countries set out to prove this hypothesis by focusing on the common needs of all industrial societies.[14] Although not explicitly cast in such terms, the lion's share of research in the 1960s and 1970s laid out the fundamentals of a full-blown *technocratic theory* of Communist politics. For one thing, this literature told us, the greater presence of technical expertise at every level of the policy process after Stalin's death seemed to contradict the totalitarian image of an irrational Communist Party apparatus dominating the realm of social decision making. For another, elite recruitment supposedly based increasingly on merit ran contrary to the totalitarian image of professional careers based primarily on public displays of loyalty and devotion to a social mission.[15]

Most important, so the argument ran, changing behavior and orientations in Communist countries went beyond the technical intelligentsia, to embrace the party apparatus itself. The clearest statement of this view is found in the work of Jerry Hough. Although Hough does not explicitly place himself in the technocratic school, his studies of policy making and implementation portray a party apparatus caught up in the details of economic development.[16] In his *Soviet Prefects*, the regional party secretary is portrayed as "a textbook example of the classic prefect in a modern setting," rather than a high priest of ideological rectitude. Furthermore, Hough's work on the career profiles of central and regional officials attempts to demonstrate how their educational backgrounds and career paths prepared them for economic functions.

Toward the end of the 1970s the technocratic model in sovietology fell out of favor. Hough's work sustained several direct attacks from authors who claimed that the regional party apparatus remained fixed on political power and ideology rather than economic development.[17] Others questioned the efficacy and goodwill of the party organs in implementing economic policy.[18] In fact, as the generalized corruption of the Brezhnev years became a well-established article of every sovietologist's knowledge, the scholarly community began to rethink some of its most cherished hypotheses and assumptions about the role of the party, its organizational evolution, and its relationship to the economy. Was this really a technocratic organization overseeing a variation of economic modernization? Any graduate student on a research trip to the East bloc understood that his or her daily encounters with universal corruption, all-pervading networks of personal connections, an obsession with secrecy, officially sanctioned public slacking, and trifling concerns with minute status gradations contradicted the notion of East European Communist regimes as somehow "modernizing." It is not surprising, therefore, that in the last decade of Communist rule Western academics drew increasingly on the language of traditionalism and oriental despotism rather than modernity in conceptualizing these societies and their rulers.[19]

East Germany and Technocracy

While these insights became part of the scholarly consensus on Communist regimes during the Brezhnev era, students of East Germany continued to present their country as an exception to the rule in Eastern Europe. Rather than an example of economic and political decay, the GDR was portrayed almost exclusively as an economically successful, albeit politically unsavory, variation on modern development.[20] As in earlier sovietology, the key to the technocratic model as applied to East Germany was the adaptation the party had made to the exigencies of economic development.

The initiator of this school among West German scholars was Peter Ludz and, among American specialists, Thomas Baylis.[21] Ludz held that the career profile of the party elite changed in conjunction with industrial progress—a trend marked by the emergence within the national leadership of a technocratic stratum (the "institutionalized counter-elite") that was gradually replacing the old, ideological "strategic clique." Baylis identified similar trends in a book that emphasized the changing orientations of the political elite to the technical intelligentsia.

Under Ludz's guidance and inspiration, a series of well-received West German studies appeared on the impact of economic modernization in the GDR on the structure of political authority and elite attitudes. Among the contributions to this school, worth mentioning here are Glaeßner's study of personnel policy and education, which maintained that personnel and training policies had changed since the 1950s to reflect the need for greater technical knowledge as opposed to mere political commitment, and Neugebauer's book on the relationship of the SED to the state apparatus—a study in the tradition of Hough's *Soviet Prefects*.[22] Taken as a group, these authors were suggesting, in effect, that there was a noncapitalist path to modernity and East Germany was just the country to prove this.

It is certainly not fair to take these scholars to task for faulty predictions. But it may be worth considering why they were wrong. Why did Western analysts of the GDR continue to find this vision of a technocratic path to socialist modernity so appealing if it did not accord with reality? How could a generation of scholars be so misguided as to the GDR's developmental possibilities? Here, one could point to a number of factors. As already noted, first on this list is Parsonian modernization theory; the influence of evolutionary and adaptationist thought in Western GDR studies was, if anything, stronger than in American sovietology. Nowhere was the logic of technocratic modernization more compelling. East Germany's relatively high level of industrialization and its unusually rigid dictatorship seemed to be the perfect case for demonstrating the supposed tension between ideological dictatorship and industrial society, and its resolution in favor of the latter. But, given the well-known bias in evolutionist thought toward stability and equilibrium, these neo-Parsonians were disinclined to identify retarding factors and impediments to adaptive responses among Soviet-type societies. Nor were they inclined to question whether adaptation at one stage of development creates obstacles to successful adaptation at subsequent stages.

Second, in attempting to avoid the anti-Communist biases that were thought to have diminished the intellectual integrity of an earlier generation of scholarship, Western analysts of East Germany appear to have been taken in by the tone of the propaganda literature they were using as their primary research materials.[23] Far in excess of what has ever occurred in Western policy debates, during the 1960s and 1970s East German political elites employed the idiom of scientific discourse in their official discussions. Discounting émigré accounts and denied unofficial documents or other reliable sources of information under the East German policy of *Abgrenzung* (demarcation), Western academics relied on the GDR's press and official East German intellectuals and, in doing so, instead of "deconstructing the narratives," committed what now appears to be the fundamental error of taking on the discourse of the culture under investigation as their own.

Neither Parsonian categories nor the contaminating effects of scientistic discourse, however, would have distorted the picture of East Germany, as it did for so long, had a further cause not reinforced the perceived predisposition to technocratic authoritarianism. Although rarely discussed in any kind of satisfactory detail, the underlying assumption of much work on the GDR was that, whatever the structural deficiencies of Leninist political institutions leading to poor economic performance and corruption in other Communist countries, the East Germans had avoided these unfavorable outcomes because they were *German*. In other words, this was a case of German culture overcoming Leninist structure.[24] It is difficult to underestimate the influence this idea had on political opinion in the West, both of the left and the right, and, while never expressed in such social scientific categories as "structure" and "culture," popular usage of such phrases as "Red Prussians" and the "People's Republic of Prussia" reinforced and was itself reinforced by the impression in the scholarly community that East Germany was somehow more honest, efficient, and businesslike (*sachlich*)—that it worked because of its Germanness.

This book sets out to explain why precisely the opposite was true: Leninist structures regularly reproduce the same bureaucratic cultures and developmental outcomes in significantly different cultural contexts. In Eckstein's sense of the term, the GDR is a "crucial case"; if for cultural reasons Marxism-Leninism worked anywhere, if anywhere there could have been a cultural predisposition to successful technocratic authoritarianism, it should have been in the GDR.[25] If historical culture were decisive, East Germany should have been a "developmental state," a Communist variation on the standard East Asian model.

The impediments to East Germany becoming a "developmental state" of the East Asian type, however, were simply too formidable. It may be instructive briefly to draw this comparison with East Asia more explicitly, for the comparison is not as far-fetched as it may at first seem. In East Asia too, elites have attempted to legitimate their less than democratic rule on the basis of superior economic performance. Scholars have explained East Asian success chiefly by pointing to the role and composition of economic bureaucracies. Although they do not usually use the term as such, their model too can be understood as technocratic. For one thing, East Asian specialists maintain, recruitment into economic bureaucracies is based on merit and educational achievement; witness, for example, the extraordinarily keen, merit-based competition for entrance to the primary educational conduits to Asia's public economic institutions. Furthermore, this literature emphasizes the businesslike and nonideological behavior and orientations of the developmental bureaucracies. Ministries of finance and state industrial planning agencies perform their tasks with an eye to growth and market control; they pay little attention to market or planning orthodoxies per se, but concentrate instead on what works. Most important, however, the literature stresses that technocratic bureaucracies work when they are "strong," in the sense of being relatively autonomous from the surrounding political environment. East Asian industrial strategies, social policies, and national budgets are worked out in relative isolation from the pressure of social forces such as trade unions, defense lobbies, political parties, and, in most cases, even parliaments.[26]

As the following chapters demonstrate, none of these characteristics of East Asian economic bureaucracies obtained for the GDR. East German bureaucrats were neither autonomous nor businesslike, nor were they recruited primarily on the basis of merit. Instead they were highly dependent on the larger political environment in which they operated and hemmed in by a seamless web of ideology and interests, which, when taken together, explain what it was about the nature of Marxism-Leninism that would keep it from being able to innovate and adapt in a way that would rival capitalism and provide an alternative route to modernity.

A Look Ahead

The book is divided into two parts. In part I, the view taken is from the top down. Our story starts in the late 1940s and early 1950s with the German Communists having come to power under the careful tutelage of the Soviet Military Administration (SMAD). Although German Communists were long considered the group of people best suited by virtue of historical experience and philosophical lineage to bring Marxism to fruition, once in power they found themselves in a difficult bind in their relationship to the German working class. Despite the presence of the Soviet Army and a formidable secret police, chapter 1 shows that even during the 1940s and 1950s, at the height of Stalinism, the SED's repeated attempts to institute a Taylorist technocracy on the shop floor faced stiff resistance culminating in the mass strikes of June 1953. Ultimately most attempts at shop floor technocracy failed. To assure the goodwill of the proletariat, the SED had to give its workers a virtual veto power over wages, prices, and work norms. Even if they did not possess an outright stranglehold on the East German economy, such concessions yielded to workers the power to restrict the range of plausible reforms at a later period.

The SED's weakness among the working class, however, did not mitigate the pressure put upon it to satisfy the rising material needs of the population. In fact, pressure on the regime intensified during the 1950s, as West Germany underwent a revolution in production and popular consumption. And while the construction of the Berlin Wall in 1961 halted the flow of refugees streaming westward, Walter Ulbricht understood that a successful resolution of the German question could only be attained if East Germany became an appealing place to live, more appealing than the West. With this in mind, East Germany initiated an in-system, technocratic reform of its economy. The GDR's reform was initiated under the influence of similar reforms begun by Nikita Khrushchev in the Soviet Union. Even so, the "New Economic System," as the reform was called, quickly took on a life of its own, surpassing anything tried or even contemplated in Moscow. The evidence offered in chapter 2 suggests that Ulbricht never genuinely understood where the reform might ultimately lead his country either politically or economically. And for good reason—nothing of the sort had ever been tried before in the bloc. Such ignorance proved fateful for Ulbricht and his reform team, as they confronted a new confining condition in addition to the already troubled relationship with the working class. From the very outset the reforms faced stiff bureaucratic resistance. Eventually, when difficult economic choices had to be made, Ulbricht was forced to square off against his own Politburo colleagues, who considered the reforms too risky, too capitalist sounding, and too ill-conceived; his erstwhile Moscow allies, who resented his attempt to solve the German question without their consultation; and a surly population, as East Germans were asked to tighten their belts one more time. Having alienated all major "interest groups" in the country, Ulbricht could safely be attacked and removed by a group in the Politburo led by Erich Honecker and backed by the Soviet leadership.

Immobilized by its own working class and unwilling to experiment with capitalist-sounding technocratic ideas, the SED settled in to a conservative consumer socialism during the 1970s and 1980s. Yet here too, the new leader, Erich Honecker, and the SED leadership confronted a third confining condition, the international political economy. As long as capital remained plentiful on international markets and the Soviets were willing to subsidize the economy of their East German allies, the GDR could consume and invest on easy terms. The respite lasted but three years. By 1974, the Soviet Union was demanding higher prices for its goods (the key item here was oil). In addition, the East German leadership found it increasingly difficult to sell its goods on recessionary Western markets. By the end of the decade, the GDR was financially insolvent. Chapter 3 examines the high politics of the GDR's debt crisis as it played itself out in the Politburo and the international arena.

Since the book examines economic decline from the standpoint of the SED, it is sensible to move the focus of inquiry outside of Berlin to the provinces where, during the 1970s and 1980s, decline was experienced not as an abstract, statistical phenomenon but as a concrete political reality. In part II of the book, therefore, I explore the politics of economic decline through the eyes of the regional and district political elites, the party secretaries. Chapter 4 asks, What kind of people are we dealing with here? How did the experience of the regional elites prepare them for addressing the growing economic crisis? What we find is an ideologically oriented group of men from the provinces, well suited to the political culture in which they operated but not inclined to change course, even in the face of crisis.

This impression is reinforced by the next three chapters. These chapters suggest that the technocratic image needs to be replaced with one that can help us understand the complex relationship between the party and economy. Chapter 5 examines the role of regional and district party organizations in implementing economic policy. As we shall see, although the regional and district organs were expected to "solve" the daily problems of the economy, they lacked the resources or the will to address the most weighty concerns. Instead the party secretaries retreated into the "campaign economy," a form of political ritual with an important political logic but little substantive economic impact.

The campaign economy reached its height on the shop floor, the subject of chapter 6. Here, ironically, the state had the least room for maneuver; it was at its weakest. In the absence of a genuine labor market and in the shadow of a continuous, yet hidden battle over work norms and wages, industrial relations in the twilight of communism evolved into a stalemate between the working class and the state. The traditional tool of productivity in the Communist world, the socialist competition, although instituted with the intention of increasing labor productivity, was robbed of its original intent in the face of working-class resistance and managerial acquiescence. It served more as a type of ritual exchange of gifts between the party-state and working class than as a stimulus to greater productivity.

Chapter 7 examines the role of the regional political elites in local politics. The two main challenges faced in this realm were in housing and consumer goods. Although the GDR's suburban housing program was mildly successful, it could only succeed at the cost of urban decay. Against this, the regional party secretaries could do little. And, as the opening passage of this chapter indicates, supplying the population with consumer goods became the real flash point of local politics. It was here that public dissatisfaction was most volatile. At the heart of Europe in 1989, shortages of basic food stuffs, consumer durables, and even luxury items were no longer accepted as legitimate. Although the regime had survived an impressive array of political challenges since the 1940s, Communists from the very top of the SED hierarchy to the lowliest district party secretary understood with remarkable clarity that the GDR faced its greatest crisis in its chronic inability to meet the material needs of the population. Ironically, the Communist system, founded on the premise of distributing abundance more justly, foundered on its inability to overcome scarcity.

Seen in this way, the explanation for the GDR's collapse offered here differs from what have become the standard cultural and political approaches to the revolution of 1989, which emphasize the role of intellectuals, generational change in the elite, German political identity, and the mobilization of civil society.[27] Of course, any account of the GDR's demise must include some discussion of the German question and political mobilization against the regime. The Monday demonstrations in Leipzig, the resignations of Honecker, Mittag, and Joachim Herrmann, the spectacle of Christa Wolf, Stephan Heym, and other East German intellectuals speaking to enthusiastic crowds in Berlin, and, finally, the dismantling of the Berlin Wall, all deserve pride of place in the history of 1989.[28] These were important, dramatic moments in German history, and they deserve to be remembered. If scholarship in the past generation has taught us anything, however, it is that revolutions have causes rooted deeply in social and political structures.[29] Mobilization is but one stage in the revolutionary process, and one that appears relatively late in the game. The following pages draw our attention back to the long-term sources of regime decay by concentrating on the political responses, high and low, to an economy in a chronic state of crisis. In doing so, they hopefully make it easier to understand why mobilization against the regime became such an appealing strategy in the first place and why unification with the West came to be seen as inevitable.

Part One The View from the Top

Chapter 1 Making Russians from Prussians

Labor and the State, 1945–1961

This war is not as in the past; whoever occupies a territory
also imposes on it his own social system. Everyone imposes
his own system as far as his army can reach. It cannot be
otherwise.—Josef Stalin

Although scholars continue to ask whether Stalin actually
wanted a separate and Communist East German state, little
doubt remains that between 1945 and 1961 the Soviet Military
Administration in Germany (SMAD) and its client party, the
SED, transferred the essentials of the Soviet-type economy to
East Germany.[1] By the end of the period, nationalized property,
centralized planning organs, industrial ministries with branch
responsibilities, and territorial party organizations with wide-
ranging economic powers—in short, all the economic institutions one would identify as distinctly Soviet—filled in the land-
scape of day-to-day economic administration.

Despite the considerable destruction of East German industry in the last months of the war and the heavy burden of
reparations to the Soviet Union, taken in the form of dismantled equipment and running production, by 1961 industrial
production had grown on average 8 percent for the preceding
five years, several badly damaged prewar enterprises were once
again running, and, most impressive, a number of newly built
industrial giants had come on line. The SED viewed such prime
examples of Stalinist industrialization as the Eisenhut Ost
Steelworks, the Schwedt Petrochemicals Combine, and the
Leuna II Chemical Works with a measure of pride.[2]

Yet looking back on the past fifteen years, SED leader Walter
Ulbricht must have been struck by a paradox. The SED had
more or less smoothly transferred the industrial institutions of
the Soviet Union to the GDR. Nationalizations in industry and
agriculture found, if not a warm reception, at least acceptance

among large segments of the population who could be convinced that the chaos of capitalism had brought the Nazis to power. Such an instrumentally employed antifascism, however, could only go so far in fostering goodwill. Although we lack systematic public opinion data for East Germany in this period, if the experience of West Germany is any indication, during the 1950s the East German regime was evaluated by most segments of the public not on its ideological pronouncements but, rather, on its economic performance, the working conditions it fostered, and the living standards it afforded its citizens. In this regard, the results were far from satisfactory. And among the working class, the one group from whom the SED hoped for the most support and feared the most resistance, very little headway had been made. The impositions of Soviet-type industrial relations on the East German working class engendered a type of resistance that was both intrepid, unexpected, and difficult to deal with.

It is important to capture the early structure of industrial relations because the choices made at this early stage determined the path of future development.[3] The purpose of this chapter is to show how the adoption of Soviet-type economic institutions in East Germany reshaped labor relations, and how these new labor relations in turn restricted economic policy and hindered structural reform at later periods. Such an analysis will hardly sound original to students of political economy. In the context of capitalist development, various studies have convincingly demonstrated the connection between labor relations and a state's capacity to formulate and implement effective economic policies.[4] It may be more difficult, however, to appreciate the nature of the constraints encountered by Communist East Germany in its early years. One might reasonably expect the presence of the Soviet Army to have hindered, if not precluded, any form of organized labor conflict and afforded the SED the leeway to reshape East German industrial relations as it saw fit. But as we shall see, in Communist contexts too, labor effectively restricts the policy repertoire of political elites. It is not my intention to provide a comprehensive history of industrial relations in East Germany. Such a topic deserves a book, perhaps several books, unto itself. Rather, I hope to show how the evolution of this relationship yielded a paradoxical sort of veto power to the East German working class over wages, prices, and work norms, and how this veto power constrained economic policy at later stages.

To anticipate the argument: between 1947 and 1953, the SED attempted to institute a rigorous Taylorist labor regime but, in the face of massive resistance culminating in the June 17, 1953, workers uprising, it backed off. Thereafter, fearing a repetition of the June events, labor peace could be bought only at the price of long-term stagnation in labor relations, wage structures, and productivity incentives. When Walter Ulbricht finally did attempt to reform the Stalinist economic structure in 1963 (the subject of chapter 2), he found himself hemmed in by the "labor pact" he had helped to fashion fifteen years earlier.

The Dilemma of Discipline

It is a commonly held belief that East Germany started with a natural advantage among Leninist regimes—a developed industrial infrastructure and a highly trained, disciplined, and *German* work force. Nowhere was this image of the German working class more deeply rooted than in the Soviet Union itself, a country that had developed intensive industrial, military, and intellectual ties with Germany in the interwar period. Stalin himself might have harbored typically Leninist doubts about the fundamental commitment of German workers to socialism, but he too deeply admired their discipline and efficiency. He admitted as much during the final stage of the war when he told Yugoslav Communist Milovan Djilas that Germany "is a highly developed industrial nation with an extremely well qualified and numerous working class and technical intelligentsia. Give them 12 to 15 years and they'll be on their feet again."[5]

But whatever the Soviets' hopes for the traditional German virtues of hard work and discipline in their own zone of occupation, the orientations and behavior of East Germans quickly changed under the impact of the difficult postwar conditions and Soviet labor practices. This is not to say that seventy years of German working-class culture could be wiped out overnight by "sovietization." It could not. Indeed, significant aspects of this culture were not at all incompatible with Soviet labor practices. Well into 1947, for example, the extensive system of vocational training developed during the Kaiserreich and extended under the Nazis continued to operate, utilizing many of the principles associated with the "company loyalty" school developed in the 1920s and 1930s by the conservative industrial pedagogue Carl Arnhold.[6]

However, "sovietization" did change things, albeit not in a simplistic way. The history of labor in postwar East Germany is less a story of implementing a master plan for "sovietization" than it is of crisis management. What we see are a series of responses to pressing problems, which, in their cumulative effect, we may more or less usefully term "sovietization." Of course, as in every country of Eastern Europe, the Soviet military authorities precluded the development in East Germany of independent working-class

Table 1-1. Daily Rations in Calories in East Germany, 1945–1949

City	June 1945	July 1946	January 1947	August 1947	July 1948	November 1948	November 1949	December 1949	Daily Requirement
East Berlin									approx. 3,500
Heavy labor	2,497		2,481	2,437	2,568	2,735	2,791	3,306	4,200
Labor	2,000		1,998	1,954	2,070	2,260	2,312	2,804	3,020
White-collar	1,611		1,617	1,573	1,736	1,869	1,919	2,066	2,200
Dresden/Leipzig									
Heaviest labor						2,275		3,220	4,200
Heavy labor					2,005	2,087		2,633	3,560
Labor					1,737	1,737		2,168	3,020
White-collar					1,526	1,554		1,790	2,200

Source: Wolfgang Zank, *Wirtschaft und Arbeit in Ostdeutschland 1945–1949* (Munich: R. Oldenbourg Verlag, 1987), 67.

organizations, especially after 1947. But suppressing working-class political organizations could not begin to solve all the problems of labor motivation and productivity. Inducing East German workers to work set off a bitter conflict over wages and piece rates. The resolution of this conflict within the confines of the command economy created a new kind of German working class with different habits and expectations—with a different moral economy—than those characteristic of its predecessor or developing in the West.

I use the term "moral economy" because, in many ways, the German worker of the postwar era finds his counterpart in R. H. Tawney's image of the peasant, "in water up to his neck."[7] In the newspapers of the day, one finds moving reports of severe malnourishment among young workers.[8] The line between survival and starvation was one easily crossed. The collapse of the financial system, coupled with shortages in every sector of the economy under the weight of reparations payments, rendered monetary wages a weak instrument for tying labor to the workplace: with almost nothing to buy, it made little sense to work for money. Where money did matter, if one had a lot of it, was on the black market. Most workers spent several hours per day in the black market and several days each month roaming the countryside in search of food.[9] Initially, then, it was a matter not so much of getting East German workers to work hard as inducing them to show up for work at all. In the two years following the war, absenteeism remained high and labor discipline lax. As table 1-1 indicates, those who arrived at the factory gates, often did so on empty stomachs or severely malnourished.

Of necessity, then, the ethic on the shop floor was egalitarian, cooperative, defensive, and geared toward survival rather than maximization of gain. The institutional expressions of this ethic were the spontaneously formed enterprise councils, which, with Soviet toleration, coordinated production and distributed equally to their employees a portion of their production and what little food and consumer goods (for barter) they could find.[10] Enterprise councils have a rich history in German industrial relations, extending back to the Weimar period and in some cases before. In the postwar years East German enterprise councils took on two new roles. First, they helped identify and root out active Nazis in industry, although in the case of management, the Soviet record on removing these officials was mixed.[11] Second, with many managers having fled to the West, councils performed the valuable service of getting production up and running again. But composed as they were of Social Democratic and Communist workers, enterprise councils could hardly have been expected to increase labor discipline with the traditional tools of differential reward and labor segmentation.

The power of the councils was undoubtedly enhanced by the neglect of the Soviet military authorities. Initially, the SMAD concentrated its energies on reshaping the East German political order and extracting war reparations. Through its various departments and provincial affiliates, the SMAD controlled nearly every aspect of political, social, and economic life in its zone of occupation. During the first year and a half of occupation, it undertook a number of delicate tasks, including the forced merger of the Social Democratic Party with the Communist Party and setting up the mechanisms for reparations payments. In the economy, it oversaw large-scale land reforms in 1945 and nationalizations of industry in 1946.[12] But both of these measures were essentially political in nature, designed more to reshape the German social structure and destroy the economic foundations of bourgeois power than to improve the health of the economy.[13] Indeed, apart from ensuring the orderly dismantling of plant and equipment, and reparations from existing production, the Soviets showed little interest in developing a comprehensive strategy for rebuilding the East German economy before 1947.

Thus the first period of the Soviet occupation, from summer 1945 until spring 1947, was marked by a general neglect of labor. Two factors finally moved the Soviets to change their thinking. First, the economic impact of reparations, land reforms, and industrial nationalizations, combined with the bitterly cold "winter of a century" in 1946–47, had depleted and demoralized the labor force. During spring 1947, many workers complained of hunger at their workplace. Absenteeism grew dramatically. In summer, the crisis reached its high point and workers began to walk off the job.[14] Even if they continued to use the Eastern Zone primarily as a source of wealth for export to the Soviet Union, growing signs of social unrest, coupled with direct lobbying by the SED leadership, probably convinced the Soviet Military Administration that some sort of centrally guided economic policy was necessary.[15]

The second and more important reason for new Soviet interest in labor discipline was the realization that the eastern part of Germany might remain in the Soviet orbit for some time to come. Over the course of 1947 the cold war began in earnest. Whereas throughout 1946 and early 1947, Stalin had assiduously avoided giving the impression of approving of a separate East German state, the announcement of the Truman Doctrine in March, the creation of the bizonal economic union between the British and the Americans in May, followed by the Marshall Plan in June, probably convinced him that the division of Germany, if not a permanent fact, at least necessitated the Eastern Zone's economic integration into the "socialist camp."[16]

Responding to these social and political crises, the SMAD called into existence what the SED leadership had been demanding for six months: a zonal economic authority. Whereas earlier, German administrative participation in the Soviet Zone had been restricted to the *Land* level administrations, following the announcement of the Marshall Plan in June, the Deutsche Wirtschaftskommission (DWK; German Economic Commission) became the first German administrative unit responsible for the entire zone.

But administrative centralization would not get to the heart of the problem—a demoralized and not very productive labor force. By the summer of 1947, East German labor productivity still lay at less than half of its 1936 level. Responding to both the crisis in labor motivation and the changing external political climate, on October 13, 1947, the SMAD issued Order 234—what the East German trade unions subsequently called the *Aufbaubefehl* (construction order). In essence, Order 234 amounted to a full-blown transfer of Soviet-style labor relations to East Germany, although initially it might not have appeared as such. The order called for a number of social measures to address the most urgent needs of workers: industrial safety, strict limits on the use of child labor, longer vacation time for workers involved in physically exhausting labor, "polyclinics" and "nursing stations" in the workplace, improved living conditions for workers, and increased wages for female workers. Most important, enterprises put on a "234 list" received special deliveries of food for the preparation of hot meals served in the workers' cafeteria and consignments of industrial consumer goods to be distributed directly at the workplace. Workers deemed to be especially productive or those involved in hard physical labor received a type "A" meal. Those evaluated as less productive or performing less strenuous tasks received a less caloric and nutritious type "B" meal. This principle was to be used in the direct distribution of consumer goods at the workplace as well.

Order 234 also contained a number of measures to improve labor productivity. First and foremost came the fight against "slackers and corruption." "People's Control Committees" were set up in enterprises to stem the tide of shady dealings and petty pilfering that were bound to occur in a shortage economy. Absentee workers who could not produce a medical excuse could now have their ration cards taken away or, in extreme cases, be assigned to clear rubble from bomb sites, which, along with construction, was among the most poorly paid work and was almost never included on the Order 234 lists of enterprises receiving extra food.[17] To aid workers in getting to their jobs, the order called for renewed attention on the part of *Land* governments to local transport networks. And since almost every enterprise reported shortages of skilled workers, the order mandated the training of a new cohort of workers under the supervision of the trade unions (Freie Deutsche Gewerkschaftsbund or FDGB). Finally, the order called for the reintroduction of piecework and other forms of productivity-based wages throughout industry.[18] To assist management in raising productivity, Soviet-style "socialist competitions" were to be employed and those individual workers who contributed most to raising productive norms were to be designated "activists" and receive financial and political rewards.

Thus began the process of "sovietization" of the East German labor force. Through a subtle combination of incentives and sanctions, the particular Soviet method of binding the worker to the factory, of refashioning the factory as a social and political, as opposed to a purely economic institution, had begun. Much of this, of course, was not new to German workers or managers. Industrialists such as Siemens and Zeiss had long understood the benefits of a *Sozialpolitik* internal to the enterprise.[19] Yet, as socially oriented as many German workers and industrialists may have been in the prewar era, they operated in a political and economic environment far different from the one confronting workers and managers in Soviet-occupied Germany in 1947. For one thing, the presence of the Soviet military authorities precluded the formation of anything like the independent employer and employee organizations that had hammered out personnel and wage policy in the Weimar era. The absence of legitimate interest representation meant that any wage settlement would be viewed by workers as suspect, as an expression of state policy or, worse, "Russian" policy, rather than as the result of wage negotiations between nominally independent parties.

Beyond the legitimacy question, which of course would persist, East German management faced a far different set of incentives than that faced by its prewar counterparts. Prewar German industry, for all the excesses of a highly organized internal market, still faced a modicum of domestic competition and the discipline of a highly competitive external market. These conditions no longer obtained for East German industry. Unlike the prewar industrialists, East German managers rarely worried whether their products would be marketed properly and ultimately bought. Pervasive shortages and Soviet reparation policy all but guaranteed that the entire productive capacity of almost any given enterprise could be sold. Rather than being determined by demand, the success of East German managers was a function of their ability to secure the necessary inputs of production, of which labor was among the most important. More than any other, this factor yielded a measure of power to the workers and ultimately determined the way in which Order 234 was implemented.

Although inclusion of an enterprise on an Order 234 list was a decision made by the provincial or central SMAD, the execution of the order fell to the SED and the protostate administrative unit, the German Administration for Labor and Social Welfare. That the Soviets assigned the utmost importance to the implementation of the order is indicated by their insistence on frequent progress reports as well as the formation of interdepartmental "234 working groups" and "234 committees." These working groups met regularly throughout 1947–48 and their reports tell a story of administrative confusion and working-class resistance.

Of course, if one were to judge from the initial reports in the newspapers, Order 234 was an immediate success. Claims of wildly improbable increases in production (based on distorted statistics) dominated the pages of *Neues Deutschand* and other official East German papers. Soon, however, orders came down from the SED economics departments to stop publishing absolute production numbers. Not only did they discredit all newspaper reporting, but with reports of 30 to 50 percent increases in production, one diplomatically inclined official warned, "workers start inquiring where the goods are."[20]

Internally it had to be acknowledged that a host of technical problems of the most elementary sort plagued the implementation of the order. For one thing, enterprises received such a quantity of repetitive questionnaires in connection with 234 that many had found it necessary to open special departments for filling them out and writing reports.[21] Apart from the problems generated within the enterprise by 234, shortages of automobiles and fuel made it difficult for representatives of the center to visit the provinces and determine whether the order was actually being implemented. When they did arrive, they often found provincial governments in considerable disarray, having given little thought to the particulars of the order. A report filed from Mecklenburg-Vorpommern by a 234 committee noted that its implementation had become the job of a lowly *Oberregierungsrat* in the provincial Ministry for Labor and Social Welfare. According to the report, in the hands of this ministry, the order took on a one-sided social flavor. "The measures taken by the [Mecklenburg-Vorpommern] government are restricted almost exclusively to implementing those aspects of the order intended to improve the situation of the workers, such as the introduction of warm meals in the workplace, the distribution of textiles and consumer goods, the introduction of a child labor protection, etc. The basic measures for raising labor productivity have yet to be utilized. The sole ministry performing systematic work toward implementing the order is the Ministry of Labor and Social Welfare, while, for example, the Ministry of Economics declares that it actually 'has little to do with the order.' "[22]

Apart from the issue of administrative competence, a litany of other, more serious administrative problems accompanied the order's implementation. The most touchy problem, of course, was that of reparations, which was also the most difficult to discuss without appearing to be anti-Soviet. East German "234 committees" and enterprise managers complained that the provincial SMAD administrations drew up the lists of enterprises to be included for food deliveries arbitrarily.[23] Left unsaid or unwritten was the understanding that the SMAD channeled resources to those enterprises producing goods to be shipped as reparations to the Soviet Union.[24]

Some portions of Order 234 could not be fulfilled with any speed or were of little use. The former characterized the calls for improved local transport or construction of apartments by enterprises: neither local governments nor enterprises had the resources to carry out these tasks in the foreseeable future. The latter applies to the "people's control committees." They tended to be staffed either by busybodies who interfered with the necessary deal making between enterprises in a shortage economy, or by corrupt elements who abused their right to confiscate illegally obtained commodities.[25] Under conditions of shortage, even a powerful enterprise such as the Leuna Chemical Works found it necessary to engage in extensive black-market trading. A report in December 1947 revealed that "an entire train with 'bartering fertilizer' had been discovered" on its way to a rural district.

> Fourteen train wagons of potatoes and vegetables that were to be transported illegally out of the Haldensleben district were sent back. No official found it strange that the Leuna works sent out an entire train with fertilizer in order to set up an exchange with the farmers in the villages of Nordgemersleben and Grossantersleben, although the farmers of these villages have not yet fulfilled their mandatory orders of potatoes and vegetables. Only the vice-chairman of the enterprise's trade-union organization did not go along with it. He approached the accidentally present minister for economics. This organized "barter trade" by the Leuna works is all the more reprehensible because this large enterprise receives guaranteed supplementary [food] deliveries through Order 234.

The report went on to note that the directors of other fertilizer enterprises in Sachsen-Anhalt had been caught trading for pork, bacon, ham, sugar, butter, and beans. Although the preceding example indicates that trade-union committees could often be counted upon to be loyal to the center in the fight against barter trade, the same could not be said for the remaining enterprise councils. Many simply refused to participate in the struggle against barter trade for fear of losing popularity among workers. In any case, the distinction between principled and unprincipled black-market behavior became blurred, and the amateurish people's control committees found themselves hopelessly overwhelmed.[26]

Administrative chaos and confusion were only a part of the problem. More important for our purposes was the resistance of workers and managers. The first signs of resistance from the shop floor reveal how easily the ethic of equality among workers could be violated by the most rudimentary tactics designed to segment the labor force. Although over one million workers were receiving warm meals and extra consumer goods at their place of work within months after the order was issued, differential access to food and consumer goods, on whatever basis, injured most workers' fundamental sense of justice. Essentially a cryptomarketization strategy to distribute rewards according to effort and political loyalty, the meal plan of the SED invited wide-ranging acts of what James Scott would term "everyday resistance."[27] Segmenting the labor force made little sense to workers when, even with the supplementary meals, average daily caloric intake remained well below daily minimum requirements. Not surprisingly, in April 1948, reports to the SED noted that workers continued to "eat from the same pot" and management still yielded to demands for the equal distribution of consumer goods despite the continued warnings from higher authorities.[28] Where management stiffened its resolve to increase wage and consumer good differentials, workers often spontaneously evened out the differences by purchasing goods for each other.[29]

The nature and scope of the egalitarian impulse are best illustrated in the reaction to the reintroduction of piecework and other forms of "productivity wages" (*Leistungslöhne*). Although the Nazis had left an unusually disorganized wage structure in industry, the tendency among enterprise councils was to level existing differences, not only among workers but between workers and technical experts. As part of the entire process of wage leveling, enterprise councils, almost without exception, opposed the reintroduction of wage practices common before 1945. Whereas before 1945, 80 percent of the work force performed piecework and other types of *Akkordarbeit*, by April 1948 the proportion had fallen to 20 percent.[30] Workers and enterprise councils spontaneously eliminated piecework and often removed time clocks at plant entrances as symbols of work speedups and other distasteful aspects of capitalist (and Nazi) industrial life.[31]

When finally introduced, resistance to piecework and productivity wages was so formidable that, within months, the SMAD and the SED worried that Order 234 had devolved into an *Essenbefehl,* a one-sided welfare measure to feed industrial workers at their enterprise.[32] Workers complained, staged slowdowns, sabotaged piecework equipment, and used every method imaginable—short of collective action—for resisting its imposition. When asked, workers voiced three further reasons for resisting piecework in addition to egalitarian sentiments. First, Order 234 came as a final blow to many workers who had seen a steady whittling away of the powers of enterprise councils and their subordination to the officially guided trade unions. The emasculation of the only truly representative working-class institution confirmed working-class fears that piecework, even if introduced by a nominally working-class party, was simply a familiar vehicle of increased exploitation. A clear indication of these fears was the revival in 1947 of the traditional German working-class dictum *Akkord ist Mord* (piecework is death) on the shop floor.[33]

Second, many workers who were in principle favorably disposed to increasing industrial discipline argued, with some justification, that any increase in productivity would flow directly into reparations and, as one worker put it, "benefit only the Russians."[34] While the total amount of reparations paid by East Germany to the Soviet Union remains a matter of scholarly dispute, the record is clear regarding the demoralizing effect that reparations had on industrial workers. The head of the SMAD, Marshall Sokolovski, had guaranteed the SED leadership on January 11, 1947, that the dismantling of enterprises would be stopped. But a string of complaints from the SED and other evidence suggest that dismantling actually increased after this date.[35] Moreover, reparations from running production continued unabated. Officially, the SED claimed to have stemmed the tide of reparations, but as trade-union chairman Herbert Warnke noted in April 1948, such claims were contradicted in the eyes of the population by the fact that the Soviets continued to walk into enterprises unannounced and take much of the production.[36]

Yet, even those workers resigned to piecework as an inevitable part of modern industry and to reparations as the cost of military defeat still protested that it made little sense to work for anything but hourly wages. Shortages in the energy sector and irregular deliveries of other raw materials virtually guaranteed each week that "after three days the raw materials are used up and in the remaining three days of the week there is nothing left to do."[37] Although the micro- and macroeconomic conditions of the East German economy had changed for good, ordinary workers could not yet have known this. To them, idle capacity was a sure sign of impending layoffs, a condition that in these circumstances might well have meant starvation.

Naturally, given the presence of the Soviet Army, the forms of resistance to piecework remained largely amorphous and disorganized—shirking, grumbling, work-to-rule, dissimulation, and other weapons of the weak. Such weapons, however, apparently proved to be quite effective. Six months after the proclamation of Order 234, the proportion of the labor force receiving piecework and productivity wages had risen a mere 3 percent (from 23 percent in October to 26 percent in April). According to SED reports from the shop floor, many foremen could not be stopped from putting all the piecework tickets into a common urn in order to ensure equality of reward.[38] Difficulty in introducing piecework is further indicated by SED's strategy for introducing it.[39] Rather than begin in the traditional centers of working-class power where it was likely to encounter stiff resistance, the SED concentrated initially on the textile enterprises of the Oberlausitz region, which employed mostly women, relative newcomers to the field of working-class politics in Germany. Not surprisingly, then, by the end of 1947 twice as many female workers received piecework wages as male workers.[40]

Corrupted Taylorism

However persistent and convincing working-class resistance to piecework may have been, the unrelenting pressure from the Soviet military authorities and the SED departments left management in all branches of industry little choice but to find a way to follow orders. East German management thus found itself in a no-win situation. Pressured on the one side by the Soviets and the SED to introduce piecework, and on the other side by the working class and its (increasingly powerless) enterprise councils to resist, management in the end did introduce piecework and productivity wages. In those cases where productivity wages were introduced honestly, wages immediately fell, and workers complained and often left for other enterprises. Fearing the loss of its workers, management responded by setting weak output norms that workers could easily meet and overshoot.[41]

The key to understanding management's behavior is the shortage economy. From the very outset of the Soviet occupation, managers were under pressure to produce as much as possible at whatever cost, a standard feature of Stalinist economic planning. Typical for the entire Soviet Zone, in 1946 only 138 of the 465 state-run enterprises in Saxony operated at a profit.[42] Here we find the origins of the East German soft budget constraint. To be sure, even without the presence of the Soviet Army, the collapse of the

German financial and transport systems at the end of the war rendered the hoarding of resources, especially labor, the sole rational economic strategy for producers of all kinds. But even after the East German currency reform in June 1948, which came as a response to the West German currency reform, the problem persisted. Hoarded labor became scarce labor, and scarce labor had more market power than if it were plentiful.[43]

Management's problem was to find a way to secure the necessary labor inputs to meet production plans. Whether the wage of a worker corresponded to his productive input was secondary. Under conditions of labor shortage and a soft budget constraint, then, management found it logical to regard the transition from time wages to piecework as a way to raise wages, through weak norms, and make their enterprises more appealing on the labor market. As such, rational managerial behavior transformed what was intended as an economic measure into a sociopolitical one.[44]

The SMAD and Communist leadership responded with a redeployment of the prewar system of norm setting, using stopwatches, production-line time and motion studies, and the other elements of German Taylorism. The SED even reactivated the old Taylorist personnel, hated as they were on the shop floor. The appeal of Taylorism to Communist labor specialists (both Russian and German) is easy to understand.[45] In the Taylorist vision, we find an image of the shop floor and industrial society that is both efficient and free of conflict. Although Taylor is best known for his principles of scientific management, within his thought there is a good dose of social engineering and an image of the shop floor that can be characterized as a technocratic utopia: as workers begin to grasp that greater efficiency means greater profits for the firm and ultimately higher wages, the culture of the shop floor and ultimately of society as a whole moves beyond the old divisions and animosities of class. As Homburg shows in her study of the rationalization movement in Weimar Germany, capitalist managers found in Taylorism the possibility of rationalizing the "human factor" in industry, hoped that it would neutralize the challenges of a labor market that was in many ways as tight as that of East Germany in the 1940s, and "create a new harmonious social order beyond class conflict, but not beyond capitalism."[46] If one removes "but not beyond capitalism," it is easy to see the appeal of a Taylorist technocracy as the answer to the labor question in East Germany.

East German labor leaders acknowledged that scientific management, time studies, and the like had been a source of labor unrest in the prewar era. They enjoyed the distinct advantage, however, of being able in effect to say: yes, in the prewar period the vision of a harmonious social order based on Taylorism was simply ideology, a mask to hide exploitation and profit seeking. But with the negation of capitalist production relations and the advent of socialism, there is no reason why methods of industrial rationalization, no matter where they were developed, could not benefit working people.

Yet, as tempting as it might have been to rely on earlier German traditions of industrial authority and management, East German Taylorism was corrupted from the outset by the environment in which it functioned. Like their prewar counterparts, East German managers could use the technocratic solutions of Taylorism neither to solve the problem of labor shortage nor to harmonize relations on the shop floor. The SED felt constrained to issue assurances that the use of capitalist methods did not imply the reintroduction of capitalism; workers were not competing against each other for their "share" of an overall wage bill. In March 1948 the SED issued orders that those who transferred to piecework or other types of performance wages were to be guaranteed an income 15 percent higher than they received previously.[47] Two months later, *Tribüne*, the official newspaper of the FDGB demanded that "the calculative and rational nucleus of REFA [scientific piecework rates] be used without the technical exaggerations and without the capitalist intensification of work."[48] Taken together, these provisos hollowed out the core of classical Taylorism and amounted to a retreat by the political authorities in the face of labor's position on the market.

In itself, paying a premium for piecework might not necessarily have been counterproductive had work norms been more closely watched. But with weak norms, piecework inevitably led to skyrocketing wage bills. The situation worsened after February 1948 with the introduction of "progressive productivity wages," which paid a premium over the piece rate for marginally greater production.[49] Although economic planning called for productivity to rise twice as fast as wages, "labor power" ensured just the opposite: wages rose much faster than productivity. In the Bitterfeld Electrochemical Combine, for example, wages rose in 1948 four times faster than labor productivity.[50] In the Maximillian Forge, 8 percent of the workers had been put on progressive productivity wages by the end of 1948, but productivity norms dropped below where they had been eighteen months before and, compared with rates in the previous year, wages had risen 60 percent while labor productivity had dropped by 24 percent.[51] Similarly disappointing results were reported in the potash, iron, and coal mining industries, as well as other key sectors of the East German economy.[52]

In spring 1948, less than six months after the proclamation of Order 234, both the Soviets and the SED sounded the alarm on wages. The East German party and state bureaucracy split on the question in a rather nasty bureaucratic battle, which drew in the entire leadership as well as the Soviets, each side accusing the other of "conspiracy" and "sabotage." Fritz Selbmann, deputy chief of the DWK for industry, argued that the working class could only be convinced to take up "productivity wages" if the remuneration remained progressive. His concern was obviously with maximizing production. On the other side, the organization most closely associated with carrying out Order 234, the Administration for Labor and Social Welfare, headed by Gustav Brack, argued that wage levels had gotten out of control.[53] Brack took his case to the Soviets. By December they agreed that Brack was right. In a letter to DWK chief Heinrich Rau, a senior SMAD labor official warned that continued wage increases "threaten the normal monetary circulation and the financial system of the [Soviet] zone."[54] On orders from the SMAD's labor department, the East Germans set to work on a new set of wage guidelines, designed to restrict the use of progressive productivity wages to essential industries and tighten norms in all branches.

The Aktivist Movement

Commitment to higher norms was one thing; implementing this in practice was something completely different. Unable or unwilling to use the threat of unemployment as a tool for increasing labor discipline, the Soviets fell back on their own particular experience of industrialization in the 1930s to demonstrate that with enough dedication, ingenuity, and effort, work norms could be raised dramatically. The "activist" and "competition" movements had been initiated under Order 234 with precisely this idea in mind, but one year later reports from the industrial provinces revealed that these movements had made little headway. East German managers had never before used socialist competitions. Most had no idea where to begin or what the fundamental organizing principles were. In many enterprises, workers were not even aware of when or in what sorts of competitions they participated.[55]

The SMAD decided that the movement needed a new push. Much as the "hero of socialist labor" Alexei Stakhanov had done as a coal miner in the 1930s, on the first anniversary of Order 234, October 13, 1948, under specially prepared conditions, Adolf Hennecke, a fifty-one-year-old coal miner from Zwickau, mined 387 percent of his normal quota of coal for his shift. Run as political campaign, the "Hennecke movement" soon spread across East Germany into every sector of the economy.[56] It is no accident that the movement began in a coal mine. Not only was coal in short supply, but with a relatively unskilled labor force and a work process that was amenable to arithmetic accounting of individual work, methods of norm breaking could be easily incorporated as political actions.

Hennecke's feat was supposed to inspire workers by demonstrating to the average person that it indeed was possible to do three and a half times the normal amount of work in a shift. Notwithstanding the spate of copycat record setting, however, one finds little evidence that the Hennecke movement actually increased labor productivity or that it convinced the working class of the need for higher norms. Most workers doubted the logic behind creating special conditions for one worker to produce faster than the norm for the simple reason that the normal work day simply did not function that way. One central committee instructor captured the attitude on the shop floor in his report of a visit to the Dresden Machine Building works during a "Hennecke Week" in December 1948. "I asked three skilled workers from the enterprise about their opinion of the Hennecke movement. . . . All three immediately agreed that the Hennecke movement would never work and would be discredited if 'Hennecke shifts' [as such record breaking shifts were referred to] continued to be prepared days in advance so that two or three workers could start well prepared."[57] In an interview with a retired steelworker, historian Lutz Niethammer confirms the general impressions one gets from the archival record. Hennecke shifts were always possible as one-time affairs, but only with a considerable loss of time for readying materials and machinery. "Only with such support was Hennecke the man. We had to clean everything in the morning and then they came in, and there stood the iron, impeccable, and they worked for eight hours, and they did something, didn't they? But it wasn't like that every day. That's not the way it's done. There is too much waste. It has to be cleaned up. You have to wash up this and that. The channels for the hot iron have to be built, don't they?"[58]

The regime, moreover, could only partially use the activist and competition movements to raise norms. As Bendix notes, the activists and other rate busters tended to be despised and isolated by the rank-and-file employees of an enterprise.[59] The evidence on this point is overwhelming, not only from the testimony of Hennecke himself, but from those who followed in his footsteps. Activists regularly suffered abuse at the hands of their fellow workers. Many were labeled "bloodsuckers," while others were spit upon; some even faced physical danger. The noted East German playwright Heiner Müller brought these passions to dramatic form in his 1958 work *Der Lohndrücker*, following a long tradition of such plays in the GDR. The play's hero, the activist Balke, addressed a member of his brigade after beginning the reconstruction of a blast furnace while the furnace is still hot, so that his factory will not shut down and the plan could be met. "You've been blathering like mad about the rate busters. You don't want to understand what this is all about. You've thrown rocks at me [while I was in the furnace]. I used them for the wall. You beat me up, you and Zemke, as I came out of the oven."[60] During the turbulent 1950s, the publication of works that had as their central theme the question of how otherwise recalcitrant workers could possibly be mobilized in support of socialist goals attests to a problem so large that it could not be ignored, even by a Stalinist cultural apparatus.

Given the frequency and intensity of resistance, in the end Hennecke shifts and production records amounted to little more than political ritual. Control over this ritual, however, constituted an important arena of working-class politics and remained so for the next forty years. The attempt to create a Stalinist East German labor aristocracy failed in the face of strong egalitarian working-class solidarity, but such evidence did not deter the continued use of Hennecke-like campaigns.[61] On the contrary, within the SED bureaucracy there was some talk of appointing Hennecke and others like him as enterprise directors.[62] Hennecke himself even proposed the wholesale replacement of management in the mining industry with activists, once the latter had gone through special remedial courses in mathematics, science, and mining engineering.[63] While none of these plans came to fruition—indeed, they were quickly slapped down at higher political instances—the Aktivist movement continued to enjoy high-level SED support, perhaps because it remained the sole device for breaking the egalitarian consensus among industrial workers, or perhaps because it nourished the illusion that workers might voluntarily produce more for less.[64]

The evidence from the shop floor, however, is that the workers would not produce more for lower wages. In the four years following Hennecke's feat, the SED employed dozens of "methods" to toughen work norms and standardize wage scales. However, the structure of the economy and the power of the working class within this structure made rate busting an unusually trying task. For all the discussion of "technically grounded work norms" (know by the German acronym TAN) and the presence of TAN-bureaus in enterprises, constant interruptions in production due to the everyday chaos of the command economy rendered nearly impossible any accurate calculation of the relationship between labor and productive output. At best, norms could be a compromise between conditions at the workplace and downtime because of supply bottlenecks. At worst, they were mere guesswork.[65]

Furthermore, as noted earlier, the shortage of qualified labor and the existence of open borders yielded to labor an "exit option" that it might not otherwise have enjoyed. If pushed too far, the more talented could pick up and leave for the West. During the economic upswing in the West following the West German currency reform in June 1948, and the economic downswing in East Germany because of its separation from the West, the problem of migration worsened.[66] Not surprisingly, every time the center attempted to reform the wage system, management catered to the egalitarian impulse of its employees and continued to even out wage differentials with funds supposedly set up for production bonuses.[67] Well into the early 1950s, despite its best efforts, the SED had still not gained control over the shop floor.

June 1953: Origins and Long-Term Consequences

The cat-and-mouse game between state and class might have carried on undisturbed had the cold war not taken a new turn. After the rejection of the second Soviet "Germany Note" by West Germany, followed by Adenauer's signature to the European Defence Community Treaty in May 1952, Stalin decided on the full integration of the GDR into the East bloc. Under Soviet orders the East Germans committed themselves to building up their armed forces and defense industry at a cost of 1.5 billion marks, to be financed from reductions in social spending coupled with higher taxation.

In July the SED quickly convened a party conference where it announced the "planned construction of socialism in the GDR." Apart from the ideological bluster, in the economy the shift amounted to a new emphasis on investment in heavy industry, forced collectivization of agriculture, and discriminatory taxation against the remaining private industrial enterprises. The economic and social impacts of these measures were felt immediately. In November 1952, West German newspapers reported sporadic riots and industrial unrest in the major industrial centers of the GDR, including Leipzig, Dresden, Halle, and Suhl.[68] As a result of the collectivization campaign, by April 1953 approximately 40 percent of the wealthier farmers in the GDR had fled to the West, leaving over 500,000 hectares of otherwise productive land lying fallow.[69] By spring 1953, severe food shortages hit the cities and, as punitive taxation on the private sector effectively shut down crucial suppliers of the state sector, consumer goods began to disappear from the shelves too.

Faced with the inflationary pressures of increased defense spending and declining agricultural and industrial output, the SED leadership had little choice but to attack industrial wage inflation. In May 1953, the SED announced an across-the-board norm increase of 10 percent, set according to strict technical standards. Such an increase might once again have been undermined at the enterprise level, and gone unnoticed, had it not been accompanied by other unprecedented measures: increases in prices for food, health care, and public transportation. Taken together, the norm and price increases amounted to a 33 percent monthly wage cut. Despite the confusion in the leadership following Stalin's death in March, the Soviet leadership retained enough internal cohesion to respond to the numerous SMAD reports that pointed to the strain these policies had put on East German society. In a series of meetings with the SED leadership, the Soviets "suggested" a number of steps for the GDR's economic recovery.[70] The SED followed most of the Soviet recommendations but, curiously, did not rescind the industrial norm increases.[71]

In any case it was too late. On June 16, 1953, workers at several Berlin construction sites walked off the job, demanding a reinstatement of the old norms. On the next day, June 17, the protests spread to 272 cities and towns throughout the GDR.[72] Wage demands quickly turned into political demands for free elections and unification with the West. In the end, public order and SED rule could only be restored with the help of Soviet tanks.

The June uprising shocked and frightened both the Soviets and the SED leadership. Across the republic, demonstrators ransacked SED regional and district headquarters and, in a few instances, physically assaulted functionaries and soldiers. On the morning of June 17, Soviet High Commissioner Semionov instructed the entire Politburo to drive to SMAD headquarters in Karlshorst. Politburo member Rudolf Hernnstadt reports that the SED leadership drove in convoy through the center of Berlin. "We proceeded very quickly in a closed convoy through the streets, which in the meantime had filled with agitated people. Several ran at the car with raised fists. Neither Ulbricht nor I talked."[73] During the first night of the revolt, the SED leadership spent the night under Soviet protection at SMAD headquarters in Karlshorst. In the early afternoon of June 17, Marshall Sokolovski, who had since become Soviet Army chief of staff, arrived from Moscow and immediately expressed an astonishment that probably reflected that of the entire Soviet leadership: "How could such a thing happen? I don't understand. Such things are not started up from one day to the next."[74]

For our purposes, even more important than the immediate shock were the long-term effects of the June events on the East German political economy. One month after the June uprising, a report to the general secretary of the Christian Democratic Union, the most important of the SED-aligned bloc parties, warned that "under a seemingly calm surface [lay] dangerous seeds of discontent," and concluded "that an external calm exists in the population and in reality the mood has in no way improved since June 17, 1953."[75] The SED could hardly have been less affected by the mood of the population than its sister party, since most public anger was directed at Ulbricht, Pieck, Grotewohl, and other leading Communist luminaries. In fact, from the testimony of his colleagues, we know that throughout the 1950s, SED leader Walter Ulbricht feared, more than anything else, a repetition of June 17.[76]

In the weeks immediately preceding and following the June strikes, Ulbricht squared off against several of his most important Politburo colleagues, including Interior Minister Wilhelm Zaisser and Rudolf Herrnstadt, the editor of *Neues Deutschland*, who insisted that Ulbricht had led the party astray by calling for the rapid construction of socialism. In a long and emotional nighttime Politburo meeting on July 7, 1953, nine members voted for Ulbricht's removal as general secretary and only two (Erich Honecker and Hermann Matern) supported him. But in a strange twist of events, Ulbricht was able not only to stay in office but, with the assistance of the Soviet Military Administration, in the following weeks managed to turn the tables on his opponents, forcing many into silence and removing the most ambitious from power altogether. Indeed, with Moscow's assistance, he emerged stronger in the SED than ever before.

How did Ulbricht pull this off? As Rudolf Herrnstadt suggests in his memoirs, the key was certainly Moscow's fear that disturbances similar to the June strikes might break out elsewhere in the Soviet orbit.[77] In explaining the behavior of the Soviet leadership, it must be kept in mind how close all of this came after Stalin's death; while in Moscow the new triumvirate of Malenkov, Molotov, and Khrushchev were in the process of displacing their main rival, Lavrenti Beria, removing an experienced and loyal Soviet ally like Ulbricht immediately after the greatest crisis socialism had seen since the end of the war must have seemed too risky. The evidence indicates that Ulbricht, who immediately after the July 7 Politburo meeting flew to Moscow for consultations, convinced the Soviet authorities during his short stay that his removal was unwise, that his opponents had capitulated to street demonstrators on June 17, and that whatever his weaknesses were as general secretary, he could be kept on a fairly short leash.[78] On July 9, 1953, Ulbricht returned to Berlin confident that the Soviet leadership in Moscow and the Soviet advisors on the ground in Germany would support him in unseating his opponents.

Having come away politically secure, Ulbricht nevertheless understood that politically charged industrial unrest had almost cost him his job and, given the clear connection between unrest and wage-price policy, he had good reason to avoid making this mistake again. It appears certain that Ulbricht feared his own working class. Not surprisingly, then, the uprising in June effectively crippled the regime on the shop floor. Norms quickly returned to the status quo ante.[79] In order to buy labor quiescence, the SED continued to corrupt the entire Taylorist apparatus set up for measuring old norms and implementing new ones. Taylorism's corruption in the East German context did not decrease the allure of the pseudoscientific and technocratic language so present in the various charts, graphs, and equations that litter the regime's labor studies of the 1950s.[80] Gradually, however, the outlines of an implicit agreement between the workers' state and the working class began to take shape: production could rise so long as norms remained low and wages high, relative to productivity. Industrial unrest did reappear sporadically throughout the 1950s, as the regime tried time and again to manipulate wages and norms. But enterprise party organizations and management had little interest in creating unnecessary industrial conflict and, in the few cases of conflict that have been studied thoroughly, both tended to acquiesce to whatever industrial demands workers might make.

Throughout the 1950s wages rose faster than productivity in virtually every sector of industry, a problem that the leadership would repeatedly attempt to rectify, albeit with little success.[81] Twelve years after the June events, for example, when the management of the Oberspree Cable Works tried to adjust piece rates in the first half of 1961, a report of the Committee for Labor and Wages lamented that "the workers declared that if new piece rates were introduced, they would take up work in another enterprise. Five workers took the discussion about the use of new rates, which would not have led to any wage reductions, as cause to quit."[82] In the same year, a member of the Economic Council of Rostock could characterize only 15 percent of the wages in his province as subject to any kind of rigorous standardized output norms.[83] Even though industrial relations could be stabilized on the basis of "high wages" (high, that is, relative to productivity gains) and low productivity (low, relative to the West), this arrangement did not in any way relieve the pressure on the regime to improve economic performance. It merely restricted one path of capital accumulation (through wage suppression) and rendered economic competition with the West that much more difficult. Wage egalitarianism remained a constant of East German industry; in fact, over the years it gradually became a social norm. Interestingly, egalitarian sentiments among workers in the GDR appear to have been replicated with equal strength in other Communist countries, leading one to suspect that the dynamics at work were inherent in Communist work experience and structures of authority rather than in any cultural particularity of the GDR.[84]

As the institutions and practices of Soviet-style economic administration took hold during the 1950s under the constraint of the implicit "labor agreement," the issue of rising wage levels constituted but one part of a larger, generalized problem of financial discipline throughout the East German economy.[85] In the first half of 1954, for example, as an unmistakable consequence of the wage concessions to the working class after June 1953, the East German money supply increased by 19.6 percent. Soviet advisors in the GDR's State Planning Commission and the Finance Ministry repeatedly complained of wage increases, industrial investment, and other sources of state expenditure being undertaken without sufficient care to the productive return on these outlays. But with little help in the way of extra consumer goods from the Soviet Union, and Ulbricht's desire to avoid a repetition of the June strikes, the confidential recommendations of the Soviet advisors quickly to "attain a level of welfare for laborers and working people of the GDR which at least equals that of the same stratum of population in West Germany" sounded comical and was largely ignored at higher levels. Similar and contradictory advice to "harden" the budget received little attention. As a result, budget deficits remained high throughout the period, and the financial capacity of the population to buy goods (solvent demand) continued to exceed that of the regime to supply them.[86]

As an older generation of East Germans resumed its place and a new generation entered the work force after 1945, both developed habits, interests, and expectations that were different from those of the working class of prewar Germany. The work ethic and culture of the East German working class had been completely refashioned. In the absence of a capitalist labor market, the egalitarian impulse developed in the early postwar years could not be broken as it was in the West. As wages lost their disciplinary and stimulative functions, however, other traditional German working-class virtues fell by the wayside. Thus, by 1960, East Germany had a higher rate of absenteeism among industrial workers due to "illness" than any other country in Soviet-controlled Eastern Europe.[87] Labor had become as much a constraint as a productive resource and, as we shall see in the next chapter, this constraint in no small way helped to restrict the scope of plausible economic reforms.

Western experts have long argued that during the 1970s and 1980s, that is, in the later years of Communist rule in the Soviet Union and Eastern Europe, an implicit "social contract" between state and society effectively restricted the room for maneuver enjoyed by these regimes.[88] The historical evidence presented in this chapter, however, suggests that this confining condition was encountered much earlier than previously thought, almost from the very outset of rule. What this has to say about the limits and logic of a technocratically oriented totalitarian rule is a subject to which we shall return later in this study. For now, it should suffice to note that, despite the imposing presence of the Soviet occupation regime and the growing power of the Communist Party, the SED, the East German working class retained an amorphous, disorganized power that, even with a good dose of Stalinist terror, could not easily be diminished. The power of the totalitarian state to shape a new moral economy, to create a new structure of consent among the working class, was extremely limited. Along with job security, East German workers had the power to demand a rough-and-ready sort of wage egalitarianism and consumer prices that remained low relative to wages. Despite this, they expected a standard of living on a par with that of their counterparts in the West and reserved the right to feel a sense of injustice when this relationship went too far askew.

Chapter 2 Reform Abandoned

The Elusive

Search for

Socialist

Modernity,

1962–1970

A short story published at the end of the 1950s in the GDR captured the way things ought to have been. Anything but a literary masterpiece, "A Man Came from the West to the East" is the work of Wolfgang Schaarschmidt, a full-time piece-rate engineer at the jointly owned Soviet-German uranium mines in Wismut and part-time *Volkskorrespondent*.[1] The story begins in 1947 with our hero, Manfred Sch., a typical West German working-class youth, finding a position as an apprentice in a paint and finishing shop. At first he is happy to have the position, but after the currency reform in 1948 life becomes difficult. The work days are long, usually twelve hours. He works hard. Just before Christmas 1952 the foreman invites him into his office and tells him that business is slow. He is laid off. Eager to find steady work, especially after his marriage in 1954 and the birth of his first child, Manfred secures a new position as a lacquer sprayer on the night shift. After three months of seeing his wife only on weekends, he comes across an advertisement for a position as a sales representative with an electronics firm. The hours are long but the salary and commission add up to far more than he made as a sprayer. The firm even gives him a car for business purposes. One evening while driving home disaster strikes. He falls asleep at the wheel, and his car crosses the left lane and hits a tree. His boss cares little for his reasons and demands payment of 100 marks every month until the damage is paid in full. Without a car he cannot compete with the other salesmen. He quickly falls into debt. His sofa, his chair, and finally his wife's radio are all repossessed. The courts begin to garnish his wages. Nine years of hard work, for what?

As one misfortune follows the next, Manfred starts receiving letters from Herbert, a friend in Mittweida, in the "Ostzone." Manfred knows nothing of communism, only that there are Communists, and he once heard that if you complain too much they send you to Siberia. The letters continue to come. The picture his friend paints sounds like nothing he hears in the West. And as his life becomes increasingly untenable, he begins to entertain the idea of resettlement in the East. Such decisions are never simple. But finally, after much agonizing, the family quietly gathers together what little it can carry, buys train tickets, and heads East. Although Manfred is warmly received and is assigned a comfortable small apartment, the resettlement is not easy. There is much to learn. He quickly finds work in his trade in a local wood-working factory. Despite the difficulties of the planned economy and the laziness of many of his fellow workers, he decides that life is "a thousand times better" in the East. He can never be fired, he is paid according to his skill level rather than his seniority, and, most important, people care. Manfred finds a warmth, a willingness to discuss problems that is lacking in the West. Within three years he has become a member of the Communist Party and an irreplaceable member of his work collective.

It is easy to see why such stories were published. While in hindsight they appear to be little more than flights into fantasy, from Walter Ulbricht's point of view this is the way things should have been—East Germans satisfied with their lot and West Germans simultaneously repelled by the hectic pace of life in the Federal Republic and attracted by the warmth and relative prosperity of the first workers' and farmers' state in German history. But as is often the case, reality was more stubborn than fiction. Throughout the 1950s, West Germany applied steady pressure on the SED by claiming to be the only legitimate representative of all Germans and solidified this notion with the "Hallstein Doctrine," according to which West Germany refused to grant full diplomatic recognition to any state that recognized the GDR.[2] Ultimately, to deflect the West's claims on its people, territory, and sovereignty, the SED had little choice but to try to make its half of Germany an appealing place to live, more appealing if possible than the West. In taking on this task, however, the SED squared off in an economic struggle against West Germany at the height of its *Wirtschaftswunder*, an era not only of impressive economic growth but also of unprecedented improvements in consumer life-styles.

The pressure to match Western living standards was unrelenting. In stark contrast to Schaarschmidt's story, between 1955 and 1957 nearly 250,000 East Germans left for the "golden West." Ulbricht must have been depressed, if not surprised, to read in autumn 1957 that, according to a prominent professor with close ties to the chemical industry, 55 percent of the workers at the Leuna Chemical Works favored the return of the prewar owners, IG-Farben, to operate the plant.[3] Desperate to stem the tide of skilled workers leaving the country, in 1958 Ulbricht declared that the next several years would prove the superiority of socialism over capitalism. The GDR's "chief economic task" was now overtaking West Germany in per capita consumption of all important food items and consumer goods by 1961. Whether Ulbricht was forced into setting his sights so high by the dominant discourse in the Communist world as set by his Soviet counterpart, Nikita Khrushchev, or whether he was genuinely committed to such a goal is not clear from the record. The timing suggests the former. But even Khrushchev, the eternal optimist that he was, had not predicted the Soviet Union overtaking the United States until 1980. Ulbricht's GDR, lacking the resources and outside support that made the West German *Wirtschaftswunder* possible, had no realistic chance of attaining its goal.

In 1960 Ulbricht admitted as much in a series of remarkably frank exchanges with Khrushchev. Writing in July, Ulbricht lamented that "the fulfillment of the main economic task is not secured.... You can be sure that we are doing everything in our powers. But West Germany has turned out to be economically powerful. In the final analysis, we cannot choose against whom we would like to compete. We are simply forced to square off against West Germany. However, the GDR does not have enough economic power to do this alone."[4] Ulbricht requested Soviet aid in the form of extra steel deliveries and a twofold increase in hard-currency credits to buy supplementary consumer goods in the West. The request was turned down. In November 1960, following the Moscow meeting of the world's Communist parties, Ulbricht once again warned Khrushchev, but this time focused the discussion on the GDR's anomalous situation of open borders with the West through West Berlin. The West Berlin problem would worsen as the city continued to develop rapidly. Once again he pleaded for economic assistance. Ulbricht worried that, given the level of Soviet support, the best East Germany could hope for was growth rates of between 6 and 7 percent. These otherwise respectable forecasted growth rates struck Ulbricht as insufficient. "To maintain a normal situation we need a yearly growth of no less than 10 percent. Otherwise we will not provide the necessities. If I cannot pay a worker in Berlin a higher salary he will go to West Berlin. This is the situation. We must improve the situation of the doctors and the intelligentsia and some workers, since the situation in West Germany is improving faster. In 1961 they already will have implemented a forty-hour working week; they will raise salaries, and we can't even think about this. Discrepancies have grown between us. We cannot achieve our goals with the help of just propaganda."[5] In a letter to Khrushchev written in January 1961, Ulbricht once again stressed that West German development outpaced East Germany's, not only in overall growth but, more important for the long run, in investment. This long-run difference in investment, according to Ulbricht, was the main reason East Germany lagged behind the West and would continue to do so in the future. "Due to this, West Germany can constantly apply political pressure. The booming economy in West Germany, which is visible to every citizen of the GDR, is the main reason that over ten years about two million people have left our Republic."[6] Left unsaid, but clearly implied, was that the population demanded Western living standards but could not be counted on to suppress consumption in order to get there.

These few excerpts from Ulbricht's communication with Khrushchev during 1960–61 strongly suggest that he was trying to force the Soviet leader into making a choice: either increase economic assistance or agree to close the passageway to West Berlin through which East Germany was losing an unacceptable number of its most highly trained people. In the end, the Soviets gave way on the trade issue probably in the hope of avoiding a showdown on Berlin. During trade negotiations with the Soviets in January 1961, the GDR received most of what it asked for, but Ulbricht continued to pressure Khrushchev. Emboldened by the Soviet "concessions," the old East German leader now considered the time right to move on the border question; surely Adenauer would avoid confrontation during his upcoming re-election campaign and Kennedy would not dare risk exacerbating relations with the Soviets during his first year in office. In addition to its evaluation of the diplomatic situation, the archival record also shows that the SED had a fairly realistic understanding of the GDR's economy and appreciated just how unattractive its economic model was to most West Germans. Ulbricht and his colleagues knew better than anyone how little hope there was in the short run of inducing people to remain in the country through superior economic performance. The logical move was therefore to push the Soviets as hard as possible for a "political" solution to the emigration problem. On August 13, 1961, with Soviet acquiescence, the SED solved its border problem for the next twenty-eight years when it built the Berlin Wall.[7]

It remains a mystery why Walter Ulbricht, a man who had spent the better part of the 1950s fighting against a technocratic form of de-Stalinization that was spreading throughout the Soviet bloc, should have adopted some of the very reformist policies and promoted some of the same people he had bitterly criticized only several years earlier. Consider the well-known case of the revisionist economist Fritz Behrens of Leipzig and his younger colleague Arne Benary of Halle. While a professor in Leipzig during the 1950s, Behrens had cultivated a loyal and talented following of young economists. Emboldened by liberalizing trends elsewhere in Eastern Europe, in 1956 Behrens and Benary dared to write about the most obvious sorts of problems that plagued the GDR's economy (overly centralized decision making, discontinuities in production, high labor costs, low quality of output, useless surpluses of goods that could not be sold) and proposed decentralization and administrative self-regulation as a remedy. In short, what Behrens called for was a technocratic substitute for market regulation. As is generally known, Ulbricht ruthlessly attacked both (as well as Günther Kohlmey, a powerful economics institute director) at the thirteenth SED Central Committee plenum in January 1957.[8] He also ordered up a special issue of the official economics journal *Wirtschaftswissenschaft* devoted to unmasking Behrens and Benary's revisionist heresies and instructed the SED science departments to hold critical discussions in the economics institutes and universities where the two had been most influential.

Ulbricht resented and feared the loyalty Behrens commanded among his students. His fears must have been confirmed when he read the report of meetings at the universities in Leipzig and Halle on February 20 and 21, 1957, that were staged to discuss the heresies of the two economists. The report of one meeting in Leipzig, written by a representative sent from Berlin, clearly indicates that Behrens's students and colleagues defended him as best they could under the circumstances. "Comrade Behrens is valued by them as a good comrade and a qualified scholar. They cannot imagine that he would have consciously written something against our workers' and peasants' power and against our party. They base this evaluation on, among other things, his very good work on June 17, 1953. If in his work comrade Behrens should, nevertheless, represent ideas that do not coincide with the party line, then this is due to the bad influence of comrade Benary. Comrade Benary comes from a petty bourgeois background and, in the opinion of the comrades, never has had a connection to the party. They portray Benary as

Behrens's Mephistopheles."[9] As committed a Marxist as Walter Ulbricht may have been, he surely saw through such a transparent attempt at saving Behrens's career. It must have confirmed his decision to force Behrens into professional obscurity.

Yet the influence of Behrens's technocratic critique of the Stalinist economic model did not end with his ouster from intellectual life. The ideas put forward by Behrens lived on as his students took up jobs in the party and state apparatus in subsequent years. In fact, given the persistence of such ideas over the years, not only in East Germany but in almost every Communist state, one is tempted to posit the immanent technocratic critique of Soviet-style planned economics as a quasi law of its development. If Behrens did not exist, someone would have had to invent him.

Caught between the devil of technocratic and market-type reforms that threatened their core values and interests and the deep blue sea of the receding, golden West, whose middle-class life-styles shaped the expectations of their own populations, Communist leaders found themselves powerless to craft an appealing socialist modernity. Nowhere was this dilemma more acutely felt than in the GDR, a country whose very raison d'être was its anticapitalism but whose population by the end of the 1950s lived in the shadow of the most rapidly developing country in Europe—West Germany. In this respect, the East German 1960s remains one of the most interesting periods in the history of the Soviet bloc. In 1963, Walter Ulbricht introduced and implemented an "in-system" economic reform designed specifically to incorporate many of the criticisms and suggestions of Behrens and Benary into economic policy. The reform was in-system and technocratic in nature because, rather than introducing markets, it attempted to simulate them through administrative measures. Rather than eliminating bureaucratic control over the economy, as we shall see, it attempted to streamline it and make it more efficient. In this way it differed from market socialist experiments tried in other East European countries. After the admitted failure of the reform in 1970, leaders throughout the bloc faced two alternatives: either retreat to a conservative immobilism or proceed down the road of gradual capitalist restoration. As we shall see in the next chapter, whereas Hungary took the latter route to 1989, East Germany took the former.

Scholarship on the rise and demise of the East German reform falls into two schools of thought. One interpretation, put forward primarily by economists, holds that the reform succeeded in its first years but ultimately failed because of flaws in its design that led to severe shortages toward the end of the 1960s.[10] A second line of interpretation argues that, by the end of the 1960s, the Soviets were in a position to back the opponents to the New

Economic System (NES), as the reform was called, and ultimately insist that the reform be brought to an end. On this view, the extraordinary degree of political dependence on the USSR explains the policies and behavior of the East German elite.[11]

While both interpretations have merit, newly accessible sources allow us to paint a richer picture. In contrast to the economics literature, I contend that an internal *political* struggle lay at the center of the reforms from the very outset. Perhaps more controversial, in contrast to the foreign policy literature I portray the political struggle not only as a contest between various hardened factions vying for Moscow's favor but, rather, as the result of differing visions of the way a socialist economy and society should work. In what follows, East German leaders are given far more autonomy than in the conventional histories of the period. Of course, along the way, the dramatis personae sought allies, domestic and foreign, but this should not blunt our sense for the fluidity of alliances or how new all of this was for everyone concerned. Views evolved and changed rapidly as the powerful themselves contemplated what they wanted for their country and calculated how they would get it. Ulbricht's economic reform appeared and disappeared, not only because Moscow wanted it that way, but also because most of the East German elite, so enthusiastic in the early years, had tired of the search for an uncertain, elusive, and risky "socialist modernity."

Designs, Designers, and Dilemmas

The NES contained two central components:[12] improving enterprise performance without introducing a full-blown capital or labor market, and upgrading the quality and qualifications of leading economic personnel without sacrificing a commitment to socialist values. Both of these ideas made eminent sense for East Germany, disadvantaged as it was with a relatively poor resource base and a labor force depleted by years of open borders with the West.[13] Good sense alone, however, will not explain why Walter Ulbricht, a man who had spent the better part of the 1950s resisting de-Stalinization, suddenly embraced ideas he had vehemently rejected only a few years earlier. One plausible explanation is the concurrent reform efforts underway in the Soviet Union. Since Khrushchev had explicitly sanctioned the reform discussion throughout Eastern Europe, perhaps Ulbricht's actions indeed were, in part, one more instance of slavish clinging to Soviet policies and discourse.[14] The extension and deepening of the GDR's reform, however, long after the Soviets had lapsed into conservatism and Khrushchev himself had been overthrown, indicates that the need for reform ran deeper in the psychology of the East German leadership than explanations stressing political dependence would suggest.

A more convincing explanation is conceivable if one keeps in mind the traumatic years before the construction of the Berlin Wall. Disappointing economic performance and mass migration at the end of the 1950s and the first two years of the 1960s created a temporary consensus within the GDR elite that the only long-run solution to the German question lay in making the GDR an attractive place to live. Even with the Berlin Wall, rationing, which had been phased out in 1958, had to be reintroduced in 1962 for meat, eggs, and butter. Secretly, the regime even raised the water content of sausage in an effort to keep up with demand.[15]

As analysts have long noted, the Wall, built in August 1961, temporarily alleviated the economic and political pressure on the regime, and afforded the leadership the kind of leeway needed to undertake an experiment like the NES. But the reform was not merely a luxury for Ulbricht; rather, he perceived it as a necessity. Consulting with the Soviet leadership in May 1963, Ulbricht reminded his Soviet counterparts that "even after the closing of the state borders, the high living standard [in West Germany] strongly affects the population of the GDR and its political attitudes."[16] The old leader believed (correctly, it now seems reasonable to say) that the long-run viability of what he considered to be genuine socialism in Germany depended on the economic performance of his half of the divided nation.[17]

After some hesitation, in 1962 Ulbricht started thinking seriously about economic reform. Toward the end of the year, he put the design of the reform in the hands of several *Arbeitsgruppen* (working groups). Some groups, most notably the one headed by Prime Minister Willi Stoph, were largely cosmetic in nature, intended to give the impression that the old guard was integrally involved in the reform's design.[18] From very early on, however, Ulbricht decided that he could not leave the reform in the hands of his old trusted political allies such as Stoph and Alfred Neumann (the head of the Volkswirtschaftsrat), but needed new faces with fresher ideas and less power.

Under the leadership of Deputy Finance Minister Walter Halbritter, the new personalities in the East German economic elite gathered in what became the most important of the *Arbeitsgruppen*. Members of this group included the new head of the State Planning Commission (SPK), Erich Apel, Ulbricht's personal economic advisor Wolfgang Berger (who had studied with Behrens), and SED Central Committee economics chief Günter Mittag. Also admitted was a new generation of economists previously excluded from high policy making and often skirting the edges of the ideologically acceptable. For example, Herbert Wolf, one of the real intellectual giants among the reform economists, and yet one more of Behrens's students, was still formally under party "probation" and had only recently been demoted from university professor to enterprise economist in Leipzig when he was brought into Halbritter's working group in 1963.[19] Safe havens of reformist thought spread from the new working groups to the state apparatus. Under the institutional umbrella of the SPK's research institute, young economists from all over the country collaborated on working out details of the reform.[20]

In one way or another, all of the ideas under consideration implicitly grappled with the classical critiques of planned economics first put forward by von Mises and Hayek. How could the center be provided with enough information on production and preferences so that capital could be wisely spent and demand for producer and consumer goods could be met? The technocratic thinking of the Communist 1960s had moved away from the shop floor technocracy of the 1950s—indeed, given the working-class resistance encountered, such a shift was logical—and concentrated instead on the "socialist board room." It was managerial in nature. It is in this context that the search began for nonmarket approaches to information processing and production forecasting, such as cybernetics and Western organization and management theory. In 1962, for example, planning chief Apel received a steady supply of synopses of West German translations of American management studies. One in particular that he read quite closely was Ernst Dole's *Large Organizations: An Analysis of the Success of American Firms*. The study outlines the organizational background behind the success of Dupont, General Motors, National Steel Corporation, and Westinghouse during the postwar period, emphasizing such factors as enterprise size, profit-loss orientations, specialty advisory groups, and control of firms through banks. Each of these considerations found a place in the reform design.[21]

By the summer of 1963 most of the important ideas were ready for dissemination and discussion. In June Ulbricht staged an economics conference attended by approximately 950 party, state, and economics officials, where many encountered the ideas and terminology of the NES for the first time.[22] The conference resulted in a series of new laws that mandated the reevaluation of enterprise capital stock, an industrial price reform, the use of profit as the primary production indicator, as well as the revitalization of contractual (horizontal) relations between enterprises. Taken as a whole, these measures added up to what was referred to in the official jargon as "a system of economic levers." The intended effects of the reform can be summarized quite easily.[23] Put simply, the reformers envisioned improved enterprise performance through a reworking of the ways in which enterprises were evaluated (enter price reform, capital stock evaluation, and profit) and encouraged (contract, capital taxation, and, again, profit distributed partially through bonuses). Planning would not disappear but would become more effective as enterprise (VEB) and association (VVB) independence freed up the planning organs from "crisis management" so that they could pursue the long-range goal of technical development. Such measures were inspired by the Soviet economist Evsei Lieberman's critique of the classical Stalinist model, and, like Liebermanism, they sought to repair the existing system through administrative and economic incentives rather than dismantle it. The difference, as we shall see, is that Liebermanism was never seriously implemented in the Soviet Union, whereas in the GDR it was.[24]

Although the reform package did not as yet amount to a coherent whole, in January 1964 Ulbricht decided to move forward. Enterprises had already partially reevaluated their capital stock and several industries implemented the first stage of the industrial price reform. The use of profit as the primary production indicator for evaluating enterprise performance became a realistic possibility with the introduction of more realistic prices. However, because all prices could not be reformed simultaneously, use of profit as *the* performance standard remained an elusive goal. Some enterprises reported profits far out of proportion to their true performance, while others quickly accumulated debts despite being genuinely more profitable.[25] Instead of simplifying planning and performance evaluation, partial price reforms made the entire bureaucratic ballet more intricate. Writing to Ulbricht in November 1964, planning chief Apel noted that planning methods from top to bottom had become "extremely complicated" and a whole series of questions as to how the reform would eventually function as a system could be answered only with "practical experience in several VVBs and enterprises . . . after the confirmation of a long-range plan [*Perspektivplan*] and the conclusion of the price reform."[26] But with the *Perspektivplan* still in its early stages and the price reform not due for completion until 1966, Apel's remarks amounted to a warning to Ulbricht that the reform road to socialist modernity would indeed be a bumpy one.[27]

External disappointments and political pressures compounded the technical difficulties of implementing the reform. The hoped-for discussion and elaboration of Soviet economist Evsei Lieberman's ideas at the November 1962 Soviet Communist Party plenum never materialized; his ideas were left for the East Germans to elaborate. Furthermore, the level of Soviet economic support for the reform remained disappointing. Already in 1963, representatives from the Soviet planning agency, Gosplan, informed the East Germans that they would not be receiving as much crude oil as planned for the next several years because of more urgent needs in Cuba.[28] Most disappointing, however, was that by 1964 Soviet economic policy took a new conservative turn. Political pressure from the Soviets remained indirect until October 1964 when, according to Günter Mittag, Brezhnev paid a secret visit to Ulbricht at Werbelinsee. During the meeting, at which Apel and Mittag were also present, the Soviet crown prince complained bitterly that the GDR had become too caught up in its own economic affairs and was neglecting the trade needs of its Soviet partners.[29]

Even before Brezhnev's visit, the Soviet Union had cut shipments of several vital goods. In 1963, deliveries of certain types of steel, cotton, grain, and meat were reduced by 25 to 35 percent.[30] It is well known that the Soviets experienced an acute economic crisis in 1963 brought on by a bad harvest and eventually resulting in food riots and industrial unrest. The East Germans paid a price for the faltering Soviet harvest too; by early 1965 a steady stream of reports crossed Ulbricht's desk, outlining the impact on domestic production of shortfalls in imports. In a rather distressed tone he reported to the Politburo that "currently there is no certainty about the willingness of the Soviet Union to supply certain types of rolled steel for industrial requirements. Until now we have always imported from the USSR without difficulties." That these kinds of trade disputes with the Soviets "could not be written about in the press" (Ulbricht) made the matter that much more difficult to explain at the enterprise level.[31]

Moscow's retreat into conservatism meant that if Ulbricht intended to continue to push forward with the NES, the GDR would have to go it alone. This sense of partial isolation was worrisome, not only because the success of the reform depended on Soviet resources and political patronage, but also because of a feeling among the designers of the reform that they had nowhere to turn for practical advice on a whole range of questions bound to come up as the reform progressed. Following Brezhnev's visit, planning chief Erich Apel pondered some of the technical issues of reform economics in a letter to Ulbricht, in particular the complexities of planning methodology, studiously noting that, "neither from the USSR nor from Czechoslovakia are there suggestions or practical ideas forthcoming for solving these problems. As in other areas, in this area too we shall be engaging in pioneer work."[32] But even with a pioneer spirit, the conservative turn in Moscow could not but have had an unsettling effect among the East German reformers.[33]

Signs of Resistance: Line versus Staff Orientations

Social scientists have offered a simple and elegant explanation for why Communist reforms fail. Notwithstanding some good intentions, reforms ultimately founder, so the argument goes, because marketization threatens the benefits accrued to rent-seeking bureaucrats who, in a market economy, will no longer be the administrators of shortage.[34] Given a choice between efficiency or power, Communist bureaucrats choose power every time. How does the theory hold up when confronted with the evidence? The archival evidence on the rise and demise of the East German reforms during the 1960s reveals motivations of a more complex nature. Middle- and upper-level officials who opposed the reforms did so not because they were afraid of losing power, but because regulating a reforming economy was so much more complicated and difficult than administering a purely Stalinist economy. Their private correspondence portrays men concerned more with a poorly functioning, half-reformed economy, than with their diminished power in the face of decentralization.

While economic performance improved by some measures during the first several years of the NES, the improvement could not be tied convincingly to the reform as such since it had yet to be fully implemented.[35] Opponents to the reform could take their cue from Moscow, but also had little trouble finding genuine economic difficulties at home. In retrospect, the problems appear very similar to those Gorbachev faced twenty-five years later in the Soviet Union when he attempted to alter its planning system. The old system of vertical bonds remained in place but had been weakened by the new system of horizontal ties between enterprises. The supply system was under strain, not only due to shortfalls in imports, but also because new incentives were causing enterprises to behave in ways that baffled planners' expectations. If profits had not yet become accurate indicators of enterprise performance, they *were* affecting aggregate revenues and bonuses. The implicit agreement with labor, hammered out through conflict and compromise in the 1950s, ensured that bonuses would only go up. Whereas the average worker bonus in centrally managed industries in 1963 was 240 marks, by 1964 it had risen to 286 marks and, had it not been for administrative intervention, theoretically could have been set as high as 486 marks.[36] The chronic problem in all socialist financial systems of high salaries chasing too few goods continued to plague East Germany and was, in fact, exacerbated by the reform. But if profit and bonus could not become the primary regulator for economic activity, continued administrative guidance remained both possible and necessary, even if the reform had made this guidance all the more tricky.

Not surprisingly, then, the first resistance to the reforms came from those officials most involved in day-to-day balancing of the financial and material plans. Consider the case of Finance Minister Willi Rumpf. In the summer of 1964 the Politburo made a number of decisions regarding prices and budgeting that were crucial in putting together the *Perspektivplan*. By late September Ulbricht was informed through party channels that Rumpf had not yet started work on implementing the Politburo decrees of two months earlier. "Apparently," wrote Mittag, "even now comrade Rumpf still has a different understanding on a series of problems." Mittag recommended that Ulbricht bring Rumpf in for a formal dressing down after the GDR's fifteenth anniversary celebrations in October.[37]

Whether the meeting took place and Rumpf received his reprimand is not apparent from the record. In any case, Rumpf was not sufficiently deterred (or had outside backing), for his opposition did not end there. Prereform methods and language continued to be used and advocated in publications and correspondence issuing from his office. Throughout 1965 Ulbricht issued instructions to keep a careful watch on all written communications from Rumpf's office and to screen it before it reached wider circles in the party or the public.[38]

What had so bothered Rumpf that he would risk being perceived as an opponent of a policy personally supported by Walter Ulbricht? Whether his resistance had an ideological basis remains unclear. He certainly did not express it this way. His concerns, while not always transparent, were cast in straightforward terms in a letter to Ulbricht in June 1964. First, Rumpf considered Ulbricht's long-range plans as excessively optimistic. Too many projects would likely be started and too few actually finished. Second, financial planning would become an even more precarious affair as production associations (VVB) grew more independent from central planners and acquired more power over their income.[39]

His points were well taken and reflected the viewpoint of a typical "line" official at odds with reformist views of his "staff" counterparts—in this case, the staff being the long-range planners in the SPK. Alfred Neumann, who, as head of the National Economic Council (Volkswirtschaftrat) was responsible for day-to-day balancing of resources, had similar concerns. Neumann's party position as a Politburo member, moreover, provided him with the opportunity and political power to express dissatisfaction with those aspects of the reform that made his job more difficult. The line-staff distinction provides us with the first clue as to the main arena of struggle over the nature and purpose of the NES. On the one hand, we have Ulbricht and his personal advisors, along with the new long-range planners at the State Planning Commission and the economics departments of the SED, who for their various reasons sought to move ahead as fast as possible—Ulbricht because he hoped the reform would help the GDR compete with the West economically and thus stabilize SED rule, and the new personalities in the party and state because they saw the reform as an opportunity to place innovative ideas and programs on the policy agenda that had been ignored or discredited in the 1950s.[40] As an inevitable cost of improvement, both were willing to accept a certain amount of disruption in the normal flow of bureaucratic procedures. On the other hand, we have veteran officials, such as Stoph and Neumann, in the state and party bureaucracies, who were mostly laymen in economic matters, but had managed to master some of the intricacies of planned economics during the 1950s and, although they welcomed improvements in planning methodology, they considered the disruptive aspects of reform as unnecessary and imprudent.

Resistance to the reform at this stage, therefore, can more readily be explained by the spontaneous reactions of officials whose traditional roles had suddenly become more complex and less familiar, than by reference to entire classes of party or state officials who sought to protect their turf from the threat of "decentralization"; this, as we shall see, would come later. Although neither Rumpf nor Neumann was ideologically well disposed to economic reforms, the resistance of both, initially at any rate, can be understood by reference to their roles within the unreformed economic structure.

Resistance to Technocracy

In addition to planning complexities, enterprise autonomy also presented some sticky political and ideological issues. Over the course of the reform, the VVB gradually received fewer mandatory plan indicators from the center and thus controlled greater portions of internal investment. What enterprises could not find from their own funds for investment, they were to borrow from the state banks. Naturally, those VVB with more enterprising managers started thinking of themselves as independent, self-sufficient entities. In this they were encouraged by Ulbricht, who on several occasions since the sixth SED party congress in 1963 had referred to the VVB as "socialist concerns."

What exactly were the limits of "enterprise consciousness"? The "Nagema" affair provided a critical test case. Toward the end of 1964, the journal

Deutscher Export carried an advertisement for the products of the VVB Nagema. Instead of using the normal appellation "VVB Nagema" ("VVB" meaning Association of People's Owned Enterprises), however, the text of the advertisement referred to the capitalist-sounding "Konzern Nagema."[41] Nagema had also begun using *Konzern* in its in-house publication *Nagema Info*.[42] The party apparatus reacted quickly. Further usage of *Konzern* could be stopped, but 7,000 copies of the journal had already been exported to seventy-eight countries. A full-blown investigation ensued, carried out by the economics departments of the Central Committee. Mittag reported to Ulbricht in February 1965 that the general director, as well as leading employees in the sales department, used the term because they thought it was "the right thing to do"; they thought it would "raise the image" of the enterprise internationally. In fact, Ulbricht himself had used the term *Konzern* at the SED plenum in February 1964, but Mittag held that it was apparent that "the comrades do not yet understand the resolutions of the fifth plenum on the development of the VVB into a leading economic organ." Mittag, as the SED's economics chief, worried that the newly powerful VVB chiefs might evolve into "captains of industry" who might someday challenge the authority of the party. He informed Ulbricht that, after discussing the issue with National Economic Council Chairman Alfred Neumann, a known opponent of the reform, the two agreed that the general director should be relieved of his position in the first quarter of 1965.[43]

From very early on, distress about the political implications of the reform went beyond the issue of the separation of economics from politics. To be sure, decentralization remained a concern and the ideologues understood as well as anyone the meaning of the popular economic saying, *Wer die Fonds hat, der hat die Macht* (he who has the capital has the power). However, the real question, the power question, was that of personnel. Several Western scholars have noted a new emphasis during the NES on professional competence in personnel recruitment.[44] The archival record supports this analysis, in part. For example, a report submitted to the Party Organs Department by the construction minister, Wolfgang Junker, in 1965, complained that only four of the eleven general directors and four of seventeen enterprise directors in the construction industry had received any education in economics, hardly the profile of managers trained to operate using economic rather than administrative principles.[45]

If previous scholarship has accurately portrayed the NES as an attempt at technocratic modernization, however, it has overlooked the timing and intensity of resistance to technocracy within the party apparatus. As early as 1965, Central Committee departments complained that the technocratic orientation had led to a neglect of traditional political and ideological concerns. Of particular concern was the October 1962 secretariat resolution restricting admission to the Higher Party School (*Parteihochschule,* or PHS) to those with some secondary education. Although many party secretaries, under the pressure of these new entrance requirements, hastily acquired some sort of secondary education, this was often not enough. "It is necessary," argued the Department for Cadre Questions, "to overcome the contradiction that, on the one hand, experienced party comrades with good knowledge of Marxism-Leninism are delegated to the industrial institutes and, on the other hand, these comrades cannot be admitted to the *Parteihochschule.*" The party personnel departments contended that if the path to the top remained the PHS, in several years the new entrance requirements would lead to a radical change in the composition of the elite: engineers and economists would dominate political life. Their recommendation was unambiguous: "The conditions for acceptance at the PHS should be altered so that those experienced in party work but without any secondary education should also be able to take up study at the PHS."[46]

The nascent conflict between potential technocrats and the more established figures in the party and state apparatus never came to a head but festered in the psychology of the leadership. The red-expert debate was never resolved to the degree hypothesized by Ludz, Glaeßner, and others. To be sure, ongoing difficulties with the reform lent credibility to the idea that younger, more educated cadres should displace the conservative and slow-moving ministers and departmental chiefs. Gradually, however, even those officials favorably inclined to technocratic solutions of administrative problems had moved in the opposite direction. A letter from Gerhard Schürer (SPK chief after Apel's suicide in 1965) to Willi Stoph written in 1970 illustrates most vividly just how far this evolution had progressed. "A way out of our problem is often presented as if we have to mobilize young scholars against the 'conservative ministers.' There will surely always be struggles against backwardness in the state apparatus. And it is good to attract young scholars. But by no means should we allow it to come to a confrontation of young scholars against the state apparatus. Many young scholars who are working in the SPK grasp very quickly the kind of difficult decisions they must confront here."[47] The lure of technocracy remained great, but as Schürer reminded his superior, economic decision making in a partially reformed system had a logic of its own that defied any easy ways to improve it. Moreover, if taken too far, its realization threatened the ideals and interests of the party and state apparatus.

A Conservative Shift: Apel's Fall

The success of NES depended on solving two key problems that had not been adequately addressed by the summer of 1965. First, the GDR remained extraordinarily dependent on an unreliable supply line from the Soviet Union of raw and semifinished goods. Second, the technological benefits of long-term planning could not be realized if the productive capacity of the economy remained unpredictable.

The *Perspektivplan* was quickly devolving into a series of never-ending planning rounds between the center and productive units. The planning organs and the Perspektivplankommision felt at sea, as they had no way of assuring the final plan would be balanced. By July 1965 the danger of serious disproportions in the long-range plan became so clear that Ulbricht held a special two-day Politburo session on the question while vacationing on the Island of Vilm. The list of invitees to the meeting included the major economic players in the GDR: Willi Stoph (prime minister), Erich Apel (chairman of the State Planning Commission), Günter Mittag (SED economics secretary), Gerhard Grüneberg (SED agriculture secretary), Gerhard Schürer (deputy prime minister), Wolfgang Berger (Ulbricht's primary economics advisor), and Siegfried Böhm (head of SED Central Committee Department for Planning and Finance).[48] Although the exact content of the discussion remains murky, the essence of the meeting was to show that both the long-term and short-term plans of the GDR could not be met at existing production levels.[49]

At the meeting Apel became the object of criticism.[50] It appears that the growth rates contained in his early draft of the *Perspektivplan* were unacceptable to Ulbricht and the rest of the leadership. Submitted in the autumn, it was immediately rejected because the forecasted low growth levels meant that the overall goals could not be balanced from the outset. In addition, Alfred Neumann criticized Apel's plan for 1966. In a report delivered to Ulbricht on November 11, 1965, Neumann explained that the level of scientific and technical progress continued to move along but did not represent a "rising curve." Moreover, for 1966 he foresaw an unbalanced domestic plan and stiffer international economic competition that would render the export plan unfulfillable.[51] This gloomy report further undermined Apel's political utility in Ulbricht's eyes.

In retrospect it appears clear that the staff of the Planning Commission faced an impossible task. The reform had indeed decentralized planning and increased the potential independence of enterprises. Yet managers still played the old, well-established game of ensuring plan fulfillment (now, of course, measured in "profit") by lobbying for more and more capital investment. According to Werner Obst, a former employee of the Council of Ministers, the amount of request for capital investments in 1965 exceeded by three times the existing material and financial capacity of the economy. Moreover, large, unprofitable, but politically prestigious enterprises continued to receive huge investments and subsidies. The brown coal combine "Schwarze Pumpe" was scheduled for the period 1965–70 to embark on a project that would retrieve natural gas so inefficiently that the expected net yearly loss came to 500 million marks. Other large enterprises continued to receive production subsidies, including the Leuna Chemical Works, the Buna Synthetic Rubber Works, the Mansfeld Foundry, Eisenhüttenstadt (the East German answer to Magnitogorsk), and the entire GDR shipbuilding industry.[52] In short, with the exception of machine building—it too would go into decline during the 1970s—the entire panoply of the SED's prestige industries continued to be capital eaters rather than capital producers.

More important for Apel, the inherent technical difficulties of planning with a partially reformed economy in no way attenuated the force of bureaucratic politics. Apel's enemies lost no time in seizing upon his difficulties to undermine his position. Sometime between early summer and midfall 1965, Apel lost Ulbricht's confidence and thereafter became fair game for others in the leadership, who were none too favorably disposed to a man who was clearly not one of them. In early December 1965, during a moment of despair, the forty-eight-year-old planning chief committed suicide with his own service revolver.

Erich Apel's death on December 3, 1965, marks a turning point in the reform. Apel's dejection and subsequent suicide are usually explained by the failed trade negotiations with the Soviets in December, after which he was forced to sign a trade agreement that eliminated any hope of fulfilling the *Perspektivplan*.[53] Perhaps this was the most proximate cause, but Apel had further reason to feel pressured. Already at the ninth SED plenum in March 1965, Ulbricht had criticized the SPK for not mastering the complexities of reform planning. The criticism of Apel and the Planning Commission picked up steam during the fall, as the Planning Commission and the National Economic Council began blaming each other for unbalanced plans.[54] At the end of 1965, Willi Rumpf once again raised the specter of imbalance in a financial plan that he himself had manipulated.[55] Indeed, the archival record clearly shows that Apel was in no way surprised by the Soviet position; he expected the Soviets to take a hard line and prepared for it.[56] In retrospect it seems reasonable to say that Apel's suicide was much more a response to stress that had accumulated over many months, even years, than a rash reaction to the failed trade negotiations.

Even Apel's friend, Günter Mittag, had deserted him. The two had been very close friends politically and personally since the late 1950s. Together they were seen to embody a new generation of economic management. Just two days before the suicide, however, the two had a bitter falling out in which they disagreed on several questions of planning. In a meeting concerning construction, the strain under which Apel was working came through. He appeared unsure of himself. Later, Gerhard Trölitzch, Central Committee department chief for construction, discussed the matter with Mittag who had already been informed of Apel's prevarication. Trölitzch reports: "After I talked with Mittag, he called Apel on the direct line. In the conversation he heaped on heavy and pointed criticism about the fully unsatisfactory conduct of the plan meeting for construction, which had just taken place. He told Apel that he was fully incapable of continuing to head up the State Planning Commission. After I was back in my office Apel called me. He obviously felt very unhappy and dejected about the argument with Mittag—and I let Apel know that I had in no way contributed to the matter."[57] Mittag's dissatisfaction with Apel was driven more by ambition than principle. He merely joined in on what others had been doing for months— blaming Apel for the growing pains of economic reform. When Apel shot himself, the GDR lost its most energetic, highly placed proponent of reform. Less than one year later, in the summer of 1966, Mittag made the jump from candidate member to full member of the Politburo. As history would show, Mittag was willing to make other alliances to save his own career.[58]

The change in personalities at the top of the economic general staff reflected a subtle but noticeable shift in policy following the eleventh SED plenum in December 1965. The plenum has been interpreted primarily as an event where the conservatives, led by Erich Honecker, reimposed their hegemony in matters of culture and the arts. Its main outcome was to limit public discussion and cultural experimentation. This interpretation is largely correct. The archival record also reveals, however, a significant economic component to the plenum, and the two are not completely unconnected. While the conservatives succeeded in ensuring that the economic reforms would not "spill over" into the cultural and political realms, Ulbricht once again was forced defend his economic reform in an awkward minidebate with Rumpf. The finance minister repeatedly questioned the advisability of allowing enterprises to invest from their own profits because "under socialist conditions the raw income belongs to the state and consequently is accumulated in the state budget. It follows that in our country investment flows primarily from the state budget." Rumpf's insistence on rigorous central control over investment stood firmly at odds with the notion of "self-financing," an integral part of the original reform guidelines of 1963 and a notion close to the reformers' hearts. Ulbricht responded with a compromise, arguing that Rumpf's ideas were "outdated." Ulbricht acknowledged the danger of what was already clearly happening—too much financing of investment from credit and not enough from accumulated profits—but assured his audience that the institutes of the SPK and the Finance Ministry could solve the problem.[59]

Despite their vigorous defense of the reforms, Ulbricht and the economic reformers felt besieged at the eleventh plenum.[60] The implication of Rumpf's words could not have been more obvious: the finance minister regarded enterprise self-financing as a threat to the power of the ministry in the economy. If Rumpf had spoken out on his own, as a renegade, perhaps the entire episode could have been shrugged off. But clearly Rumpf could not have acted alone. He would never have spoken as he did (nor could he have survived so long, given that his resistance started as early as 1964) without a good deal of support at the highest political instances, in this case his boss, the chairman of the Council of Ministers Willi Stoph as well as Erich Honecker.[61] Rumpf, we can infer, represented a number of constituencies within the party and state apparatus who felt threatened by the reforms. Coupled with the conservative attack on cultural policy led by Honecker, the attack on the core features of the NES left Ulbricht little tactical choice but to speak of the NES in a way that would allay the fears of his fellow Politburo members. Thus, his report to the eleventh plenum no longer stressed the differences between the classical Stalinist economic system and the NES, but concentrated instead on elements of continuity in economic policy.[62]

In the final analysis, however, the impact of the conservative attack at the plenum went well beyond the changes it forced in cultural policy and economic ideology. Honecker's criticism of the cultural liberalization and its warm reception at the plenum effectively ended any widening of the public sphere and, in doing so, prevented the possibility of the economic reformers calling on the cultural intelligentsia at a later date for support in their struggle. In short, the return to political conservatism precluded developments of the sort that were slowly starting to take shape in Czechoslovakia.[63]

Policy after the Eleventh SED Plenum: Diverging Trends

Throughout 1966, policy advanced along two tracks simultaneously. On the one hand, Ulbricht's own team, along with significant parts of the economic bureaucracy, continued to work out the main elements of the NES—price reform, capital charges, investment by credit, and the like. On the other hand, an increasing number of officials called for more decisive central intervention to coordinate investment and production.[64]

The reduction of centrally handed-down production indicators during 1966 and 1967 reflected the first trend.[65] This signaled a movement toward an economy operated on the basis of economic rather than administrative criteria. One must note, however, that the reduction of indicators initially confused the planners at the SPK who were increasingly unsure of the proper mix in their work between long-range forecasting and yearly planning. Ministers, for their part used to accepting coordinating instructions from the SPK, were now expected to do much of their own plan coordination but were unsure exactly how to do this.[66]

The problems extended beyond that of administrative competence. Once again, implementing such a key element as price reform proved more troublesome than first anticipated. Even before the eleventh plenum, the Council of Ministers had considered the need for moving beyond industrial prices into the sensitive realm of consumer prices. The problem was quite simply that, in many cases, consumer prices remained lower than production costs and would have to rise. Most officials felt that this would have to be done slowly. But many in the economic elite agreed with the head of the State Bank, Grette Wittkowski, who asserted quite bluntly at a meeting in the Presidium of the Council of Ministers in July 1965, "In the area of consumer goods prices we need a plan and we have to get rid of the idea that consumer goods prices will stay unchanged." Apel agreed with her. Although he foresaw a solution to the problem only in the future, he predicted that many prices would have to change, and soon, if the price reform was to provide useful information to the planners.[67]

Even after Apel's death, the issue of consumer goods prices did not disappear. In February 1966, Stoph informed Ulbricht that it would soon be necessary to start thinking about making "corrections" in consumer prices because of the impact of the industrial price reform.[68] Ulbricht, however, did not yet feel confident enough to broach the question of consumer prices in public. He personally oversaw several drafts of the official *Argumentation* for the third and final stage of the industrial price reform, making sure that it was clear that consumer prices would not be affected.[69] Ulbricht, of course, was not alone. In both the party and state bureaucracies, many felt that for political reasons the burden of reform could not yet politically be shouldered by the public. The memories of June 1953 were still too fresh.

Such a constraint on policy making merely underlines the fact that the reforms were restricted by the tacit agreement with labor, hammered out in the shop floor struggles of the 1950s, just as much if not more than by bureaucratic infighting at the middle and upper levels of power. From the standpoint of economic reform, the GDR never recovered from the trauma of the June strikes. Once the leadership decided on a strategy of reconciliation rather than conflict with labor, it became extraordinarily difficult to deviate from this path. The evidence for this is quite overwhelming, for, apart from consumer prices, industrial relations also remained off limits. Investing according to profitability ultimately would mean closing down or scaling back many unprofitable enterprises. Such a radical departure would entail, at a minimum, tens of thousands of "socialist transfers"—the retraining and relocation of workers. In 1966–67 this process was due to begin. Those threatened with transfers to new work put up stiff resistance. Coal miners and their managers in Zwickau brought the situation to the edge of revolt. In the face of these prospects, plans to close down certain parts of the coal mine were quickly dropped. Supported by the conservatives in the party, the Central Committee quietly withdrew the entire plan for restructuring the deployment of labor.[70]

Furthermore, the issue of piece rates and wage levels continued to plague SED labor specialists. Despite the relative peace on the shop floor in the years after 1953, in 1960 the trade unions (FDGB) still recorded 166 work stoppages or strikes, due mostly to administrative adjustments in wages or piece rates.[71] After the construction of the Berlin Wall in August 1961, the SED leadership initially considered it safe to raise piece rates and exert downward pressure on wages through an imposed *Produktionsaufgebot* (production levy). Thanks to this, as well as a series of policies designed to "soak up" excess earnings, the relationship between labor productivity and wages improved temporarily.[72] But trade-union reports of 135 strikes in 1961 and 144 strikes in 1962 dashed any possible hopes among SED labor specialists that the Wall would decisively alter industrial relations or working-class attitudes.[73] Within several years, all ground gained had been lost. The Finance Ministry reported in April 1966 that wages were outpacing productivity in seven of eight mining VVBs, three out of five VVBs in metallurgy, and in nine of fourteen in machine building.[74] Considerations by the Council of Ministers toward the end of 1965 and the beginning of 1966 of instituting the five-day workweek, every other week, in what would have simply been a ratification of already spontaneously occurring practices in many enterprises, suggests that labor continued to represent as much of a constraint as a resource.[75]

Despite Ulbricht's determination to concentrate on industrial prices, by

June 1966 the third stage of the price reform was already six months behind schedule. More important, his main economic advisor, Wolfgang Berger, advised him of a further complication: even if the industrial price reform were completed by the new estimated date of January 1, 1967, the new prices would soon be obsolete "if they were not continually kept in harmony with the development of labor productivity and costs."[76] Berger had raised the prickly issue of continual and decentralized price flexibility, a possibility that would certainly be unwelcome in Finance Minister Rumpf's office. But if this were not done, then profit based on prices linked to neither scarcity nor labor productivity would continue to be a poor indicator of enterprise performance.

In retrospect, it seems puzzling that three years into the reform Ulbricht and his reform team had yet to give this crucial aspect of the NES any serious thought. But the quandary is easily understood when one keeps in mind that the reformers had little help from the outside or from countries that had undertaken similar reforms in the past. Furthermore, like other reformers in the history of Communist Eastern Europe, Ulbricht had a very small window of opportunity to act before the reform consensus collapsed both in Moscow and at home. Ulbricht found it necessary, then, to place the implementation of the specific measures of the reform in the hands of officials bound to oppose them and to go ahead with measures well before their implications were fully understood. In this respect, too, Ulbricht's dilemmas appear not unlike those faced by Mikhail Gorbachev twenty-five years later.

This sense of not yet having figured out the reform and things spinning dangerously out of control was reinforced by the Council of Minister's evaluation of the economy for the first half of 1966, which brought very little good news. If the level of production remained constant, the current yearly plan for 1966, the plan for 1967, as well as the *Perspektivplan*, could not be fulfilled. Ulbricht announced at an SED plenum in April that NES had, in fact, not yet been fully introduced and that it would probably take two more years before the "system" was in place.[77] The main trouble areas were construction, export, and technical development. The report predicted that the balance of payments would remain manageable only through decisive intervention to reduce VVB imports. In construction, the plan had to be reduced by 200 to 300 million marks for the next yearly plan, and the reductions needed to be continued for the next 2 to 3 years, which, the Council of Ministers warned, "discredits the entire planning process as well as the directives of the Council of Ministers."[78]

This development, as well as other sobering news from the industrial ministries and the economics departments of the Central Committee, gradually led to increased intervention in the economy at the very moment when some of the more advanced measures of the NES, such as the capital charge, were implemented. The contradictory tendencies in economic thinking could hardly have gone unnoticed. Throughout 1966, for example, Willi Rumpf sustained his resistance to the price reform—implementing the measures as he saw fit, excluding his own reform-oriented deputy minister from important discussions and decisions, as well as holding information back from higher government bodies, including the Politburo and the Perspektivplankommission.[79] He was kept in check through continuous reports to the top by the Central Committee economics departments, especially the Department for Planning and Finance.[80]

The bureaucratic opposition Ulbricht faced during the first several years of the reform, however, did not prevent him from choosing policies that suited him. Notwithstanding many unforeseen technical difficulties, most of the NES measures had been implemented. Despite continued interference in the planning and management of the VVB, many enterprises had become more independent since 1963. But bureaucratic victories did not automatically amount to economic success. Price reform, enterprise autonomy, and the like were means to an end. The primary goal of reform was to overcome the yearly plan mentality that neglected long-range structural changes in technologies and production processes. But try as they might, the designers of the NES had not managed to overcome the short-term perspective of "plan fulfillment." The *Perspektivplan* remained bogged down in endless plan rounds and bureaucratic infighting. Critics of the reform could easily point to its failure to deal with the very problems it set out to address.

In some respects the conservatives were right. Enterprises left to their own devices would not necessarily invest in projects that served the long-term goals of the planners. Here we see the limits of technocratic reform, as well as the gulf between it and market reforms. If the center had dropped its seemingly hopeless long-range plans and simply allowed enterprises to adjust to consumer demand, the reforms might have worked, or at least changed the structure of production. Such an arrangement, however, would no longer be "socialism" in the way that Ulbricht and most of the SED understood it. In such a system, planners and party would no longer be setting production goals and could no longer be sure of output. Ulbricht seems to have picked up on this criticism. At the seventh party congress in April 1967, the appellation "New Economic System" was dropped in favor of the "Economic System of Socialism" (ESS), with the emphasis on "socialism." Under the ESS, the reforms of the previous period were carried forward and even intensified—for example, in the credit system. In those areas, however, where the leadership saw that economic instruments and incentives were not having the desired effect on technological innovation, the planning organs and the ministries stepped in directly. Structurally important projects in the economy were singled out and given special administrative attention and preferential access to supplies and labor.[81]

These so-called structure-determining projects initially received wide support among all groups within the economic elite.[82] Although the reinstitution of tight bureaucratic tutelage over selected projects gave the impression of a return to preform methods, if the number and size of the projects remained modest, there was no reason why enterprise independence could not continue to grow. But easy access to supplies proved to be too strong a temptation to the ministries. The number of structural tasks began to multiply.

Ulbricht's and Mittag's thinking in intensifying structural policy in the summer of 1967 was straightforward. By pouring considerable amounts of resources into selected projects, they hoped to catch up with and overtake the West in several economically important areas. Thus the contradictory sounding strategy of "overtaking without catching up" (*Überholen ohne Einzuholen*), overtaking the West in chemicals, machine building, and electronics before actually catching up with its economy as a whole. With this selective "great leap," so the argument ran, the GDR's labor productivity would increase faster than the West and eventually its living standards could pull ahead as well.

The paradox of the decision to introduce the structure-determining tasks was that, at the very moment when most of the significant bureaucratic obstacles to enterprise autonomy had been lifted, a new force of central direction emerged.[83] As bureaucratic politics took over, and demands of the specific forecasting groups flooded the SPK and the ministries, the percentage of total investment allotted to the structure-determining tasks rose from approximately 26 percent in 1968 to 41 percent in 1969. In several other industries the increase was even more dramatic.[84] Enterprises found themselves increasingly obliged to fulfill centrally handed down orders, while their formal freedoms became increasingly empty for lack of resources or time to meet normal contract obligations.

The East German economy fell victim to its leader's own ambitions. It had become overburdened and brittle, subject to severe shortages when placed under any strain at all. Why is it, we may ask, that Ulbricht failed to see or appreciate the contradiction between intensified central intervention into enterprise decision making, on the one hand, and a deepening decentralization, on the other?[85] Did he not see that political intervention undermined technocratic self-regulation? Although no definitive answer can be given to these questions, we may speculate that given his original reasons for instituting the reform in the first place, Ulbricht had grown weary of waiting for the slow progress promised by the original tenets of the NES. The idea of a great push to propel the country past its rivals found sympathy in the mind of an aging leader who could look back to what must have seemed like simpler days. However far he might have come since 1963, in a very important way Ulbricht remained a product of his formative years as a Stalinist revolutionary.[86]

The Economy and the National Question

In 1968 Ulbricht's old rival and ally, Anton Ackermann, wrote him a ten-page letter on the economy, which amounted to a conservative attack on many of the most cherished assumptions of the reformers. Curiously, although Ackermann wrote "personal" and "confidential" at the top and, although the letter was critical of the NES, Ulbricht decided to circulate the letter among his Politburo colleagues. Ackermann reminded his old comrade that in Socialism "the plan, with the use of the price-value mechanism, is the decisive regulator, and under no circumstances the other way around." He continued, with an attack on several of the "economic levers" of the NES, warning of the dangers inherent in increased social differentiation. "Profits that are the product of assortment or price speculation are extremely harmful. . . . In the present situation, where the class enemy concentrates from outside on discrediting the socialist planned economy, on stimulating 'convergence theory' and the change from a socialist economy to a so-called 'socialist market economy,' must we not wage a struggle, not only against the open but also against hidden forms of this ideological diversion?"[87] Had Ulbricht begun to reconsider his earlier positions and revert back to an earlier way of thinking? Had he passed on the letter to his Politburo colleagues as a tangible sign of this change? The record provides few answers.

Besides troubles in the domestic economy, Ulbricht worried about the political and economic changes underway in Prague. At every level of the economic bureaucracy, the events of spring and summer 1968 across the border had given rise to new fears of marketlike mechanisms devolving into "market socialism." The name Ota Šik, the architect of the Czech "third way," became an official synonym for counterrevolution and was best left out of polite conversation altogether.[88]

Still, if Ulbricht had clearly eliminated the market from the policy repertoire, he had not given up the goal of overtaking the West. The ideals of the reform were not dead, at least not in Ulbricht's mind. The lessons he drew from Prague diverged sharply from those drawn by Brezhnev and other members of his own leadership, for the Prague Spring reinforced in Ulbricht's mind the idea that long-term political stability could only be attained through superior economic performance. Speaking to Soviet Ambassador Abrassimov in March 1969, Ulbricht asserted: "We assume that it is only possible to raise our influence over the working class in West Germany, first by continuing our peace policy and, second, if we prove the superiority of our social system. Part of this is the superiority of our economic system." One month later, Ulbricht wrote Brezhnev before the April 18, 1969, meeting of the Perspektivplankommission, illustrating his continued preoccupation with outperforming West Germany. "Corresponding to the directives of the seventh party congress, we assert that the main task of the *Perspektivplan* in the all-round strengthening of the GDR consists in putting the superiority of our socialist society over that of West Germany to proof. This requires us to overcome the lag in labor productivity, still holding at 20 percent for the last several years. Only in this way can we increase the influence of the GDR over West Germany."[89] Influence over West Germany? What could Ulbricht possibly have meant? Here we have a clue to the connection in Ulbricht's mind between the economic reform and the national question. It appears that he still had the dream of unifying with the West, on his terms, and understood that the only possible way to achieve this goal under socialism was to make socialism appealing, not only to his own population but to the population of the West as well.[90]

Ulbricht's desire to see his "half" nation succeed politically by exceeding his rivals on the economic front explains his continued interest in the petty details of comparison with the West.[91] Such comparisons did not please everyone. They were bound to prove that, given realistic growth rates, the GDR would never catch up to the West and, furthermore, they encouraged comparisons of degree rather than comparisons in kind. A good number of leading officials had come to believe that socialism could not succeed if it evaluated itself by standards set in the West. The day before the Perspektivplankommission meeting on April 18, 1969, for example, Alfred Neumann sent Ulbricht a letter from his weekend house in Liebenburg. His letter illustrates just how far many top officials had evolved in their thinking on economic performance and the national question. Whereas only three years earlier, Neumann argued that "The main question is how does [the policy] affect our economic competition with the West,"[92] now he wrote on comparisons:

I have read much and know of our main economic problems. It is correct from time to time to compare the state of achievement in the GDR with West Germany or with international results. But all these comparisons with the capitalist performance always give rise to an aversion in me which has to do with the doings of Ota Šik. We should really think over politically and ideologically the type and manner of comparison with those capitalist states. Maybe it is better to assume from the outset the advantages of the socialist GDR over other leading capitalist industrial states. I have in mind not only the advantages of the socialist mode of production vis-à-vis the capitalist regimes. . . . I am also against us making such one-sided comparisons with other foreign top achievements as it is often done, expressed as if for two boxers—whoever has the longer reach must win. Whoever has the most plastic per person is the best. If this kind of one-sided argumentation were valid, then the Americans would have long ago won in Vietnam. I am against this kind of comparison of the socialist GDR with the capitalist West Germany. Should we put up the slogan: "The GDR must become better than West Germany in the economic area?" That will not do! That does not fit into our constitution, or our socialist national and state consciousness.[93]

In this passage we see the essentials of the counterreform program and the groundwork for a new set of policies after Ulbricht's departure in 1971. Overtaking the West is no longer a goal; gone are dreams of unification; even the notion of one German people is downplayed and replaced with "socialist national and state consciousness." Ulbricht's strategy of winning over all Germans through superior economic performance is cast aside as a hopeless and dangerous dream.

Neumann, Stoph, Honecker, and others worried that Ulbricht remained so intent on catching up with the West that he would take the country deep into debt in order to buy the necessary equipment. Their suspicion would have been confirmed had they been party to a conversation between Ulbricht and the deputy chairman of the Soviet Council of Ministers, Nikolai Tikhonov on June 25, 1970. When it was already clear that the Soviets would no longer subsidize Ulbricht's programs in any way, he informed a concerned Tikhonov of his logic for accumulating debt in the West:

It is straightforward: We get as much debt with the capitalists, up to the limits of the possible, so that we can pull through in some way. A part of the products from the new plants must then be exported back to where we bought the machines and took on debt. In a short time we must pay for the equipment. . . . We are, therefore, now correcting the lags from the time of open borders. We will make a leap forward, but with exact measurements. We know the plan will be upset by it. Comrade Schürer can not really balance the whole thing. But in interest of the structural policy it was necessary to act the way we did.[94]

Ulbricht's plan, it appears, amounted to little more than what the Polish government tried only a few years later: massive borrowing from the West with the promise of repayment from the profits earned.

Clearly by 1969 Ulbricht had grown either bold or reckless, depending on one's point of view. Whereas earlier he had hesitated to criticize the Soviet Union for what he viewed as too little economic assistance, now he called for open criticism. Whereas earlier Ulbricht had reassured the Soviets and his Politburo colleagues that increasing trade with the West would be balanced by deepening ties with Comecon, now he underlined that trade with the West would increasingly supplant trade with the East. Whereas earlier he had hesitated to place the burden of reform on the population, now he seemed quite ready to do so. And, finally, whereas earlier Ulbricht had not bothered to play up the doctrinal differences between his country and the Soviet Union, now he pompously raised his country's experience to a model for the Soviets to follow.[95]

Ulbricht predicted in 1970 that the next three years would be difficult ones, but was confident that at the end of this period the GDR would have made it over the hump and be competing on a equal footing with the West.[96] Whatever his strategy, Ulbricht never had an opportunity to put his ideas to a full test. During 1969 and 1970, shortages in consumer goods and the energy sector quickly led to mass discontent. The monthly reports of the first secretaries from the various *Bezirke* or regions, starting as far back as early 1969, attest to the growing level of public (as well as official) dissatisfaction with existing economic policy.[97] In Berlin, First Secretary Paul Verner reported incomes far outpacing supplies. In Cottbus, as far back as January 1, 1969, First Secretary Walde complained that the *Strukturpolitik* had placed extraordinary strain on territorial and branch resources.[98] In Dresden, First Secretary Werner Krolikowski implied in his March report that the problems in the economy threatened to undermine the upcoming party elections.[99] Throughout 1970 the central authorities, faced time and again with shortfalls in deliveries, found it necessary to institute *Sonderschichten* (extra shifts) in several branches of the economy, the most essential being machine building, metallurgy, and transportation.[100] With work stoppages and industrial unrest having shaken the foundations of Communist rule in neighboring Poland in December 1970, the GDR's leadership was now forced to consider whether shortages, bottlenecks, and *Sonderschichten* at home might soon lead to the kind of politically charged industrial protest that had not been seen in East Germany since 1953.[101]

The fourteenth SED plenum in December 1970 provided a dramatic public forum opportunity for criticism of Ulbricht's economic policy. But the ground for the December plenum had been prepared well in advance, for the reform consensus had fallen apart. During 1970, Politburo meetings were often long and raucous. Apart from Honecker, Stoph, Neumann, and his other antagonists in the political hierarchy, even some key reform economists at the State Planning Commission had turned against Ulbricht's economic policies.[102] In June 1970, serious questions about the economy were raised at the thirteenth plenum.[103] The culminating moment, however, came in a Politburo meeting on August 25, 1970. The meeting, led by Honecker and conducted in Ulbricht's absence, started off diplomatically enough, but within minutes Honecker had assessed the situation in the economy as tense and called for less "modeling and more strict management." He was followed by Stoph who called for "operational measures." Finally, Alfred Neumann, a man known for his straightforward, honest, and orthodox views, laid out the essentials of the counterreform agenda:

> Everything is disorganized because of the structure-determining tasks. With structure-determining tasks, we also have to consider what will no longer be developed and produced. Structural policy yields growth in some areas. This must, however, lead to a narrowing in other areas. This has not been completely planned and balanced. . . . I can't understand how the system of balances no longer plays any role in the SPK, and in the ministries these departments have been reduced to one or two men. The economic organs are working according to the principle of economic accounting and not according to state and national economic standards.[104]

With these words, the groundwork for recentralization had been laid; "economic accounting" (a market principle) had been contrasted with "national economic standards" (a principle supposedly denoting economic planning). A resolution was drawn up that limited itself to correcting the accumulated disproportions and raising the wages of ordinary working people. In September, it was issued without Ulbricht's approval.[105]

How such an important decision could be issued without Ulbricht's approval can only be understood in light of the increasing self-confidence of his enemies and the support they were receiving from abroad. Honecker and company received a steady stream of advice and encouragement from Brezhnev. Already in July, the Soviet leader let Honecker know of his deep disappointment with Ulbricht's domestic and foreign policy. Only weeks before, Ulbricht had traveled to Moscow and asserted that the GDR deserved the respect of a "genuine German state. . . . We are no Byelorussia, we are no Soviet state." The Soviets now openly acknowledged that they were fed up with Ulbricht's dream of securing East Germany's future by overtaking the West economically, while simultaneously accumulating debt with it. Brezhnev informed Honecker that the Politburo would like to see Ulbricht removed from office and would appreciate being kept informed of events on a day-to-day basis.[106]

Brezhnev resented Ulbricht, not only because the old man held up his country as a model for others, including the Soviet Union, but also because he suspected that Ulbricht was prepared to sacrifice relations with the Soviet Union and the rest of the communist world in order to settle the German question. A letter from Honecker to Ulbricht written after the fourteenth plenum explained quite clearly where the two leaders differed.

> We work with the Soviet Union not just because we possess only a small quantity of raw materials or because we are a small country. We would also cooperate if we were a large country and had sufficient natural resources. The main point is to tell clearly the party and the whole population that our cooperation with the Soviet Union is conducted on the basis of Marxism-Leninism, proletarian internationalism, and that it corresponds to the class interests of everyone in the CMEA [Comecon], the united socialist countries. That is why we take the path of socialist integration. Only from this standpoint can we justify cooperation in all areas. At the same time, we can prove how powerful the possibilities are to further build socialism in the GDR. From this position it is also necessary to conduct the struggle against appearances of a "pull to the West" [*Westdrall*], against the idea of a special relationship between the GDR and the FRG.[107]

With the Soviets dissatisfied on all counts and the SED provincial and district leadership fearful that the economy was headed for the rocks, Ulbricht's rivals in the Politburo felt secure in preparing his ouster. In doing so, they were driven not only by a blind desire to please their Soviet masters, but by the conviction that Ulbricht's economic policies (domestic and foreign) and his implicit vision of a successful socialism, were both unnecessary and unrealistic.[108] By December, the fix was in. At the plenum, Ulbricht's economic policies came under attack from all sides. Willi Stoph warned of accumulating debt to the West. More serious, he argued that Ulbricht's economic plans simply did not make sense. "We cannot set as our goal a leap of 10 percent in labor productivity and production per year without having the real conditions for its fulfillment at hand. . . . This leads to serious disproportions in various branches of the economy and to political complications."[109] Those opposed to the reform for practical reasons could now find common ground with those opposed to it for principled ones. Bureaucratic resistance, so bothersome in the early stages of the reform, had become political opposition.

Over the course of the next several months, Ulbricht lost his power. He was permitted to retain his position as ceremonial head of state and eventually given a newly created and powerless position as "chairman" of the party. But Ulbricht did not leave the historical stage gracefully. During 1970 and 1971 the Politburo had its hands full trying to kick Ulbricht upstairs and head off his attempts to influence personnel and policy. Politburo decrees carefully regulated his work schedule and severely restricted his communication with district first secretaries and other party luminaries around the country.[110] Ulbricht's refusal to leave the political stage and his determination not to be excluded from political life in the manner of Khrushchev were characteristic of a man who had ruled so long, who had survived so much, that he simply could not imagine himself out of power. Perhaps this provides us with a clue as to why Ulbricht refused to move away from his technocratic dream of overtaking the West, even after it was abundantly clear that the Soviets, his own party, and even the East German working class—in short, all three major "interest groups" in East German politics— had little interest in continuing down the bumpy and uncertain road of technocratic reform.

With Ulbricht's departure, dreams of unification based on economic superiority no longer guided policy. The leadership under Honecker moved to a new ruling formula, one that sought to establish a separate GDR identity on the foundation of a qualitatively different socialist life-style from the capitalist West. In the long run, for the new formula to work, not only did the leadership have to give up hopes of catching up with and overtaking the living standards of the West, but the population of East Germany had to as well.[111] Although the "unity of economic and social policy" (the watchword of Ulbricht's successors) stabilized SED rule for a number of years, as we shall see in the next chapter, the idea that economic comparisons with the West could be halted in the minds of the population simply because the leadership willed it was deeply flawed.

Chapter 3 Communism and Capital Markets

We know what motivated Ulbricht. In a conversation with State Planning Commission Chairman Gerhard Schürer during his last year in power, Walter Ulbricht predicted that the GDR would catch up with West Germany sometime between 1977 and 1980. In 1969 he confidently predicted that by 1975 the GDR would be selling computers in the West.[1] He based his forecast on a yearly accumulation-investment rate of between 22 and 30 percent of national income over the next six years. Ulbricht understood and accepted that such impressive rates of investment would necessarily eat into the resources available for consumption. Whereas earlier he had hesitated to call for sacrifice, by the end of the 1960s, not only was Ulbricht prepared to endure the distortions and disproportions that come with unnaturally high rates of investment, he was also ready to place the burden of forced savings more squarely on the shoulders of ordinary East Germans, in the form of higher prices for public transportation, consumer goods, and living accommodations.[2]

But what about his successor Erich Honecker? How did this man, who had played second fiddle for so long, understand the future of socialism in Germany? Like many in the top leadership, Honecker concluded from the difficult years at the end of the 1960s that the long-term stability of the GDR depended not on making his country more powerful economically than West Germany and thus resolving the national question. On the contrary, stability depended on giving up unification, separating his country's political fate from the West, and constructing an appealing socially oriented consumer society based on a realistic assessment of the GDR's economic possibilities. Instead of resolving the national question by surpassing the West German standard of living in the future, Honecker wanted to shore up the regime's legitimacy by raising his country's stature in the international community—made possible after the signing of the Basic Treaty in 1972—and by granting his population a decent standard of living in the present. Gone were Ulbricht's dreams of unifying Germany under socialism. "The GDR is not part of the FRG [Federal Republic of Germany]," Honecker declared in 1973, "and the FRG is not part of the GDR."[3]

Of course, Honecker's choices would entail costs too, and it is these costs that form the subject matter of this chapter. Unwilling to entertain ideas of reform that might complicate or diminish party control over the economy, curtail Communist consumerism, or threaten the welfare state, Honecker settled into a politically pleasing conservative socialism. Such a strategy seemed not only viable but wise, as long as the regime could live off accumulated investments from the Ulbricht era and be kept afloat by Soviet largesse and easy terms on international capital markets. The revolutionary changes in commodity prices and terms of trade during the 1970s, however, rendered such a strategy unworkable. The worldwide recession and credit crunch in the mid-1970s and early 1980s ultimately forced Honecker and his economics chief Günter Mittag to look for ways to improve economic efficiency without sacrificing the ideological and social commitments that constituted the foundation of Honecker's conservative socialism. The response, "the combine reform," appeared to render the planning system more manageable in the short run but, as we shall see, it could not forestall the decay of the capital stock, the rising indebtedness to the West, the decreasing international competitiveness of industry, and, ultimately, falling living standards of ordinary East Germans relative to their counterparts in the West.

Conservative Socialism and Institutional Uniformity

Already before Ulbricht's downfall, Honecker's faction in the Politburo had succeeded in pushing through wage increases for several classes of workers. According to the monthly reports of the regional administrations or *Bezirksleitung* (BL), the increases found a warm reception among the working class during political discussions on the shop floor. But higher wages could not cure shortages; in fact, they exacerbated them. In 1971 shortages of basic goods continued to threaten the smooth flow of party elections at the enterprise level. "Twenty-five years after the end of the war," commented the workers of one Leipzig enterprise in preparation for the local party convention, "there should no longer be any problems in consumer supplies. Too much is being exported and there is nothing left for us."[4] Not surprisingly, when he finally deposed Ulbricht as first secretary just before the eighth party congress in June 1971, one of Honecker's first acts was to reduce the level of investment and import a sizable quantity of food and clothing from the West for direct sale to the public in the major industrial centers of the country.[5]

Beyond these populist measures, Honecker and his faction in the Politburo dismantled the entire technocratic edifice of Ulbricht's New Economic System. Toward the end of 1970, the Council of Ministers issued several resolutions changing the direction of economic policy. This shift can best be termed a deliberate recentralization. For one thing, the resolutions diminished the importance of financial indicators. Higher authorities once again set enterprise manpower levels quantitatively. The bonus fund was disentangled from profit and relinked more firmly with total commodity—that is, physical—output. Over the next several years, the number of production indicators sent down to the enterprises from above rose by at least twofold. Enterprises lost their right to accumulate capital for investment and the procedures for securing credit were (formally) tightened up and recentralized.[6] Price reform was abandoned and, as of January 1971, the Office of Prices and the Council of Ministers once again set the prices for all new goods centrally. Most important, several key members of Ulbricht's economic reform team, including Wolfgang Berger and Herbert Wolf, were removed from positions of power. Others, grateful to have temporarily landed on their feet, kept as low a profile as possible.[7]

It should be noted that Ulbricht's successors were concerned primarily with dismantling the reforms and unseating the reformers. At no point was there a critical discussion of the economic reform itself, what exactly went wrong, or the proper lessons to be drawn from the experience of the 1960s. In this sense, Western academics were correct to describe the GDR's recentralization of the 1970s as "directionless."

Quite apart from policy, the ideology of technocracy, *cybernetics*, came under attack. Here is not the place to examine in detail the rise and demise of cybernetics in East Germany. As already noted, Ulbricht admired cybernetics because he viewed it as a nonmarket solution to the problem of economic and social coordination. Since 1962 he had promoted this new organizational science as a nonthreatening way of conceiving the New Economic System (NES) in doctrinal terms. But despite the relative innocuous (and, to most East Germans, indecipherable) nature of cybernetics, complaints gradually began to emanate from the party apparatus. In his monthly report in January 1969, Paul Verner, the first secretary of the Berlin party organization (and one of Ulbricht's chief antagonists) warned that among students "the impression is growing that cybernetics, operations research, and other similar disciplines take the place of Marxism-Leninism and scientific socialism."[8] Verner's concerns presaged ideology chief Kurt Hager's well-known attack on cybernetics, which was published as an article in the SED's theoretical journal *Einheit* in November 1971: "As important as cybernetics and systems theory are and remain, we cannot allow them to take the place of dialectical and historical materialism, the political economy of socialism, scientific communism, socialist management science." Hager warned of the danger "that the language of this special science is becoming the language of our party," and with it, "the party will cease to be a Marxist-Leninist party."[9]

What these changes in policy and ideology amounted to was a new departure in the SED's thinking on socialism in the modern world. Honecker was determined to tie his country's fate more tightly than ever to the Soviet Union, and in Leonid Brezhnev the new East German leader found a kindred spirit, a man who, like him, sought popularity by raising the living standards of ordinary people without sacrificing his commitment to traditional Stalinist values of state property, centralized control, and a strong military. Like other European socialist leaders, Honecker regularly visited Brezhnev at his vacation home in the Crimea. But the relationship between the two leaders was especially close, cemented as it was by their collaboration in unseating Ulbricht. Honecker owed his political fortune to Brezhnev and, by all accounts, during these visits he sought to please the Soviet leader, to flatter him by asking for fatherly advice on a wide range of questions, and, most important, to assure him that in the GDR the Soviet Union had a steadfast ally.

One way to demonstrate this was to make the GDR's economic structure look even more like the Soviet Union's than it already did. To be sure, a certain amount of institutional uniformity was always expected among the socialist regimes of East Europe. This, after all, was the main reason for the 1968 invasion of Czechoslovakia. Honecker, however, sought to restore a uniformity that had not been seen since the mid-1950s, an era when the East Germans slavishly imitated every minute change in Soviet ideology and organization. Obviously, dismantling Ulbricht's reforms partially contributed to this end. Yet the difficulty in completing the project of institutional standardization stemmed from a peculiarity of East German development, the continued presence of over 11,000 small and medium-sized private and semiprivate enterprises (the latter were referred to as "enterprises with state participation").

Unlike the Soviet Union, with its confusing array of federal, republican, and local enterprises, East Germany possessed a relatively simple industrial structure. Eleven industrial ministries controlled the vast majority of productive assets, with the remainder of production divided among smaller enterprises that were subordinated to provincial and district councils. In 1971, however, East Germany's private and semiprivate enterprises still employed 470,000 people, accounted for 11.3 percent of production in the GDR and, according to East German efficiency expert Harry Meier, constituted the "secret weapon" of the economy.[10] These small, highly flexible enterprises produced specialty machines and consumer goods on short order for large state enterprises and for direct export to the West. To the extent that East German industry remained internationally competitive at all, it was due in large measure to the goods produced in this sector.

The SED derived political as well as economic benefit from the retention of the traditional German *Mittelstand*. In the fifteen years prior to Honecker's ascendancy, the East German elite presented the *Mittelstand* as proof of the diverse social coalition on which power was supposedly based in the GDR. Most of the owners belonged to one of the bourgeois bloc parties, the Christian Democratic Union (CDU), the National Democratic Party (NDPD), and the Liberal Democratic Party (LDPD), which, nominally at any rate, represented their interests in the national parliament. Of course, control remained a concern. To this end, a rigorous tax policy as well as a comprehensive system of police surveillance prevented these remnants of the old order from turning their control over productive assets into political power. One did not get rich or become influential as a businessman in East Germany. More important, as the appellation "semiprivate" indicates, since the late 1950s, most privately owned enterprises had taken on the state as a partner and, over the years, the total portion of state ownership had increased; by 1972, the average state ownership in semiprivate enterprise amounted to 70 percent. Most owners welcomed this arrangement because partial state ownership guaranteed access to capital and more favorable treatment within the state-controlled supply system.[11]

As objectively convenient as this arrangement might have been to both regime and entrepreneur, the twin political and economic crises of the late Ulbricht years tilted the balance of those in favor of getting rid of these capitalist remnants. During 1969 SED first secretaries from various *Bezirke* (regions) filed a series of complaints, too well coordinated and timed to have been coincidental, about the behavior of semiprivate enterprises. First, the

Bezirk secretaries complained that semiprivate enterprises, because they could pay illegally high wages for overtime and extra work, drew labor away from the state sector. This competition for labor, in turn, drove up wages illegally in all sectors.[12] Second, under Ulbricht's reform, especially in its latter stages, the legal capacity of all enterprises, semiprivate included, to accumulate profits for investment reduced the capacity of the state to control production profiles through selective access to capital. Instead, the semiprivate firms structured their production to maximize profit which, after all, was the purpose of the reform.[13] Finally, and most distastefully to the provincial barons, semiprivate enterprises supposedly booked profits out of proportion to their productive contribution to the economy as a whole.[14]

In December 1970, the SED and the Council of Ministers responded to these complaints with a new decree raising taxes for nonstate enterprises. But one year later planning chief Gerhard Schürer gave a speech to the fourth SED plenum in which he claimed that the problem had yet to be adequately addressed. Many private craftsmen and enterprise owners, noted Schürer, "still attain an income significantly higher and, to some extent, rising faster than the income of comparable groups in the economy." Of course, Schürer's own confidential reports to the Politburo on entrepreneurial incomes, which showed that they were largely "earned" and usually no higher than that of directors in comparable state enterprises, received no mention.[15] Instead, he suggested that the party establish "the conditions so that in the course of the five-year plan . . . the process of socioeconomic rearrangement be carried out to the benefit of socialist development for the strengthening and enlargening of nationalized property [Volkseigentum]." This rather arcane phraseology may sound like typical "party Chinese" to the untrained ear, but to Erich Honecker it was pure music. Barely able to restrain himself, the record notes that Honecker responded to Schürer's suggestions by blurting out, "For overcoming the capitalists!," to which the audience replied "quite right!"[16] The nationalization of the remaining semiprivate firms had now formally been put on the agenda.

Although the SED justified the 1972 nationalizations as an economic necessity, Honecker's uncharacteristic enthusiasm at the fourth plenum provides us with the first indication that the motives for nationalization were political and not economic.[17] The manner in which the SED executed the nationalizations provides the second clue. The official order for nationalization came down in a Politburo decree of February 8, 1972. According to the decree, the nationalization was slated to occur gradually, only after thorough discussions with the concerned parties and a series of test runs in the Apolda district.[18] Soon, however, the entire program devolved into a campaign. Local party organizations competed with each other for the honor of being the first to complete the nationalization in their respective districts. Owners were brought into local councils and forced to sign over their property after being informed that their compensation would be deposited in special accounts from which only a small fraction of the total sum could be withdrawn annually. By July, the "knockout" of the *Mittelstand*, as one historian has put it, was largely complete. Apart from some token resistance, the nominal representatives of the owners, the CDU, NDPD, and LDPD, proved worse than useless. None of the leaders of these organizations protested and, in at least one case (the LDPD), they used the nationalizations to have a portion of the seized property transferred to their own organization.[19]

Honecker's communication with Brezhnev on the matter indicates an unusual degree of Soviet interest in wiping out semiprivate ownership in East Germany. Here we find the most compelling proof that the nationalizations had more to do with Honecker's drive for institutional standardization than anything else. In his memoirs, the former head of the LDPD, Manfred Gerlach, notes that in January 1972 Honecker informed the bloc party chairmen that the impetus for the nationalizations came from Moscow, which, while understanding the peculiarities of the GDR, saw in these enterprises a preservation of capitalism "that could become a danger for the system."[20] Whether Honecker said this in order to demonstrate to the bloc party chairmen that the nationalizations were inevitable ("Once Moscow wants something, it is useless to oppose it"), and thus make his own position more palatable, remains unclear. Given Honecker's enthusiasm, it is safe to say that he and Brezhnev saw eye to eye on the matter. Whatever the line of causality, on July 18, 1972, Honecker sent Brezhnev a letter thanking him for his interest in the GDR and including an extended report on the nationalization campaign. Its tone is unusual for communication between the SED and the Soviets, indicating more than anything else the completion of an assigned or mutually agreed upon task:

Time and again we confirm with happiness that, despite your great burden of work as general secretary of the Central Committee of the CPSU, you constantly devote a great deal of attention to the development of socialism in the GDR. It is pleasant for me to inform you, as assigned by the Politburo of the Central Committee of our party, that, as is evident from the included information, the transformation of the enterprises with state participation, the private enterprises, and the industrial cooperatives of craftsmen into state enterprises has been successfully completed.[21]

As we shall see, the destruction of the semiprivate enterprises and their full integration into the operations of larger industrial units contributed in no small way to the economic decay of the GDR in the 1970s and 1980s.

Despite some hard feelings among the old *Mittelstand*, little serious resistance to their integration into the state sector could be expected from this group. The same could not be said from the economic bureaucracy. Although they did not oppose the nationalizations, economic officials, especially those in the planning organs, understood that such a move marked the end of any distinctive German path to socialism. Fearing resistance to a reimposition of Stalinism in a "purer" form from leftover reformist elements in the Planning Commission, Willi Stoph laid down the law at the end of March 1972, in a meeting of the Council of Ministers. Stoph argued, first, that planners should cease spending so much time on long-range forecasting. Instead, they should get on with their real job, the tried and tested methods of monthly and yearly planning and balancing. No matter what the actual results, the five-year plan would in any case be adjusted to make it feasible. In returning long-range plans to their position as symbolic rather than working documents, Stoph laid to rest one of the key parts of East German reform economics and started the bureaucracy down the road of economic self-delusion.

His second criticism of the planners was more subtle but, in its own way, equally important. Stoph declared that he was uncomfortable with several aspects of economic discourse as it had evolved in the GDR, especially the use of the term "satisfaction of buying power" (*Kaufkraftabschöpfung*), which simply referred to the common concern among financial planners that enough desirable goods be available to prevent income being squirreled away for a day when something really worth buying appeared, thus forestalling hidden or latent inflation.[22] In turning planners' attention away from consumption and back to production, Stoph was reinforcing orthodox "physical output" orientations over reformist "financial" ones. This otherwise trivial attempt to restrict the language of internal bureaucratic discourse reflected a general concern at the top that the economic and social program might encounter resistance from the very officials charged with implementing it.

Economic Ideology and the Costs of *Sozialpolitik*

Honecker's main interest in the economy was in the sphere of social policy. The consensus among former SED officials is that Honecker's vision of socialism was shaped by his experience with poverty and party work in the late Weimar period. Socialism thus meant guaranteed shelter, clothing, and food; other "needs," by definition, were superfluous. Doctrinally, because of the peculiarities of German history, East German social policy was particularly interesting. In the 1950s the SED still considered *Sozialpolitik* to be a West German remnant of Bismarck's Germany, totally superfluous in a socialist state where, by definition, workers receive protection from the vagaries of the market. Only in the late 1960s did SED theorists begin discussing the matter and, in a fascinating dialectical twist, came up with an idea that appealed especially to the disaffected members of Ulbricht's Politburo—not only can there be a *Sozialpolitik* under socialism, but only under socialism can it be said to exist at all.[23]

Western scholars agree with their East German counterparts that the social turn in East Germany began with the eighth SED party congress in June 1971, Honecker's first as head of the party. Starting in 1972, the SED raised pensions, reduced the number of mandatory hours in the work week, rolled back apartment rents below the already paltry one mark per square meter, and introduced fairly impressive systems of day care, child support, and maternity leave. When discussing economic policy, Honecker referred to it as "the main task" (*Hauptaufgabe*) but, after 1976, was always careful to follow it with the expression "in its unity of economic and social policy," a qualification that in effect promised the population that production increases and higher standards of living went together.[24] In 1976 the SED initiated a massive housing program with the goal of building three million apartments over the next fifteen years. The SED had taken on the task, in its own words, of "solving the housing question as a social problem," and comparisons were frequently drawn to the situation in the larger American and West European cities. Finally, the cornerstone of social policy became the comprehensive subsidization of costs for a wide range of basic goods, such as food, apartments, and children's clothing. Whereas in 1970 subsidies amounted to 8 billion marks per year, by 1988 it had climbed to an astronomical 53 billion marks per year and, as we shall see shortly, became sacrosanct—a policy whose alteration could not be seriously considered.[25] By identifying all of the measures as essential parts of "the unity of economic and social policy," Honecker was effectively taking what he considered to be a condition of stable SED rule and raising it to a matter of principle.

It is worth noting that well before the SED publicly announced the specific provisions of the social policy in the middle of 1972, the State Planning

Commission (SPK) submitted a lengthy paper to the Politburo in January arguing that the GDR simply could not afford a welfare program as ambitious as the one proposed by Honecker. The effect, the paper argued, would be increasing indebtedness to the West and a ballooning domestic monetary overhang, as well as declining rates of capital accumulation. The SPK proposed an alternative, more modest social program that promised to pay off most of the debt to the West by 1975. The paper was discussed during the January 7, 1972, Politburo meeting. Planning Chairman Schürer immediately came under attack. Hermann Axen, SED Foreign Department head, argued that the paper put into question the resolutions of the eighth party congress. Of course, it was right to be concerned about the debt, Axen argued, but was it not possible "to get long-term credit and to find other countries besides the FRG from which to borrow?" Other Politburo members reacted less politely. Paul Verner was angry that the SPK report had circulated widely in the party. Honecker stated flatly that SPK was "making propaganda" and criticized it for concentrating so heavily on the debt question.[26]

Whether out of a sense of duty to his office or concern for the long-run viability of his country, Schürer pressed on with his concerns in the Politburo for two more months, until March 1972, when the social program was publicly unveiled. He also continued to present two alternative five-year plans, one more realistic but with lower production and consumption, the other with higher production and consumption but with rising debt. In the end, his colleagues chose the second variant. Schürer warned that "this will mean living with a hole," but was merely told to cease "sowing panic" and instructed that there was to be no more discussion of the matter. Schürer complied for the time being.[27]

In his public rhetoric, of course, Honecker sought to strike a balance between consumption and production. Lower levels of investment and a labor force that had been shrinking since the mid-1960s meant that growth would increasingly depend on a better utilization of the existing factors of production and technical progress—what socialist theoreticians called "intensification." At the tenth party congress in 1981, Honecker spelled out the "strategy of intensification" in ten doctrinal principles. The list is rather typical of Honecker's public statements on the economy.

1. A new stage has been reached in the connection between socialism and the scientific-technological revolution, which has become the main source of growth and efficiency.
2. Labor productivity must grow faster than production.

3. A more rational use of raw materials, energy, recycled materials, and equipment.

4. Higher standards of quality in production.

5. Raising the efficiency of labor.

6. Comprehensive intensification.

7. Concentration of investment on rationalization.

8. Increasing the production of consumer goods on the basis of inputs produced at home or imported from other East bloc countries.

9. The growth of production and national income with the help of "qualitative growth factors."

10. Intensification of production becomes the determining signature of the planned economy.[28]

Clearly such a "strategy" was more of a wish list than a path to its attainment. Ulbricht's strategy, after all, envisaged many of the same goals. One is, in fact, unavoidably struck by Honecker's clearly articulated and quickly implemented social welfare policies, especially compared with his vague economic formulations. This was no accident. Unlike Ulbricht, who had been involved in East German industrial and agricultural planning at every stage and relished debate over the smallest of details, Honecker remained until the end a dilettante in economic matters, notwithstanding his commitment to social policy. Before becoming first secretary in 1971, Honecker had spent his entire career until that point in political and security matters, making his real mark as head of the Communist youth league, the FDJ (Freie Deutsche Jugend), the East German equivalent of the Soviet Komsomol. Most evidence suggests that Honecker was bored with the economics of production. He considered it a no-win policy realm (unlike the high-profile prospects of international diplomacy) and, for the most part, preferred to leave planning and management in the hands of a few chosen favorites, the most prominent one being Economics Secretary Günter Mittag.

Over the course of the 1970s, Mittag and his team tinkered with the economy. Certain production indicators and producer prices were altered. Several programs for increasing the uptime of imported machinery were introduced. None of these measures, however, dealt with the system-determined problems of enterprise behavior. Enterprises continued to hoard labor and materials and seek soft plans. Plan fulfillment continued to be delayed due to shortages in small amounts of critical supplies. Capital continued to be spent too broadly and construction times too dragged out.[29]

The first half of the 1970s was nevertheless probably the best period of the GDR's history. Apart from its successes in attaining diplomatic recogni-

Table 3-1. GDR Trade with USSR, 1970–1977 (in billions of valuta marks)

Year	Imports	Exports	Balance
1970	8.2	7.3	−0.09
1971	8	8.1	0.2
1972	8	9.6	1.6
1973	8.6	9.9	1.3
1974	10.1	10.2	−0.02
1975	14	12.4	−1.6
1976	15.1	13.1	−2.1
1977	17.1	14.4	−2.8

Source: Jochen Bethkenhagen, "Entwicklung der Wirtschaftsbeziehungen zur Sowjet-union," in Hans-Adolf Jacobsen, ed., *Drei Jahrzehnte Außenpolitik der DDR* (Munich: Oldenbourg, 1979), 391.

tion, the SED could also point to expanding personal consumption and basic improvements in the overall quality of life for most East Germans. All economies have inefficiencies, and the inefficiencies of the Soviet type might not have been so fatal were it not for the economic and political crises of the late 1970s. In particular, the delayed twin oil shocks of 1973 and 1979 and rising prices for other imported commodities, a world recession starting in 1974, and increased armaments spending after 1975 all contributed to a decrease in the GDR's export earnings relative to its import requirements. As table 3-1 shows, after years of relatively balanced trade, in the mid-1970s the GDR began to run large deficits with its most important trading partner, the Soviet Union. More ominously, as table 3-2 indicates, in the same period the GDR's trade imbalance with its most important Western trading partner, West Germany, began to grow. The numbers in both these tables are far from perfect but they do demonstrate the trend. Perhaps most telling, after 1976 the GDR stopped publishing separate import and export totals and issued only aggregate trade figures. East German industries needed imports from the West, and the leadership continued to import large quantities of Western goods to satisfy consumer demand, part of the now explicit social contract. Under these conflicting pressures, net indebtedness to the West during the second half of the 1970s increased by more than 20 percent annually.[30]

Table 3-2. GDR Trade with West Germany, 1961–1976 (in millions of Deutsche marks)

Year	Exports	Imports	Balance
1961	941	837	68
1962	914	853	62
1963	1,022	860	163
1964	1,027	1,151	−124
1965	1,260	1,206	54
1966	1,345	1,625	−280
1967	1,264	1,483	−219
1968	1,440	1,432	7
1969	1,656	2,272	−616
1970	1,996	2,416	−420
1971	2,319	2,449	−180
1972	2,381	2,927	−546
1973	2,660	2,998	−338
1975	3,250	3,671	−419
1975	3,342	3,922	−580
1976	3,877	4,269	−392

Source: Horst Lambrecht, "Entwicklung der Wirtschaftsbeziehungen zur Bundesrepublik Deutschland," in Hans-Adolf Jacobsen, ed., *Drei Jahrzehnte Außenpolitik der DDR* (Munich: Oldenbourg, 1979), 466.

The Debt Crisis

Some turning points in history, such as wars and revolutions, are dramatic, others much less so but nonetheless important. Quiet changes in policy do not always make headlines, but they often bring about the events on which we eventually cast our brightest analytical light. Such is the case with East Germany's international debt. If under Ulbricht the primary challenge to East Germany's leaders came from the working class and the debate over economic reform, during Honecker's tenure the most formidable challenge came from the GDR's precarious position in the international political economy. Whereas European Communists originally desired to avoid contact with capitalism altogether, over time nearly every Communist regime found it necessary to deepen and multiply such contacts. The GDR was no exception, since it relied both on Western capital markets to borrow money and on Western product markets to buy and sell an increasing portion of its goods. Contact and interdependence with capitalism, however, ultimately entailed a degree of economic competition that brought the viability of Honecker's social policies into question.

The irony is that the first bad news came not directly from the West but from the GDR's Soviet allies, who were beginning to feel their own vulnerability on international markets. In spring 1974, less than two years after Honecker initiated his social program, the Soviets informed the SED Politburo that, due to skyrocketing prices for raw materials on world markets, a series of price increases would soon come into effect. As an importer of raw materials, in practice this meant that East Germany would be expected to deliver more finished products to the Soviet Union for the same or less raw materials. The Politburo took up the issue in earnest on August 9, 1974. Mittag reported that the matter demanded careful attention because it could easily affect the living standard of ordinary East Germans. Honecker, hearing this, retorted that there was no need for panic, but declared emphatically that under no circumstances could the Politburo permit external changes to affect living standards. "Otherwise," he noted, "we can all resign immediately, and naturally *that* is something we don't want to do."[31]

In the end, the minicrisis was settled through high-level negotiations. The Soviets and East Germans agreed to higher prices if the increases could be phased in over a five-year period and funded on the basis of credits amortized over twenty years. It is interesting to note, however, that before signing off in December 1974, Honecker let Brezhnev know that he did not believe this decision to be in the interest of the GDR. In his letter to Brezhnev, Honecker reminded the Soviet leader that Soviet support for the East German welfare state was essential because the Basic Treaty had increased contacts between citizens of the two German states. Indeed, the numbers of visitors from the Federal Republic and West Berlin nearly tripled between the years 1971 and 1973. "Under the conditions of mass visitation of the GDR by citizens of the FRG," Honecker noted, "we believe it necessary to solve a whole range of social questions (increasing pensions, raising the minimum wage, promoting families, help in child care, speeding up the construction of apartments, hospitals, schools)."[32]

If the debt in the East remained a matter of mutual flexibility, debt to the West required a kind of adaptation that challenged the essence of Honecker's ruling formula. In fact, the story of the GDR's debt to the West offers an interesting vantage point from which to view responses and nonresponses to economic crises. Whereas Ulbricht was sharply rebuked for daring to run a hard-currency debt with the West as high as 2.2 billion marks in 1970, by 1975 the debt load had increased to 11 billion, by 1980 to 25.3 billion, by 1985 to 30 billion, and by the time the Wall fell to over 46 billion marks.[33] As students of American politics know, it requires a good deal of political ingenuity to keep such an important issue off the political agenda. Avoiding discussion of the matter in weekly Politburo meetings was no mean feat. Yet, by all accounts, Honecker and Mittag managed to do this. Questions of fundamental economic policy were hardly ever discussed in Politburo meetings and, when they were discussed, this occurred only after careful preparation of materials by a "small circle" in which the line was decided. According to the former first secretary of Berlin, Günter Schabowski, the Politburo actually debated very few substantive issues. When the question of exports, imports, and debt came up, it was more a matter of information than discussion.[34]

Honecker and Mittag deflected discussion of their country's rising debt through a combination of political intimidation, institutional engineering, and a measure of good luck. True, in addition to Schürer, several leading officials warned of rising indebtedness to the West. In early 1972, for example, as the new social program was being discussed in the Politburo, president of the Staatsbank, Grette Wittkowski, added her voice to Schürer's, but received little outside support. Werner Krolikowski, brought in temporarily as Central Committee economics secretary in 1973, drew up a secret report in April of the same year, outlining the growing disproportion between the rate of consumption and investment. Upon showing the report to Honecker, however, the first secretary responded with his usual epithet, calling him a "panic monger," ordering him to destroy every copy of the report and, thereafter, marginalized him from economic decision making.[35]

In 1977 Schürer once again attempted to sound the alarm on debt, this time in collaboration with Mittag. In the six years since the eighth party congress, he warned, hard-currency debt had increased fivefold. He advised that measures be taken immediately to decrease the rate of debt accumulation. Again, however, Honecker responded with a firm "no." Any such moves might affect price stability or some other aspect of the social policy, a result unacceptable to the party at large as well as the population. As his response to Schürer demonstrates, raising prices or scaling back the social program undermined the position Honecker had staked out for himself, in contrast to Ulbricht.

We can't change our entire policy from one day to the next. What is suggested [by Schürer] means deep changes in policy. We'll have to step up before the Central Committee and say—we didn't foresee, or we lied to you. . . . In [Schürer's] material it looks as if the policy after Ulbricht was wrong [*falsch gemacht*], as if Ulbricht didn't do anything wrong and

Honecker has? What should our policy have been? The policy of raising prices would have solved nothing. . . . It also says that the deficit came about because of import surpluses between 1971 and 1975. So, now everyone is going to say, before there were no debts. Honecker made the debts.[36]

Despite the logic of Schürer's position and the force of his analysis, by June 1977 Stoph, Krowlikowski, and Verner all sided with Honecker. In retrospect, it seems surprising that the 1977 exchange did not cost Schürer his job.

Even the Soviets cautioned Honecker that the maximum debt burden his economy could possibly live with was 6 billion hard-currency marks.[37] But by 1979 the GDR owed over 39 billion marks and the accounts receivable were primarily to countries of the second and third world that shared the common trait of being unable or unwilling to pay their debts. Throughout the 1970s, critics in and around the top leadership repeated their warnings that the GDR's productive capacity was simply inadequate to support Honecker's social program.

By the end of the decade, the debt could no longer be ignored. The background material for a Politburo resolution of June 27, 1980, declared that, even with increased exports, the GDR was no longer capable of servicing the interest on its debt. Interest payments alone were higher than yearly hard-currency export earnings. More troubling is that, unlike Poland, whose otherwise larger debt was increasingly spread out among two consortiums of Western governments and banks, East Germany's debt remained overwhelmingly in the hands of several hundred Western banks, who were less willing and able to grant easy terms of repayment.[38] If for some reason capitalist banks refuse to increase the GDR's credit line, the background report warned, in a very few months the GDR would be insolvent and, more ominously, be forced to halt all imports from the West. As we shall see, this day would come a mere two years later.[39]

Yet despite these warnings, Honecker still managed to keep the topic off the Politburo agenda. One way he did this was to route all economic decision making through an appointed economic commission of the Politburo. Formed in November 1976 and headed by Mittag, its members (about thirty-five in number) were made familiar with the real size of the debt and given responsibility for dealing with the crisis. A further method of depoliticizing the debt was to set up a special organization whose sole task it was to gather as much hard currency as possible. This assignment was given to Alexander Schalck-Golodkowski, who ran an agency called "Commercial

Coordination," a shadowy and highly secretive body charged with finding ways of raising hard currency outside the official foreign trade channels and often in violation of Western-imposed trade restrictions. Schalck reported directly to Mittag and Honecker, bypassing the Politburo altogether.[40]

Although Schalck enjoyed remarkable success in devising new, if sometimes ethically questionable, methods of shoring up the GDR's hard-currency reserves, he fought an uphill battle. The combined effect of the oil shocks and world recession was to reduce the hard-currency intake per mark spent on production for export to the West from 0.536 valuta marks in 1970 to 0.454 valuta marks in 1980.[41] In other words, the GDR had to export 20 percent more goods to the West just to keep even.

Within the central organs, the first panicky meetings about the debt took place toward the end of 1978. In consulting with Schürer on the contents of his speech to the ninth SED plenum in December, Honecker advised the planning chief to highlight the difficulties caused by the price changes within Comecon and that the speech should make quite clear the differences in oil prices from ten years earlier. Honecker wanted Schürer to discuss the reasons for new measures designed to save foreign currency, including a strict regime of import licensing and efforts to substitute domestic and Comecon production for goods usually purchased in the West. Becoming uncharacteristically excited, he blurted out, "the sociopolitical program is to be implemented exactly as it has been decided and not piled up higher. In supplying the population, we are certain of stable retail prices. It should be emphasized what this costs us in 1970 compared with the situation in 1979. . . . In no country are needs completely satisfied; that comes only under [full] communism. Satisfying all needs today, that will not happen!"

At the enterprise level, it is more difficult to pinpoint a date when the balance-of-trade crisis began to show its pernicious effect. In 1979, however, one finds a pattern of alarmed reports from the party apparatus.[42] According to the Berlin regional party office, in September shortages threatened the fulfillment of production goals for the "socialist competition" in honor of the GDR's thirtieth anniversary.[43] In Dresden, rumors of price increases for gasoline and other consumer goods spread quickly as the leadership scrambled to reassure the local party activists of the regime's commitment to a stable price policy.[44] Reporting to the tenth SED plenum in 1979, Foreign Trade Minister Gerhard Beil admitted that "compensating for the burden on the economy due to the price development of raw materials can no longer be done on the basis of increasing exports."[45] And finally, at the eleventh SED plenum in December 1979 Honecker spoke on the subject with unusual semipublic candor. "In fulfilling the plan for 1980, mastering the problems of foreign trade will play a decisive role. It is necessary to evaluate thoroughly the experience of the past, especially of 1979. This year, far more than in the past, we have been occupied with questions of our foreign economic relations, securing needed imports, fulfilling the export plan and the requirements of the balance of payments." Honecker predicted that in the year ahead the GDR would confront continual shortfalls in imports, which would put the country "in a difficult position."[46]

Debt and the Polish Crisis

The SED leader could hardly have missed the paradox. In unseating Ulbricht, Honecker had tied his fate to the Soviet Union, but it was Soviet unwillingness to underwrite his social program that contributed in no small part to the mounting debt. In the context of this slowly building crisis, we find the first signs of a subtle but noticeable shift in Honecker's thinking about his relations with the West. The shift was subtle because in matters of foreign policy the GDR continued to mimic the Soviet line in almost every matter. The keen observer, however, could easily perceive a distinct difference in Moscow's and East Berlin's reactions to such an important matter as the NATO two-track decision to deploy Pershing and Cruise missiles. Whereas the Soviet propaganda machine heated up for a long-term "peace offensive," the official SED line was to express regret at the West German decision. Throughout 1979 and 1980, both Honecker and Mittag expressed their hopes that good trade relations could be sustained even through times of international tension.[47] The culmination of this minisplit between Moscow and East Berlin over the Euromissles came during summer 1984, when the planning for a historic visit by Honecker to West Germany was already well underway. In Moscow the Soviet Politburo (now lead by Konstantin Chernenko) told Honecker and other visiting SED Politburo members in no uncertain terms that such a visit would not occur in the near future. Under the circumstances, Honecker had no choice but to postpone the trip indefinitely.[48]

Even before the showdown over the state visit, however, the Soviet leadership was quick to react to minute changes in orientation on economic questions. In March 1979, on a trip to Moscow, Schürer met with Soviet Premier Tikhonov. After some time, Tikhonov asked the translators to leave the room, so he could talk with Schürer face to face. Immediately, the Soviet premier told Schürer of the CPSU's concerns of "weakening economic cooperation" between the GDR and the Soviet Union. Armed with five pages of cases, he used as his prime example secret negotiations between the East

Germans and the French (of which, naturally, the Soviets had gotten wind) for the purchase of Citroën automobiles as limousines for the highest GDR officials. To those not familiar with the Communist elites, it may seem odd that Tikhonov chose such a trivial matter as several dozen automobiles to illustrate the importance of the CPSU's worries. After all, a "weakening" of trade ties should imply much more. In the Communist world, however, more than any other perquisite or privilege, cars were a sign of status, and status was all-important. Where one chose to purchase the signs of ultimate status indicated one's loyalties.[49]

It is in the context of the conflicting imperatives of economic support from the West and political support from the East that the GDR's behavior during the Polish crisis is to be understood. On the one hand, Honecker and company had an immediate interest in quashing Solidarity. During 1980 and 1981, Poland ceased to meet its trade obligations with the GDR, as the series of strikes in Polish coal mines under Solidarity's leadership brought Poland's coal industry to a grinding halt. It is understandable, then, that of all East bloc leaders, Honecker was the most vociferous supporter of a quick and decisive Warsaw Pact invasion to restore traditional party rule and, although Honecker considered the political threat presented by Solidarity to be paramount, he could scarcely have ignored the economic dimension. Energy imports constituted an irreplaceable element of the GDR's economy. On the other hand, Honecker was determined to prevent the Polish crisis from damaging relations with the West, and throughout 1980 and 1981 he made several attempts to let the West German government know that the relationship could continue to develop despite the most serious crisis in Eastern Europe since 1968.[50]

The game of pleasing both East and West became far more complicated than Honecker might have liked. He ran the real risk of pleasing neither the West Germans, whose appreciation for the SED general secretary was always limited, nor the Soviets, who expected East Germany to be the most loyal of allies. But if Honecker worried about a potential spread of the Polish crisis to the East German population, he must have also been heartened by the extent to which it reconfirmed his value in the eyes of the Soviet leadership, thus bolstering his own position at home. During 1980, East Germany's rising debt to the West led to critical discussions among the pro-Moscow members of the SED Politburo, those very members who had brought Honecker to power in the first place. Council of Ministers Chairman Stoph, his deputy Krolikowski, the head of the armed forces Heinz Hoffmann, and the state security chief Erich Mielke worried that Honecker talked a good anti–West German line, but in fact the GDR was becoming more economically and thus politically dependent on the West with every passing month. In fact, they were right. Honecker had decided on a more Western-oriented economic policy and on the occasions that he took a hard line on relations with West Germany, such as his speech at Gera in 1980 when he demanded diplomatic recognition from the West, it amounted more to a political tranquillizer for Moscow than a reliable guide to future practice.[51] But even with reports of Honecker's double-dealing in hand, the Soviet leadership did not waver in its support.[52] Satisfied with a promise from Honecker during a visit to the Crimea in summer 1981 that the GDR would reduce its debt to the West by half before 1985 and incur no further debts from the Soviet Union, Brezhnev hesitated to criticize the East German leader at a time when the Soviet Union needed his help and support in dealing with a far more dangerous situation in Poland.[53] Without Soviet support, Honecker's potentially troublesome fellow Politburo members lacked the power and courage to move against him.

Yet if Honecker remained a trusted ally, Soviet actions during the Polish crisis drove the GDR into the hands of Western creditors more quickly than ever. Honecker probably found it somewhat distasteful to have to cozy up so closely to Western financial institutions. He had always profited politically by turning his country to the East. But by 1981, the Soviets were no longer in a position to do what they had always done when necessary—bail out the SED. In 1953 to finance the new course, in 1958 after the events in Poland and Hungary had adversely affected the GDR's foreign trade, and again in 1960 when the SED faced mass emigration and a threatened cutoff of trade with West Germany, the Soviets had stood by the SED leadership with credits and extra deliveries at every turn.[54] Now, not only would the Soviets no longer help the GDR through this latest foreign trade crisis, they made matters worse. At the end of August 1981, Brezhnev informed Honecker that, as a result of three consecutive poor harvests, the CPSU leadership saw no other choice but to reduce oil supplies to the GDR by almost two million tons annually. In the next several weeks East German officials scrambled to convince the Soviets to change their decision. Honecker wrote Brezhnev, pleading with him to reconsider. The letter clearly shows that the national question remained open in Honecker's mind no matter how often he publicly denied it. The reduction in oil deliveries, Honecker warned, "undermines the foundation of the GDR's existence."[55] Whether Honecker reflected on the irony of this statement—that the continued existence of his country depended on the delivery of a mere two million tons of oil per year—is a question probably best left for psychohistorians to answer.

Quite apart from the psychological dimension, Honecker did have very practical reasons to be extraordinarily distraught over the Soviet decision. Since the first oil shock in 1973, a significant portion of the GDR's hard-currency income came from the reexport to the West of Soviet oil purchased at prices well below world market levels. This source of easy foreign income, furthermore, constituted a growing portion of overall hard-currency receipts. Even more painfully, since the mid-1970s the GDR had invested over a billion hard-currency marks in imported equipment for oil refineries, thinking that even if the Soviets raised prices for their oil, they would do so at a rate less than that of the world market. Cuts in Soviet oil deliveries meant that, if the East Germans wished to avoid the shortfall, they would have to do it in hard currency. Otherwise, such a large investment in foreign equipment would have been misspent. It is thus easy to understand that, whereas every other country in the East bloc gave its immediate, if reluctant, approval for the cuts in deliveries, Honecker refused.

Brezhnev responded by sending a delegation from Gosplan to East Germany, led by its chief Nikolai Baibakov, to discuss the matter with his counterpart Gerhard Schürer. Baibakov informed Schürer that the answer they had received from Honecker was not "the answer they expected" and Baibakov's job was not to discuss "whether" but "how" the GDR would manage with less Soviet oil. Over the course of the meeting the discussion became increasingly impassioned. Schürer, a man usually not inclined to stray far from technical matters, told Baibakov: "I assume that a healthy, stable, socialist GDR plays an important role in the strategic thinking of the USSR. Imperialism stands right at the door of our house with its hate on three television channels. Now we have the counterrevolution in Poland at our backs. If the stability were endangered here, it could not be restored with 3.1 million tons of fuel."[56] Under these circumstances, Schürer advised Baibakov that the GDR would have no choice but to incur an additional $3.5 billion of debt by 1985, which would violate the agreement made only weeks before in the Crimea. To this, Baibakov could only respond that more debt to the West was inadvisable. Instead, he suggested, the GDR should reduce investment. This, at any rate, "is what is being done in the Soviet Union." Schürer's plea for Baibakov to consider once again the importance of the GDR was met by a response that reveals only too well the frustration of the highest economics official in the overextended empire the Soviet alliance had become. "[I have to think about] the People's Republic of Poland! When I cut back on oil there (I am going there next week) that would be unbearable for socialism. . . . And Vietnam is starving. We have to help. Should we just give away South East Asia? Angola, Mozambique, Ethiopia, Yemen. We carry them all. And our own standard of living is extraordinarily low. We really must improve it."[57]

Not surprisingly, the GDR simply had to accept the Soviet position; but Honecker's resistance, on this issue unique within the Soviet bloc, alerted the Soviet leadership to the gravity of the situation. But there was little Brezhnev could do. During consultations with Honecker on the Polish crisis in October 1981, Soviet Central Committee Secretary Rusakov tried to console an obviously agitated Honecker with a message from Brezhnev. "When you talk with comrade Honecker," the aging Soviet leader told Rusakov, "tell him that I cried when I signed [the order]."[58]

For its part, the Soviet leadership accepted that the GDR could not get by solely on reduced investments but would also need to borrow more from the West. But Soviet willingness to let the GDR take on more debt from the West would not ensure that Western creditors would be willing to lend. In the wake of the Polish crisis, international financial institutions hesitated to increase their exposure in what appeared to be an unstable Eastern Europe. In 1982 the situation had reached crisis proportions. Reports of shortages of basic goods now constituted a regular feature of the monthly SED Bezirksleitung reports. The first secretary from Cottbus reported that soldiers from the army and members of the *Volkspolizei* had to be deployed in the coal mines to increase production.[59] The Politburo issued a number of secret emergency measures for ensuring the GDR's liquidity, the most important of which was a series of approvals for "temporary" releases of weapons, ammunition, and raw materials from the two "state reserves" for sale against hard currency.[60] Honecker and Mittag felt so anxious about the trade deficit that the crisis team was required to report daily on the net flow of hard currency. Yearly, the head of the foreign trade bank looked for new sources for the 5–6 billion marks in credit required to ensure East Germany's solvency.[61] Only in 1983, after a secret meeting between Commercial Coordination frontman Schalck-Golodkowski and Franz Josef Strauss, chairman of the West German Christian Social Union (CSU), did West German banks receive government guarantees and resume lending to the GDR.[62] With West German banks now lending to the GDR, other foreign banks resumed their lending as well.

The crisis of the late 1970s and early 1980s had taught the East German leadership that some sort of innovation in industrial administration was necessary. Directionless recentralization could not adequately address pressing economic problems. The oil shocks, rising interest rates, and skyrocketing commodity prices laid bare the weaknesses of the economy. Furthermore, the technological revolution that picked up steam after Western economies adjusted to the 1973 oil shock impaired the capacity of the GDR to compete in export markets—a key reason for the growing balance-of-payments crisis.

Mittag and the Combines

In its search for a solution to the problems of industrial administration, the East German leadership was hamstrung by its rejection of market ideology. Günter Mittag had taken it upon himself to impose a sterile orthodoxy on the entire economics profession. With the exception of a three-year hiatus (1973–76), brought about by power considerations in the Politburo and known affectionately among East German economists as the *Mittags-Pause* (a play on the German expression for "lunch break"), Mittag had run the economics departments of the Central Committee since 1962. As we saw in the last chapter, he had been a supporter of Ulbricht, writing (with others) the old leader's treatise on economic reform, *Politische Ökonomie des Sozialismus,* and this close association had brought him temporarily into disfavor with Honecker and other Politburo members—hence, the *Mittags-Pause* three years after Honecker came to power. As if to atone for his sins, Mittag developed into a centralizer par excellence, and upon his return to the post of economics secretary in 1976 he accelerated the recentralization measures initiated under his temporary replacement, Werner Krolikowski.

Mittag tightly controlled economic discourse in the GDR. In 1983, he closed down the relatively nondogmatic biweekly economics magazine, *Die Wirtschaft* (the German equivalent of the Soviet *Ekonomicheskaya Gazetta*). Mittag brought the main economics publishing house (also called Die Wirtschaft) under his tight control. According to one source, every book published under the Die Wirtschaft imprint had to receive the go-ahead personally from Mittag before being sent to press.[63] The sole academic journal for economists, *Wirtschaftswissenschaft,* ceased to publish articles of any intellectual value. As a matter of policy, economists could no longer get access to official statistics or production figures unless they agreed in advance that the work would remain confidential.[64] Economic discourse thus acquired a sterile, factless character, dominated as it was by officially promoted dogmatists such as Otto Reinhold, Helmut Koziolek, and Harry Nick.

Behind the scenes, however, these otherwise colorless economists were preparing the doctrinal and organizational underpinnings for what would be the SED's final answer to the inherent problems of Soviet-style economic administration—combine formation.[65] Before the combine reform, the East

German industrial structure had been ordered in a three-tier hierarchy. At the top of the hierarchy came the branch ministry. One level down came the production association or VVB, an administrative organ grouping together enterprises with similar production profiles. At the head of the VVB stood a general director who was not really an economic- or production-oriented official. It was Ulbricht's idea to turn the VVB into large socialist concerns, but, with the failure of the NES, the VVB reverted back to an intermediate-level administrative organ. Finally, at the bottom of the hierarchy, came the individual enterprises, each subordinated to a VVB. Within a VVB each enterprise manager enjoyed more or less the same status and each lobbied for inputs and plan targets that would allow him to complete his task most easily.

Large enterprises called combines had existed in the GDR since the 1950s. They tended to be operations specializing in chemical production or raw materials extraction, essentially horizontally integrated production units. A combine of the 1980s, however, was organized primarily on the principle of vertical integration. Since the early 1960s, a process of creeping industrial concentration had been under way. One East German source notes that by 1982 the number of enterprises in the GDR had fallen to 23 percent of the 1960 level.[66] But although most East German analysts in the 1980s tried to portray combine formation as a continual process since the 1960s, only with the dissolution of the VVBs in the 1970s did vertical integration become the preferred form of industrial administration. By 1986 over 90 percent of all industrial production took place in 133 centrally managed combines with an average of 20 to 30 enterprises and 20,000 employees, and 93 smaller Bezirk-led combines with an average of 2,000 employees.[67] What made the general director of a combine different from his VVB counterpart was that the former was also the manager of the "main enterprise" (*Stammbetrieb*) of the combine and was nominally responsible for the day-to-day operation of the combine as an economic unit.

What are we to make of this process? The essence of the combine reform was to raise an objective tendency of enterprise autarky in the economy to a matter of principle. East German officials proudly proclaimed that combines constituted a "relatively closed reproduction process." As other scholars have noted, the strategy of Soviet-type economies can be thought of as an extreme form of import substitution or autarky.[68] However, given constant shortages and supply constraints, managers continually employ a form of "import substitution" within the economy, that is, between firms, in order to avoid depending on deliveries from enterprises over which they have no control. Seen from the industrial manager's point of view, the do-it-yourself approach to solving the supplies problem has great appeal even though the lack of specialization it produces may not be very efficient for the economy as a whole.

In a sense, the combine reform corresponded perfectly to the political preferences of the relevant actors. At the top, Mittag relished the possibility of greater centralized control offered by fewer productive units. It also offered the SED economics chief the opportunity to promote more effectively such pet industries as computer hardware and brown coal production. The combine reform found additional support among economists who saw in it the possibility of creating powerful economic counterparts to the ministries and planners in Berlin.[69] It also won favor among the managers of the large enterprises (ones that would become "main enterprises" of the combines), who likewise expected to enjoy a newfound status within the system. Most important, the SED elite was pleased. Traditionally, the SED had considered its political strength to reside among the workers of the large (socialist) industrial complexes. By contrast, it felt politically weaker among the workers of smaller enterprises. There was a logic to this. Larger enterprises had a far greater capacity to provide goods and services to their workers than smaller ones. Whatever the accuracy of this estimation, the Ministry of State Security (the Stasi) devoted an inordinate amount of its resources to watching a supposedly unreliable work force at small enterprises.[70]

With the formation of combines and the elimination of the VVB, the three-tier structure of industrial administration was reduced to two, ministry and combine. A former Central Committee department head notes, however, that often the formation of combines actually changed nothing.[71] Directors of main enterprises found themselves so overwhelmed managing the combine that they put the operation of the main enterprise in the hands of a subordinate. At the microlevel many combines thus remained little more than paper entities. Notwithstanding these limitations, the combine general director managed his enterprise and the combine as a whole according to the Soviet principle of one-man management, setting the production profile of his entire combine and possessing the power to shift capital and investment between enterprises attached to the combine.

General directors enjoyed a considerable degree of political power and prestige in the system, and this potential for power led many East German economists to believe that they would be able to assert their interests against the center. To a certain extent the economists were right. General directors had a vast empire of resources at their disposal. But their relatively small numbers also permitted a remarkably high degree of centralized control. This centralized control was institutionalized in the Central Committee seminar for directors, which started in 1978. Twice yearly, before the start of the Leipzig trade fair, all general directors of centrally guided combines, together with the party secretaries of the main enterprises and other economic luminaries in the country, would gather for a Central Committee seminar led by Mittag himself. Being invited to this meeting was a matter of pride and prestige, and being personally attacked and humiliated by Mittag a matter of course. At the seminars the general directors discussed specific problems of combines in smaller sessions of panels but were always careful never to bring the overall structure of the economy into question.[72]

Apart from the capacity for self-supply, one of the most heralded benefits of the combine's autarky was its ability to integrate the latest innovations into the production process, an issue that had never been satisfactorily addressed in any socialist economy. As a matter of central policy, combines possessed their own rationalization departments. Between 1980 and 1988 the amount of in-house machine construction and rationalization in the combines increased almost fourfold, and the amount of resources channeled through these divisions climbed to 25 percent of all investment.[73] Their record, however, was mixed. Not only was it irrational for an enterprise to spend time making a machine that should otherwise have been bought from mass production, but there is also evidence that the rationalization divisions increasingly used their resources for other functions within the enterprise. According to one East German source, the rationalization divisions spent 20 percent of their time modernizing machinery, 20 percent on repairs, and the remaining time was devoted to substituting for unavailable imports.[74] Thus, although the initial impact of the rationalization divisions was rather impressive, the marginal returns decreased dramatically after very few years.

Combines also conventionally had their own research and development divisions, and were encouraged to come up with their own innovations. This policy may sound reasonable and, indeed, it appeared rational to most managers, but one can imagine the results if each combine derived its own software solution to the same problem and then did not necessarily share it with other combines.[75] With each combine expected to reinvent the wheel, as it were, the scientific capacity of the country turned into a fragmented set of service organizations for industrial production. Not surprisingly, the research and development divisions of enterprises spent increasing amounts of time on repairs and upgrading existing equipment, rather than on basic or applied research. As overall investment declined, the capital stock deteriorated and the use of scientists as repairmen intensified.

A further innovation receiving much official fanfare was the linking up of a foreign trade enterprise directly to one or perhaps two combines, subordinated to both the combine management and the Ministry of Foreign Trade. Under conditions of especially unfavorable terms of trade and a rising deficit, planners forced combine directors to concentrate on increasing the amount of their production for export to the West. Given the importance of foreign trade for the GDR and the GDR's dismal performance in this area in the late 1970s (leading to the trade crisis at the end of the decade), it was thought that attaching trade and sales organs directly to the combine might improve the trade balance.

However, geographic or administrative proximity of the foreign trade organizations to the combine management could not make East German products any more attractive to the West. Throughout the period of the combine reform, the capacity for productive innovation in the GDR's industry declined. Apart from the distorted image of the process of industrial innovation inherent in the combine idea, the virtual monopoly enjoyed by each combine of the goods it produced on the domestic market provided little incentive to modernize the vast majority of goods. The most "famous" East German product, the Trabant automobile, stood as a testimony to the impact of combine formation on product innovation.[76]

Falling rates of innovation under conditions of a racing world technological revolution could not but cut into the ability of the GDR to maintain old markets and conquer new ones in the West. Desperate for hard currency, enterprises were encouraged to export at any price and preferably for cash. Already in 1979, Gerhard Beil, the minister for foreign trade, complained during an SED plenum that the GDR's export markets for cranes had largely dried up because of competition from Swedish, Austrian, and Finnish firms, whose products were 30 percent lighter, more energy efficient, and easier to service. Customers thus demanded lower prices, a demand that Beil thought the GDR had little choice but to meet.[77] But perhaps the most telling sign of the GDR's decreasing competitiveness on Western markets came in its traditionally strong machine-building industry. Whereas in the first half of the 1970s, 75 percent of its industrial machines were exported to Comecon countries, by 1980 this figure had risen to 85 percent. In 1985 the machine-building department of the State Planning Commission reported that the decline in exports to the West continued unabated and the prices obtained per mark spent on production continued to fall as well. "Export of tool and processing machines," lamented the department, "has become ineffective." Under such conditions, the amount of foreign currency earned per mark spent on production dropped dramatically across all industries, from 0.454 in 1980 to 0.275 in 1985.[78]

The GDR's export structure in the 1980s indicates a distinct trend. To the

Table 3-3. GDR Exports to Western Industrial States (in percentages)

Export	1975	1980	1988
Raw materials	31.2	38	40.3
Machine tools, electronics	30.6	34.4	27.8
Light industry and food	38.2	27.7	31.9

Source: Günter Kusch et al., *Schlußbilanz—DDR: Fazit einer verfehlten Wirtschafts- und sozialpolitik* (Berlin: Duncker & Humblot, 1991), 46.

Comecon countries of Eastern Europe, the GDR exported products typical of a highly developed country. To the West, on the other hand, as the figures in table 3-3 on trade during the 1980s indicate, the GDR was a country undergoing a process of Latin Americanization. Exports increasingly consisted of an array of low-value-added products, including raw materials, food, textiles, and semifinished goods. Those goods that were exported were often done so at prices far below their cost of production in order to keep the supplies of hard currency at acceptable levels. Further evidence of East Germany's Latin Americanization can be found in its pattern of economic cooperation with the West, which consisted largely of *maquiladora*-type enterprises utilizing cheap East German labor in assembly plants for goods exported abroad.[79]

The Final Crisis

Notwithstanding these disturbing trends, the SED continued to announce the fulfillment of its yearly plans. Officially announced growth rates held steady at 4 percent. But the figures were patently untrue, the books cooked in Mittag's office.[80] All evidence to the contrary, the combines continued to be praised as "the backbone of the socialist planned economy." Naysayers within the economic elite were either forcibly silenced, or their reports never made it to the Politburo.[81] Economists, managers, or even ordinary workers who expressed views to the contrary were simply denied a public forum. Gravely discouraged, several leading economists and economic functionaries left the country during the 1980s.

In 1985, when Gorbachev came to power in the Soviet Union, proponents of change found a new source of hope. Finally, the GDR would face up to its problems. They understood the irony of the situation. The SED had always been ideologically dependent on the Soviet Union, and no one had proudly proclaimed this dependence louder than Honecker. Nevertheless, the SED leadership under Honecker, Mittag, and Hager refused to give in. The Soviet Union faced a crisis, so the SED argued, because the Soviet economy had not yet undergone "comprehensive intensification" (which could be a reasonable translation of Gorbachev's first tentative campaign—*uskorennie*, acceleration), a task already completed in the GDR.[82]

In the hope of eliciting Gorbachev's support for some kind of move against Honecker, at the end of May 1986 Prime Minister Willi Stoph gave the Berlin KGB station in the Soviet embassy a packet of materials for Gorbachev, outlining the real economic situation in the GDR, that was directly critical of Honecker and especially Mittag.[83] Anticipating his policy of noninterference in the affairs of other Communist countries, which would be announced officially at a November 1986 meeting of the party chiefs of the Comecon states, Gorbachev refused to take sides.[84] In fact, from Gorbachev's praise of the GDR's economy in his speech to the eleventh SED party congress in 1986, it initially appeared to Honecker and Mittag that they had found an admirer and an important external source of validation for their assertions that the GDR had already completed economic intensification. But as a former provincial first secretary, Gorbachev probably understood the Potemkin village–quality of most East German claims. During the presentation of the prototype of the much heralded East German one-megabyte computer chip, the Soviet leader nearly spoiled the entire event. Upon seeing it, he asked when it would be produced en masse and was quickly led away.[85]

Whatever the twists and turns of his thinking on the GDR as a potential model, shortly after attending the eleventh SED congress Gorbachev must have changed his mind because his laudatory speech was never included in later collections. From this point on, relations between the Soviet Union and the GDR steadily worsened. Honecker understood very early and quite clearly that Gorbachev was a destabilizing force for European communism. After the first few reform plenums of the Soviet Party, especially the January plenum of 1987, the SED took several measures to shield the GDR from the reformist thinking emanating from the Soviet Union. Honecker set up a special committee headed by Hanna Wolf, the former head of the Higher Party School of the SED, to comb the Soviet press in search of offensive reformist articles and prepare critical commentaries for Politburo members.[86] In a sharp break with past practices, the SED drastically curtailed the yearly contingent of its brightest stars sent to the prestigious Higher Party School of the CPSU in Moscow, which was developing a reputation as a breeding ground for Gorbachevian revisionists. On orders from the Politburo, the GDR postal service interrupted the delivery of some Soviet publications to East German subscribers, such as the reformist digest of the press, *Sputnik*. *Bezirk* (regional) and *Kreis* (district) level first secretaries continued to receive Gorbachev's speeches by encoded telegram, but the SED's stance on most of Gorbachev's pronouncements was official silence.[87] To the extent that it published Gorbachev's speeches, the GDR press did not print them in their entirety and usually left out the parts calling for greater candor in political and economic discourse. And as a counterpoise to Gorbachev, in 1987 the SED began to reprint articles from the Soviet press that were critical of Gorbachev, including the infamous Nina Andreeva piece. It also initiated a press campaign praising the economy of the Honecker era. All the standard East German "mouthpiece" economists were dragged out for this. As a final measure, *Neues Deutschland* began simultaneously to run a series of articles written by visiting Soviet general directors who supposedly admired the East German economy.[88]

Yet if the real state of the East German economy could not easily be hidden, Honecker and Mittag lacked the political nerve to call for the kinds of policies that might change the situation.[89] For one thing, Mittag justifiably felt that any discussion of the GDR's economic problems might weaken its position on international capital markets. For another, it was far from clear that the East German public would tolerate the kinds of steps that would have been necessary to change course. One plan calling for just that was Gerhard Schürer's final attempt to coax Honecker into thinking through the implications of his economic policies. In April 1988, the planning chairman sent Honecker a report on the economy entitled "Thoughts on Further Work on the National Economic Plan 1989 and Beyond." Schürer predicted a "rapidly rising foreign debt." In order to stop the rate of debt growth, he explained, the GDR would have to run a 6.5 billion Deutsche mark surplus with the West per year. But even given Schürer's optimistic projected export surplus of 4.2 billion marks, the GDR would still have to come up with an additional 2.3 billion Deutsche marks per year. Schürer called for a halt to the GDR's expensive and not very successful microelectronics program, a pet scheme of Mittag's, which alone had cost the state 15 billion marks in the three-year period from 1986 to 1989.[90] Far more controversially, he recommended a drastic reduction in subsidization of consumer prices.[91] This last suggestion went to the heart of the matter. The GDR had been living beyond its means for years, and the only way out, Schürer implied, was a drastic cut in living standards for most East Germans.

The Politburo meeting in which Schürer's paper was discussed provides a sad commentary on the final stages of a political economy in crisis. Gone was the energy of the late 1970s and early 1980s, which at least stimulated a vigorous reaction to the growing crisis. Honecker, who seemed already to be preparing an excuse for future historians, referred wistfully back to his 1981 letter to Brezhnev that warned the Soviet leader of the dangers associated with reduced oil deliveries, and informed his colleagues that he had recently told Gorbachev the same thing but the Soviet leader offered absolutely no help.[92] Other Politburo members denied the need for any change at all. "No one has achieved anything with so-called economic reforms," claimed Werner Jarowinsky, Central Committee secretary for trade and supply questions, "they all have debts too, but at the same time the basis of trust and optimism is destroyed. We must keep the GDR stable."[93] Jarowinsky's few words were backed up by a lengthy refutation of Schürer's paper issuing from Mittag's office. Once again, Mittag accused Schürer of violating the letter and spirit of the 1971 SED program that had formed the basis of economic and social policy in the Honecker era.[94]

In retrospect, it is easy to understand the concerns of the core Politburo members. Since the regime had never put itself to a popularity test, the sole perceived basis of political continuity remained stable consumer prices, a centrally planned economy, and the comprehensive social program—in short, all the features of what the SED called "really existing socialism." This was the defining logic of the Honecker era, and the logic appeared sound. Who, after all, really needed a second capitalist Germany, given that one was already so successful? The only compelling reason for existence of a second German state is if it were fundamentally different from West Germany. Schürer's attempt to question the viability of socialism in East Germany unless the SED introduced what must have sounded like a restoration of capitalism was bound to fall on deaf ears.

As late as May 1989, with the debt completely out of control (Schürer predicted that it would rise to 57.7 billion valuta marks by the end of 1992 and 64 billion by 1995) and elements of the economic elite already discussing the necessity of some kind of confederation with West Germany, the core Politburo members still refused to act.[95] Meeting to discuss the 1990 plan on May 16, 1989, most members acknowledged that the debt had become so large that something needed to be done. But the question remained, What? The SPK argued that consumer prices had to change and suggested that the regime start with something as innocuous as cut flowers. Werner Krowlikowski agreed that consumer prices had to be put on the agenda, but warned against doing anything "hasty." Trade-union chief Harry Tisch counseled continuity. Jarowinsky stuck to the same line he had in previous years. "If we start fiddling with prices now, we lose all credibility."[96] That the regime had in any case been losing credibility for years is something that Schürer tried in vain to get across to his colleagues.

Why institutions fail to stave off their own demise, through change in the face of crisis, constitutes one of the more interesting questions of social science and history. This chapter provides us with some insights into a possible answer. The SED elite believed that it faced an extreme version of the Tocquevillian paradox: unpopular governments become unstable when they start to reform themselves. It is of course doubtful that any members of the Politburo had ever read a page of the French master, but their conversations in the final years reveal an intuitive understanding of their predicament. Reform seemed to be both necessary and unimaginable. For forty years, the SED had struggled to survive and devise a formula for socialist modernity. In the 1970s, buoyed temporarily by easy credit and the high levels of investment during the Ulbricht years, the SED appeared for a brief moment to have accomplished this, to have found a viable route to a distinctively socialist modernity. This helps explain the peculiar unwillingness of the leadership to change course in 1988–89. The preceding narrative suggests, then, that part of the reason that human institutions fail to save themselves through appropriate action is that their members develop cultures of deception, not only in their dealings with others but, more important, in regard to themselves. They look back on contingent successes as defining moments that will last indefinitely. They convince themselves that they will survive into the future because they have survived until the present. They delude themselves into believing that change is always more dangerous than continuity. This last pathology, so common in all ruling groups and political organizations, appeared with remarkable regularity in the culture of ruling Communist parties in twentieth-century Europe, and seemed to inform most SED deliberations in its last years of existence. The SED did not change course because it was perceived as too risky and because it made no sense to deviate from what had worked for almost two decades.

Such an explanation, however, is only partial at best; for even if Honecker and company had wanted to "reform" the economy, even if they had understood what all seems so obvious today, the evidence presented thus far indicates that they would not have had an easy time of it. They were hemmed in by the choices both they and their predecessors had made at critical junctures in their state's history. Having compromised with the working class in the 1950s, Ulbricht had little chance of making his economic reform succeed in the 1960s. Having come to power on a program of institutional conservatism and consumer satisfaction in the 1970s, Honecker could neither slip the bonds of his own economic institutions, turn the tables against his own working class, reduce his political dependence on the Soviets, nor diminish the power of international capital markets over his own domestic policies in the 1980s. If the history of the GDR is as I have described it here, it suggests that institutions fail not only because of their cultures of deception, but also because the way they adapt to their environments may be rational in the short run but irrational over the long run. The SED's pattern of adaptation, as it had evolved since the early 1950s, while conducive of short-run stability, ultimately meant compromising with, rather than conquering, the confining conditions of its political environment.

Part Two The Campaign Economy

The preceding three chapters have shown the formidable, perhaps inescapable, constraints faced by the SED elite in shaping an effective structure of consent on the shop floor, in fitting the Soviet model to their own production needs, and in adapting to the changing international political economy in the 1980s. In retrospect, it is perhaps not so surprising that "really existing socialism" collapsed when it did, but that it lasted so long. But such a retrospective view is flawed because it fails to account for the pattern of decline—political stability amid economic decay. Failure to devise and implement effective policy from the center constitutes but one part of the story of the politics of economic decline, and perhaps not the most interesting part. For all the difficulties they faced, the SED elite administered the decline in relative isolation from the society in whose name they ruled. Each day, Politburo members could be seen driving back and forth on the "protocol road" between East Berlin and the enclosed (and well-supplied) estate in Wandlitz. The decline they faced was distant and abstract. It was not in the State Planning Commission, the ministries, and Central Committee departments in Berlin, but in the industrial provinces and on the shop floor where the SED confronted the mundane problems of making Soviet-style socialism work.

The second half of the book therefore shifts the focus from the national level of decision making to the regional and district level. This shift makes sense because it was at the local level where people experienced socialism; it was here where the regime would either succeed or fail. More than any other officials, the regional and district Communist Party secretaries were responsible on a day-to-day basis for keeping Marxism-Leninism afloat in the GDR. The SED had an extensive apparatus of 15 *Bezirksleitungen* (BLs or regional administrations) and 261 *Kreisleitungen* (KLs or district administrations). Local party organizations were formally responsible for every aspect of political, economic, and cultural life within their administrative competencies, but memoirs and archives reveal that these overburdened party secretaries and instructors spent most of their time on what can broadly be termed economic matters. Who these officials were, how well they were equipped to handle the challenges they faced, the kinds of activities they engaged in to overcome the day-to-day problems of the command economy, and their orientations toward their action constitute the subject of the next four chapters. What we find is an intricate web of relationships that simultaneously reinforced the authority of the party in the economy and forestalled total economic collapse, yet doomed economic life in the GDR to a never-ending series of politically directed economic campaigns of extremely limited effectiveness. As we shall see, the "campaign economy" justified and established the careers of hundreds of officials, but, in doing so, it also helped to cut off most genuine public consideration of what truly ailed the East German economy.

The following chapters, instead of proceeding chronologically and from the top down, proceed analytically and from the bottom up. Most of the discussion focuses on the 1970s and 1980s. What is gained by this focus is a richer understanding of the identity-defining, everyday experiences of the regional and district political elites, and why they continued to propose and implement the same kinds of inappropriate responses to economic decay, even in the face of a growing crisis, instead of trying to save the system (and their jobs) by calling for and implementing change. In fact, although proceeding with a different tempo, there is a "story" in part II as well, but it must be understood in theoretical terms. The story is one of microrationality at odds with macrorationality; of politics at odds with economics; of an organization whose formal attributes and practical behavior did not express any kind of superordinate economic logic but, rather, reflected the cultural milieu in which the party and state organizations operated. As we shall see, many of the procedures and programs nominally intended to enhance economic efficiency spread quickly throughout the GDR, not because they actually improved efficiency, but because as myth and ritual they enhanced the SED's organizational integrity, promoted the careers of regional and district political officials, and reinforced a set of culturally constructed notions of how an economy and society should be administered.

Chapter 4

Reds and Experts

The Retreat from

Technocracy

One of the main tasks of this study is to reexamine the use of technocratic imagery by students of Leninist politics. The previous chapters examined the search for technocratic solutions to industrial relations, economic structure, and foreign trade. All proved elusive. However, my characterization of the policies themselves as technocratic may have been misleading. Technocracy is as much a question of who rules as how rule is carried out. As we have seen, Erich Honecker and his allies were at least as concerned with the effect reformist policies would have on the structure of power—on who would rule—as they were with the disequilibrium generated by Ulbricht's economic experiments.

This chapter focuses on the changing personnel policy at the middle levels of power from Ulbricht to Honecker. In doing so, it places important parts of the East German power elite into sociological perspective. What kind of people ran the industrial provinces in the GDR? How were they chosen? How did their background and training prepare them for the economic challenges they faced? What kinds of ideas did these people bring to their work and what kind of cultural milieu did they operate in? Contrary to what conventional sociological wisdom would lead us to expect, in important ways the structure of authority in East Germany actually became more ideological and less technocratic over time.

This latter point deserves further explanation. The word "technocracy" broken down into its parts means literally the rule of those who know and understand technique or technology. At the heart of the technocratic model lies the simple postulate: as social processes become more complex, those who possess specialized knowledge relating to the task at hand will obtain a larger share of social power. Although the technocratic ideal can be traced as far back as Saint-Simon, the real inspiration in North America has come by way of Weberian social theory. Weber notes of the early modern world that "The absolute monarch is powerless opposite the superior knowledge of the bureaucratic expert," and in the modern order, "The 'political master' finds himself in the position of the 'dilettante' who stands opposite the expert."[1] Put simply, Weber predicted a secular trend away from politics as the clash of values and interests, and toward politics as technique. Neither Weber nor his disciples implied that the rule of the expert would be any more democratic than that of the parliament or the monarch, but because of his knowledge the expert would be more efficient and rational.[2] In the more elaborate of these theories, the greater efficiency and rationality of rule by experts is not only in fact more rational, but, more important, it is understood as such by wide sections of the public. This understanding therefore forms the basis of a qualitatively new type of legitimacy and a new structure of authority in modern industrial society.[3]

Of course, Weber was not the first social theorist to examine the relationship between knowledge and power. It has, in fact, been a staple of political discourse since the ancient Greeks and, given the fundamental nature of this question, political theorists from the Renaissance to the present have carried on the tradition of grounding authority relationships in a theory of knowledge. One finds in Marx's work more of the same. Marx dealt with the problem of knowledge and politics under the rubric of class consciousness. In its struggle with the humiliating conditions of capitalism, Marx believed the proletariat would acquire the necessary wisdom and insight to become a class "for itself" and not merely "in itself." On the question of political leadership, though, and its relationship to knowledge, Marx is uncharacteristically silent.[4]

Lenin attempted to fill this gap in Marx's thought by drawing a clearer picture of the relationship of knowledge to political leadership. Firmly in the Kautskyite tradition of the Second International, Lenin argued that the working class left on its own would never become revolutionary. The proletariat would never have the knowledge to justify its own political leadership; at most the proletariat might demand economic or "trade-union" concessions from employers and the state. This fatal flaw would ultimately divert it from fulfilling its true historical mission: revolution.[5]

Lenin solved the riddle of class consciousness by creating his well-known party of dedicated full-time revolutionaries who would mediate historical truth to the working class. But how could the party guarantee that its agents would possess the proper knowledge? Lenin solved this by effectively decoupling the agency of the revolutionary from the source of the revolutionary's knowledge. The professional revolutionary would not know historical truth by virtue of superior intellect, but by devotion to the ideology and political line of the party. It is the party, not the cadre or ordinary member, that is the repository of political wisdom. In this way, political membership (which can be maintained only through loyalty) and "knowledge" become conceptually interchangeable, and both yield the right to political leadership.

To some extent, Lenin had a technocratic vision of politics, not only in the prerevolutionary order but also in the postrevolutionary order. He understood politics not primarily as a problem of reconciling conflicting values and interests, but of finding the best way to implement historically necessary measures. Value conflict and the formation of the public will cease to be problematic in the postrevolutionary order. Completing the revolution, then, is a technical task, pitched, to be sure, in the idiom of world historical significance, but not a matter for heated public debate. Postrevolutionary politics resolves itself into administration, but this too is rather curiously developed. As A. J. Polan skillfully demonstrates, Lenin's thought, as typified in *State and Revolution*, shows a simultaneous disdain for politics and an unusual naiveté regarding the prospects for simplifying administration in the postrevolutionary world.[6]

It is here that Lenin parts ways with Weber and the theorists of technocracy. Whereas Lenin considered state administration to be a relatively simple task unworthy of serious study, Weber viewed it as complex and eminently worthy of scholarly consideration. Whereas Lenin believed that staffing the state is a relatively mundane affair, a matter of finding enough loyal workers and party members to carry out duties not more complex than the postal service, Weber considered the staffing of the modern state with competent personnel as a process that could be successfully accomplished only under very particular historical conditions. And, whereas technocratic legitimation has its roots in a belief in natural science and method, Leninist legitimation is tied to a teleological world view.

Reds and Experts

Given the prominence of technocratic thinking in early postwar American social theory, the potential contradiction between political loyalty and professional competence in Leninist regimes was a continuous object of scholarly attention. The literature on the subject is too large to explore here in detail. The essential part of the argument for our purposes is that, in staffing its bureaucracy, every political order faces the dilemma of choosing between the most loyal and the most competent, and rarely can one find in a single person both traits in equal and strong proportions.[7] Because of their commitment to a radical ideology, Leninist parties face this problem in its most acute form.

As in other areas, the SED's way of dealing with these dilemmas was largely derivative of the Soviet experience. Two terms form the heart of the Soviet contribution: cadre and nomenklatura. The word cadre was originally a military term, referring to a commanding officer or the "frame" of staff officers. In line with the frequency of other military analogues in his thought, Lenin saw in the professional revolutionary a soldier of the vanguard.

It was Stalin, however, who saw in cadres the "command central of the party," who because of their loyalty and understanding of ideology should have exclusive right to command. In his own words, "Cadres decide everything."[8] They are the kind of people "who understand the party line, who consider the party line their own, and who are prepared to translate it into deed, who understand how to put it into practice, and who are capable of defending the line and fighting for it."[9] Stalin's formulations outlined the ideal transformation of the professional revolutionary into the professional Communist state functionary. Above all, according to Stalin what determines success in work is ideological commitment and loyalty to the party of the working class:

> The higher the political level and the more conscious the Marxist-Leninist attitude of the functionary of the respective branch of the state or party apparatus, the higher the level of the work, the more fruitful it is, the more effective its results. And contrariwise, the lower the political level and the less Marxist-Leninist the attitude of the functionary, the more probable are mistakes and failures in his work, and the more probable is it that the functionaries themselves are superficial and become little do-gooders. . . . One can say this with certainty. When we understand how ideologically to arm our cadres in all branches of work, and politically armor them so that they can easily orient themselves in the international and domestic situation, when we understand how to make them into full fledged Marxist-Leninists who are competent to decide the questions of leadership of the country without serious mistakes, then we will have reason to think that we have solved nine-tenths of our problems.[10]

The exclusivist cadre principles of the Stalin era were integrated into the SED almost unchanged. When the SED became a "party of a new type" in 1952, several Soviet books on the subject were translated into German. Shortly thereafter, East German party specialists on cadres started to publish their own renditions of the general principles.[11]

After Stalin's death, especially during the late 1950s and the 1960s, a trend in the literature on cadres appeared that more or less widened the meaning of cadres policy to stand for "personnel policy." The designation cadre no longer referred solely to employees of the party apparatus or even party members. One finds, for example, frequent use of the term "nonparty cadres." The first extensive and relatively systematic East German treatment of the subject, published in the 1960s, considerably widened the scope of cadres policy. The authors, Richard Herber and Herbert Jung, define cadres as "a group of people who on the basis of their political and professional knowledge and capacities are suitable for being assigned to lead other people in carrying out assigned tasks."[12]

Western academics latched onto to this loosening of the cadre concept.[13] Rather than simply encompassing political categories and characteristics of employment, the concept started to be aimed especially at the intelligentsia. Thus, one West German study cites the following passage from Herber and Jung's work. "The concept of cadre encompasses both the management and functionaries as well as scientifically educated professionals, who with respect to their activities significantly differ from one and other, but who have in common the fact that they have to be developed and deployed systematically, in a planned fashion, and corresponding to social needs."[14] Beyond the change in discourse, one also finds a new departure in policy during the 1960s, the most important of which was a much cited Central Committee directive of 1965 that dealt with the educational level of party and state personnel and called for increasing the technical qualifications of personnel in all areas of social life.[15]

In at least one respect Western academics were correct in their assessment. One does find a technocratic bent to the literature on cadres policy in East Germany. Starting from the late 1950s, this trend permeated not only political writings and speeches, and internal political communication, but also the enterprise novel of the period.[16] The debates are written in a language that is unusually vigorous and specific for SED literature.

Despite all the fanfare surrounding the issue of administrative competence, however, it remains unclear how much of a difference the discussion or the directive ever made on the structure of power. Even granting the importance of the debate, the East German political writings on the subject are far less transparent on the subject than the conclusions of most Western academics would warrant. I believe that a second reading of the materials from earlier studies reveals a far more muted and tentative technocratic tendency in the 1960s than is usually maintained. For example, according to one East German publication on cadres, enterprise managers should have some expertise in the following fields: philosophy, political economy, pedagogy, organizational science, cybernetics and computer science, mathematics, psychology, and sociology.[17] However, at least four of these subjects, as taught in the GDR, can be classified as ideological education, with little connection the operation of an enterprise. And concerning cybernetics and systems theory (the most "technocratic" of all subjects), East German informants note that it was generally the object of ridicule among middle- and lower-level enterprise personnel, as few could understand what they were studying or how it would apply to the production process.[18]

Regarding the education and training of public officials, one Western scholar uses the curriculum of the Edwin Hoernle School of Public Administration in Weimar as an example of technocratic training. This school specialized in the preparation of midlevel provincial officials for positions in the state apparatus. The following subjects were taught:

1. Foundations of Marxism-Leninism, with minicourses in dialectical and historical materialism, the political economy of capitalism and socialism, scientific communism, and the history of the workers movement.
2. The theory of state and law.
3. Law of state management and planning.
4. Selected problems of economic, labor, agricultural, and family law.
5. Economic policy of the SED, basics of management and planning of the socialist economy and of territories.
6. Scientific organization of socialist state management.
7. Economic geography.
8. Culture and aesthetics.
9. Russian.
10. Physical education.
11. Civil defense.[19]

Once again, at least six (the first two and the last four) of these courses cannot really be counted among those that might help future administrators perform their tasks more efficiently.

The approved curriculum for engineers provides a further example. According to the GDR's Ministry for Higher Education, a typical engineering course of study included 300 hours of training in Marxism-Leninism. This figure put ideological study in second place behind mathematics (352 hours), but ahead of engineering, in total class time spent on a subject.[20]

After 1971, the regime made a conscious effort to reverse any earlier technocratic trend. GDR political specialists had read Western studies of their country, especially the work of Peter Ludz, who was the first West German social scientist to posit a "systemic need" for the increasing power of the technocrats. Interpretations of cadres policy as technocratic became their first object of attack.[21] According to one publication, "As earlier, bourgeois ideologists direct their attacks and slanders, above all, against the leading role of the working class and its party. They assert that under the conditions of the scientific technical revolution the intelligentsia takes over the revolutionary impulse from the working class, and themselves become the main producer of social wealth. The working class [read party] loses its revolutionary elan and, therefore, its right to rule."[22] In a 1978 speech to the Kreisleitung (KL) first secretaries, Erich Honecker underlined the point quite clearly, "Our society does not need 'pure specialists,' but professionals with a political and scientific profile."[23]

In some respects the shift in orientation was subtle. Reading the literature of this later period carefully, one could still come away with the impression that the stress on ideology was purely formalistic in character. Statements, such as "The decisive proving ground for managers . . . is the work process. Especially here cadres show how seriously they take their political responsibilities," seem to show continuity in attitudes to the proper mix between red and expert. However, several policy moves served to underline the shift in orientation. In 1977 the Central Committee Secretariat issued a new directive on cadres policy, which replaced the 1965 directive.[24] In its preamble, the new directive lamented that in recent years ideology had been neglected and demanded that the situation be remedied.[25] It instructed party organs to ensure that sending cadres to party institutions of higher learning was not merely a formal act, but one that was well thought out.[26]

Furthermore, in a conscious attempt to prevent the intelligentsia from reproducing itself and dominating the party, the leadership renewed its concern with its own social composition, and the kinds of people who would receive a chance to rise up through its ranks and have access to higher education. So, for example, in 1979 Honecker reported that 56.9 percent of all party members were workers, and called for still higher numbers.[27] Greater emphasis was placed on recruiting young workers into leadership positions. According to one source, in 1981 over 90 percent of KL first and second secretaries, 87 percent of ministers, 68 percent of ambassadors, 92 percent of mayors of Bezirk capitals, and 71 percent of general directors came from working-class origins.[28] Of importance here are not the numbers themselves, for without more specificity they cannot be meaningfully interpreted, but the general concern of the regime to legitimate itself by reference to its working-class origins, rather than general level of technical expertise.

Selection of Personnel: The Nomenklatura

Given the relatively small size of the SED party apparatus, the control over personnel selection through the nomenklatura became the most important way the party kept a hand in administrative and economic life. In its essentials, the nomenklatura consisted of a list of positions that a particular level of the party or state apparatus had responsibility for staffing. The distribution of the positions within the levels of nomenklatura of the party vary in their numbers and posts. The size of the nomenklatura for the Berlin Bezirksleitung (BL) in 1982 was approximately 1,100.[29] Both the numbers and positions were subject to frequent change and negotiation.

The party, state, and economic nomenklatura can be seen in table 4-1. The picture may be deceiving in that it shows separate hierarchies for each of the three areas. In fact, the SED apparatus—that is, the party—completely controlled the other two hierarchies. In an interview, the party secretary of Rostock University insisted that the main role of the university party organization was selection of personnel. When asked about the "nonparty" personnel department of the university, he smiled and said that it did not really make the decisions but merely registered them.[30]

Of course, this observation holds true only insofar as the position under question was not on the list of a higher level of the nomenklatura than the local party organ. For example, the first secretary of a Kreisleitung did not have the power to remove the director of a large enterprise subordinated directly to a ministry in Berlin. The only recourse available to such an official was to complain to a higher level in the party hierarchy. But, regarding personnel decisions within his or her own nomenklatura, the powers of a KL first secretary were essentially unlimited.

As to how local party organs actually made personnel decisions, the picture is differentiated. An example may be illuminating. In 1978 the head of the technology division of a local milk factory in a southern GDR district died suddenly and a replacement had to be found. Since the enterprise was subordinated to the local council, the KL first secretary asked the director of the enterprise to suggest a replacement in consultation with the enterprise party organization and the trade union. From there the personnel

Table 4-1. SED Nomenklatura of Party, State, and Economy

Level	Party	State	Economy
Politburo	Central Committee members, Central Committee secretaries, BL first secretaries, directors of Central Party institutions	State Council, Council of Ministers, chairman of SPK	
Central Committee	Central Committee department heads, BL secretaries, Central Committee party organizers in combines, KL first secretaries	Ministers, deputy ministers, Bezirk council chairmen, deputy Bezirk council chairmen, director of Bezirk ABI, Kreis council chairmen	General directors of combines, directors of major construction projects, Bezirk economies council chairmen
Bezirksleitung	KL secretaries, secretaries of important enterprise organizations, directors of Kreis party schools	Department heads and section heads of staff organs, Bezirk council department heads, Kreis council members	Combine department heads, directors of medium-size enterprises (1,000–5,000 employees), chief accountants
Kreisleitung	KL employees, secretaries of enterprise party organizations	Kreis construction directors, city construction directors, Kreis council department heads	Small enterprise directors, medium-size enterprise department heads, foremen

Source: Gert-Joachim Glaeßner, *Herrschaft durch Kader* (Opladen: Westdeutscher Verlag, 1977), 240.

department of the enterprise sent the candidate's dossier to the Kreisleitung for confirmation.[31] In this case the person seemed right for the job, had a clean political record, and was routinely confirmed in the position by the Kreisleitung.

In situations where a suitable replacement could not readily be located or a candidate who otherwise looked good had politically damaging information in his or her dossier, the Kreisleitung would get more deeply involved. The picture here becomes somewhat confusing. At least two divisions of the local party apparatus would officially be encouraged to let their opinion be known. The second secretary and his men in the party organs department (the personnel section of the KL) would write a report, as personnel decisions that affected the SED naturally fell within their competence. In addition, the secretary responsible for economics would have his say as well, since the personnel of the milk plant would influence the performance of an area for which he was held responsible.[32] Amid the bureaucratic to-and-fro between the factory director, the economics department, and the cadres department, the first secretary would step in and make the final decision if necessary.[33]

Perhaps in order to avoid bureaucratic uncertainty and overlapping competencies, after 1963, party, state, and economic units were ordered to plan personnel replacements five years in advance. The "cadres program" supposedly played an integral role in the life of every enterprise and territory. In the Kreis Eisenberg in 1981, for example, it was determined that by 1990 the Kreis would need thirteen mayors and an even larger number of enterprise officials. According to a report made by the KL second secretary, the party organization arranged a program to find and train replacements. First it directed the enterprise party organizations, together with enterprise directors, and members of the local council to hold meetings in the enterprises with the chosen members to advise them of the decision. During a *Kadergespräch* (a formal political interview) an evaluation was quickly made of their suitability from a political point of view, separately from how they looked on paper. Thereafter, the necessary training and educational measures were worked out with the enterprise and/or the local administrative council.[34]

Each level of the party developed its own list of candidates to fill positions in its nomenklatura at a moment's notice—its cadre reserve (*Kaderreserve*)—and to bring along a new generation (*Nachwuchskader*) of potential members, whether in the party, state, or economic apparatus.[35] In the Honecker era, young people destined for careers in the nomenklatura of the Politburo or Central Committee customarily started their careers as full-time youth league (FDJ) employees and had some higher education under their belt. From there these young cadres spent three or four years at the Higher Party School in Berlin, or, better yet, at the Higher Party School in the Soviet Union.[36] It is certainly no accident that Honecker's own career went precisely along these lines.

Although planning cadre selection and training rationalized personnel policy to some extent, for political as well as technical reasons cadre planning did not always function smoothly. Making long-term training and planning of replacements for existing employees of the party, state, and economy amenable to central supervision threatened to reduce the effectiveness of an important instrument of power available to the provincial first secretary—the power of discretionary appointment. That the party press constantly featured articles criticizing formalism in cadres work, and describing in excruciating detail the "ideal" cadre selection and planning procedure, indicates that central authorities faced fairly stiff resistance in rationalizing personnel policy.[37]

But even when the will to cooperate with the center was present, local political authorities often confronted a simple shortage of appropriate personnel for politically and economically important positions. In Landolf Scherzer's unique diary of his month spent with a KL first secretary in the mid-1980s, Der Erste, First Secretary Fritschler is clearly not satisfied with the new director of a chain enterprise but, unable to find a suitable replacement, decides to tolerate him. Several days later, the mayor of small town has to be replaced. Fritschler has trouble finding a replacement and is forced to order the mayor of Merkurs, another small town, to take up the position against his will, since he has no suitable replacement lined up.[38]

As Jerry Hough notes in his study of the Soviet Communist Party, this second, informal aspect of personnel selection played just as large a role in the function of the local party organs as the planned deployment of nomenklatura cadres.[39] Local party organs often assisted factories in locating employees for important positions. They also acted as clearing agents for enterprises. When important employees did not work out in one position, KLs and BLs spent a great deal of time finding new jobs for unsuitable workers and managers. In discussing this question, the SED literature regularly cites Lenin: "One can be the most able revolutionary and agitator, and yet be completely unusable as an administrator." The trick of good personnel work is to find the right place for every one.[40]

Although the first secretary often lacked the formal power to replace personnel through the nomenklatura, especially if the official in question was in the nomenklatura of a higher level, the secretary could still exercise considerable influence over some of the directors within the region. One variation on this theme is illustrated by a further example from Der Erste. In 1986, Horst Mosche, the director of the glassworks in Dermbach, was on temporary sick leave. He called the first secretary of Bad Salzungen to say that he felt well enough to return to work.[41] The first secretary, however, had in the meantime decided to remove him from his post (and, since the position *was* in nomenklatura of the Kreisleitung, this was fairly straightforward), but did not want to let on because he had yet to find Mosche a new job. Instead the first secretary replied, "Horst, go for a walk and take it easy.

For the last sixteen years you've had no time for that. In two weeks come here and we'll talk about it."

Little did Mosche know that First Secretary Fritschler had already decided to use Mosche's dismissal to exert pressure on the other managers in the Kreis to fulfill the plan. During a visit to the local aluminum works he informed its director, Bernd Radtke, "The director of the glass factory has been relieved; tomorrow early I'll tell him about it." Radtke replied shocked, "Relieved? The man fought in the trenches for years; he never took a break— and now relieved?" The first secretary responded, "He was not forward thinking enough, that was perhaps his biggest mistake," to which Radtke said dejectedly, "Forward thinking! What do I have to do to be forward thinking?"[42] Noteworthy here is that the Radtke's position was in the nomenklatura of the Bezirksleitung, and Fritschler, therefore, did not have the immediate authority to remove him from his position. From Radtke's reaction, he nevertheless understood that Fritschler's word carried considerable weight with his superiors in the Bezirksleitung.

Two weeks later, when Mosche returned, he was offered the position of a division chief in the aluminum works. Although, as a party member, First Secretary Fritschler could have ordered him to take the position, Mosche explained that after so many years trying to supply the aluminum plant there was no way he could work under Radtke, its director. The first secretary agreed. Eventually, in consultation with the KL economics secretary, all parties agreed that he would take up the directorship of a new brewery.[43]

The removal of an official from the nomenklatura altogether rarely happened. The procedures necessary to remove someone under most circumstances were cumbersome. A major exception to this rule involved personal conduct. The literature on cadres was quite explicit in its expectation that public officials will lead exemplary personal lives and were expected to have their immediate families do the same.[44] Notwithstanding the usually generous interpretation of the rules, midlevel party and state employees (those lacking high-level political clout) would immediately lose their position if, for example, a family member tried to flee to the West.[45]

The Sociology of the Party Apparatus

The pattern of actual personnel decisions can be detected in the profile of the provincial elite. Even proponents of the technocratic thesis do not dispute the fact that, at the time they were writing, the top positions were still in the hands of the old guard. What they argued, however, is that rational-technical officials would increasingly occupy leading positions. Baylis, for example, doubted in 1974 that, "having been admitted to the leadership as consultants, advisors, and even participants in decision-making, the technical strategic elite will or can be turned out again."[46] In the Soviet context, Hough notes that this trend had already permeated the party itself. During the postwar era, Soviet regional and district first secretaries tended to have industrial backgrounds, either as engineers, factory directors, or as employees of the economic apparatus of the party (or agricultural careers if the region where they worked was agricultural).[47] Hough makes his case most forcefully when he says, "if the secretaries of the local party organs were all to be men with careers in agitation and propaganda work, then the local party organs would surely have a different role in practice than if all the secretaries were former factory directors."[48] In fact, as we shall see shortly, Hough was wrong on two accounts if one extends his model to East Germany. Not only were provincial first secretaries mostly drawn from ideological (and not production) work, but they still carried out the same kinds of functions in the economy as Hough's more technically trained "prefects."

What does this mean? First, it suggests that one did not need industrial expertise to be a good prefect. Second, given that expertise was not necessary, the activities of the local party secretaries in the economy were not simply or even primarily about economics, but were laden with other meaning. Finally, it suggests the limited value of inferring role and orientation from raw sociological data. Nonetheless, such an exercise does appear to have some use, in that it can give us a better idea of the kind of experience these officials gained before becoming powerful.

Apart from career profiles, we do have some fragmentary knowledge of the role orientations of local politicians in the late Ulbricht and early Honecker period. Even after the considerable efforts of the 1960s to make the members of the provincial and district apparatus more aware of the issues of industrial modernity, a confidential poll of the reading habits of 124 KL secretaries (of whom 109 were first or second secretaries) taken at the end of the Ulbricht era in 1970 suggests that these officials remained primarily "politicians." Almost all first secretaries started their day by reading *Neues Deutschland*, heading first for the lead article, turning then to articles dealing with international or all-German matters and other issues of "topical political importance," and only after all this would they take up pieces considering "economic problems." Whereas 94 percent of the group claimed regularly to read the remarkably dull organizational journal *Neuer Weg*, and 85 percent read the theoretical journal *Einheit*, only 9 percent claimed regularly to read the more industrial and technically oriented newspaper *Tribüne*, and only a single member of the group bothered to read the highbrow *Sinn und Form*. And although 74 of 124 party secretaries claimed to have bought the treatise on reform economics, *Politische Ökonomie des Sozialismus* (the so-called Mittag bible), only 11 had actually read it.[49]

Upon coming to power in 1971, Honecker reinforced the political (as opposed to the earlier economic) orientation of the party. At the eighth party congress in 1971, all members of the Politburo were reelected with the addition of two new full members, Werner Lamberz, an organizational, ideological, and cultural specialist, and Werner Krolikowski, Honecker's partner in overthrowing Ulbricht, also an ideological specialist.[50] Harry Tisch, first secretary of Rostock, and Erich Mielke, head of the Stasi, were made candidate members as a reward for their participation in the Ulbricht affair. Major demotions at the top came only at the eighth plenum of the Central Committee in October 1973, when Walter Halbritter, an economics specialist and the architect of the price reform under the New Economic System (NES), lost his position on the Politburo. Günter Mittag was also replaced temporarily as economics secretary. A third technocrat from the Ulbricht era, Günther Kleiber, stayed on the Politburo temporarily as a candidate, but his star was also on the wane.[51]

Regarding the composition of the main party organs, the secretariat remained the realm of pure ideological and organizational specialists, and the number of economic specialists in the Central Committee was reduced. By the time of the tenth party congress in 1981, only five representatives of the economic apparatus were members of the Central Committee.[52] In short, whatever technocratic trend there was in the composition of the Central Committee under Ulbricht had been curtailed by Honecker.

As opposed to the mild changes made at the top, large-scale turnover occurred at the provincial level. Shortly after the eighth party congress in 1971, five of the fifteen BL first secretaries were changed. Honecker chose men for these positions with careers and orientations similar to his own. The patronage based on career background is obvious. Like Honecker, four of the five new applicants had played an important role in the FDJ, and three had been close collaborators of Honecker at the FDJ while he was its chief.[53]

Honecker seemed to have a good idea of the kind of first secretary he wanted to run his provinces. By 1987, thirteen of the fifteen BL first secretaries had careers exclusively in the ideological, youth league, and organizational wings of the SED apparatus. Of the two that did not, one BL Schwerin first secretary, Heinz Ziegner, had extensive experience (six years) in the apparatus of the FDJ while Honecker was youth chief, and the other, Hans Albrecht, the only "technocrat" in the group, was widely regarded even among East Germans as one of the most corrupt and brutal provincial officials in the country. The "ideal" career for becoming a BL first secretary included some time spent in the youth league apparatus, a stint as ideological secretary, and then a longer period as second secretary of the same Bezirk in which one became first secretary.[54]

The picture at the Kreis level looks much the same, although here my data is far from complete. Of the sixty-five first secretaries of Kreisleitungen for which I have fairly complete biographical information, forty had made their careers primarily in either the youth league, the ideological apparatus, or the SED's organizational bureaucracy. The careers of these officials indicate a replication of the Bezirk-level experience.

Once Honecker had settled on the type of officials he wanted, he let them remain in office largely undisturbed. Long tenures in office were not only an informal practice, but a matter of policy. In the case of chairmen of Bezirk councils, a midlevel administrative body, Bräuer and Conrad recommended leaving them in their jobs for twelve years.[55] By 1985 the average tenure for sixteen BL first secretaries[56] was 13.6 years, with six first secretaries having served more than 15 years, two for 22 years, and one for 27 years. Eighteen BL economics secretaries[57] in 1984 averaged 13.9 years in office. Seven had served over 15 years. Similarly, BL agricultural secretaries averaged 13.9 years at the same job. As long as they maintained political stability and ideological conformity in their territory, and did not publicly oppose the policies of the center, first secretaries were not fired. Based on the declining economic performance of all Bezirke, their positions were obviously not tied to any strict economic performance criteria.

Like Hough's prefects, local SED secretaries were men of the provinces. In 1987, of the thirteen BL first secretaries for which I have birthplace data, ten were born in small towns (none of which are among the twenty largest in East Germany) as the sons of workers in provincial industries. Noteworthy is that the three who do not fit into this category, Horst Schumann of Leipzig, Werner Eberlein of Magdeburg, and Günter Jahn of Potsdam, were all sons of prominent prewar Communists.

By 1987, the average age of a BL first secretary was just over sixty years old, which meant that for the most part they were too young to have participated in the risky business of underground activity during the 1930s, but were old enough to have witnessed and understood the final collapse of the Third Reich. By contrast, the men whom they replaced in the 1960s and 1970s had led completely different lives. The earlier generation, which included such men as Honecker, Stasi chief Erich Mielke, and ideology czar Kurt Hager, as well as most of the provincial secretaries, participated in the drama of illegal activity under the Nazis. Most had spent their childhoods in large cities. Following the Nazi seizure of power in 1933, many had spent time on the run, living under false identities or, worse, in prisons and concentration camps. Thereafter, they administered the transformation of social relations and the construction and reconstruction of an industrial base on East German soil, and they were still at the helm when the Berlin Wall went up.

This older group, "the men of 1909," were intelligent political entrepreneurs, who certainly could have prospered in any social system, including the one against which they struggled, but chose instead to play for higher stakes, a game in which the potential payoff was high, but failure meant paying the ultimate price. Their replacements, "the men of 1929," by virtue of background and life experience were conservative men who valued the merits of stability. Although such a generalization is hazardous, as sons of the provincial proletariat growing up in Nazi and then Soviet-occupied small towns, they probably did not respond well to new ideas, but thrived in a situation where everyone knew their place and what was expected of them. The endless cycles of socialist economic campaigns and rituals, and the propaganda that surrounded the East German productivist culture, built the existential nest in which these officials made their political homes.

Based on career training and social background, then, the officials who controlled the provinces in the Honecker years were not technocrats. Although Bezirk-level economics and agricultural secretaries generally had considerable experience in some branch of the economy before entering the apparatus, from the standpoint of his career a Bezirk economics secretary had reached the end of the line. In the GDR, the generational transition in the provincial leadership was not from ideologue to industrial administrator, but from revolutionary political entrepreneur to ideologue. In this sense, as time went on ideology became more and not less important. One should not, however, dismiss these officials as "mere" ideologues, as practitioners of a kind of socialist scholasticism, or doubt their own special kind of hard-headedness. Their backgrounds prepared them well for the rugged political road in the 1980s, when both the GDR's economic and political arrangements would come under attack, from friend as well as foe.

An agitprop specialist in East Germany had to be an unusual kind of person. Such an official encountered political attitudes and difficulties far more intractable than in other countries of the Soviet bloc. Day in and out the agitator knew with absolute certainty that the better part of the GDR's population went home in the evening and received a far more convincing political education on West German television than could possibly be provided in party meetings and public gatherings. In a way, to be a professional propagandist meant daily to engage in a constant struggle against the popular cultural tide of Western civilization. To survive long at such a job, the propagandist most likely had to be both resourceful and a true believer.

As noted earlier, the debates on cadres policy revealed a muted technocratic trend in the 1960s and a swing back in the direction of ideological orientation in the 1970s and 1980s. Certainly, the insistence on party membership for assuming an important post in 1975 had a far different meaning than it did in 1952. Furthermore, after 1963, the system of specialized institutions of higher learning vastly increased the academic experience of the party and state apparatus. According to one source, by 1981 all secretaries of Bezirksleitungen, and 98 percent of secretaries of Kreisleitungen had received diplomas of higher learning.[58]

But the content of the curriculum at most educational institutions attended by full-time party workers suggests that their educational experience was as much one of socialization into a given way of thinking, a "grammar of life," as it was of technical training. This went especially for visits to the party schools, an obligatory step for any ambitious manager.[59] And for those pursuing a purely "political" career, for the young party secretaries, an extended stay in Moscow at the Higher Party School often meant coming away with little more than the rudiments of the Russian language.[60] A perusal of the *avtoreferati* (detailed abstracts in Russian) of dissertations written by SED members at the party school of the Communist Party of the Soviet Union (CPSU) reveals dissertation topics mostly on how to conduct ideological and organizational (cadres) work.[61]

One should not conclude, however, that the political education of cadres was a pointless exercise. On the contrary, the cultural immersion in the ways of the Leninist world at the *Parteihochschule* in Berlin, the newfound friendships among their fellow members of the elite, or, alternatively, the shared trials of an extended stay in Moscow, the capital of the Communist world, was a formative experience for many officials. The "knowledge" they received helped them do their job, it helped them secure the power of the party, and it prepared them for the kind of institutions in which they would work.

It is in this light that the renewed importance of ideology after Ulbricht's fall from power is to be understood. The interpretation of ideology as unimportant is absurd, for if it did not matter at all, why did the leadership not simply dispense with it and the entire institutional infrastructure for propagating it? For the SED, ideology was the code of power, and while economic processes undoubtedly required technological know-how and skill to take place at all, such processes were preferably administered by people who could interpret them as part of a larger vision, whether it be building communism or competing with the West. When, in 1971, Kurt Hager attacked the proponents of cybernetics, he did so because they were trying to substitute their language, the language of cybernetics, for that of Marxism-Leninism in understanding economic processes.[62]

These brief observations on elite socialization under communism inevitably lead to comparisons with similar processes in liberal democratic countries. Is it not the case that liberal democracies do much the same thing? After all, we too have institutions that serve as conduits to the higher levels of power. One need only think of Harvard, Princeton, the Navy, or a dozen or so law and business schools in order to compile a fairly comprehensive list of such socializing institutions in the United States. The difference is that most people living in liberal democracies, including those who attend the elite institutions, receive remarkably little *formal* political socialization. What they do receive they acquire informally through exposure to the media and the limited number of hours spent in elementary and high school civics classes. Western governments spend very little time ensuring that their bureaucrats learn and explicitly accept the main values of the institutions in which they work, and almost none at all at inventing a language or a cultural code to express the values of the system. Perhaps this is so, as most postmodernists would argue, because the values and discourse of Western modernity are reproduced so insidiously and unconsciously. Even if such an evaluation is accurate for liberal democracies, in East Germany, as in other Communist countries, cultural reproduction was a conscious act that had to be repeated over and over. The SED therefore took ideas, political socialization, and the myths and rituals associated with communism very seriously. Anyone who desired a successful career at the middle and upper levels of power had to spend many months in classes that were specifically designed to provide a systematic understanding of the "socialist situation," a language in which to express it, and an armor to protect themselves from capitalist interpretations of it.

The priority that the SED assigned to ideological education helps explain why, despite the visible signs of corruption and self-serving behavior at the top of the political hierarchy, the kind of spectacular corruption seen in Poland, Hungary, and Romania during the 1970s and 1980s was largely absent in the GDR, especially at the middle levels of power. Notwithstanding (or perhaps because of) the challenges posed by the proximity of West Germany, the SED was an organization consisting of a remarkable number of true believers. Party secretaries at the Bezirk and Kreis level lived fairly modest lives. Since 1989 very few of them have been charged or even accused of abusing their public office for private ends. Even more important than the relative absence of corruption, however, the SED's commitment to ideological education also contributes to our understanding of why the vast majority of the East German elite remained loyal to the ideas of socialism, and the SED as an organizational vehicle implementing these ideas, long after the visible signs of economic decay had set in. How the socialist economy helped to institutionalize these biases is the subject we turn to next.

Chapter 5 The Campaign Economy

Unwilling to reform its economy or revise its understanding of socialism, the SED found itself atop a classically Stalinist economy well into the 1980s. Day-to-day management of economic decay ultimately fell into the hands of the regional and district party elite. How did party secretaries and instructors respond to the environment in which they operated? What kinds of measures did they take to stave off economic crisis during the 1970s and 1980s? This chapter begins a three-part analysis of the behavior of the regional, district, and shop floor party organs in an era of economic decline.

In a command economy, it is generally acknowledged that all sorts of supporting and coordinating functions necessary to the effective functioning of enterprises somehow fall through the bureaucratic cracks. Enterprises may be formally subordinate to ministries in the capital but most are located in the industrial provinces, far away from the caring, watchful eye of the center. The more complex an economy, the more difficult and intricate becomes the act of bureaucratic coordination. East Germany, the most industrialized country in the Communist world, arguably faced this contradiction earlier and more squarely than any country in the Soviet bloc.

In his pathbreaking study of Soviet industrial administration, *The Soviet Prefects*, Jerry Hough argued that historically the local party organs played a crucial role in addressing this problem. Stepping into the bureaucratic breach left by central planners and administrators, the local party organs constituted, in his words, an essential element of "development administration" within the Soviet model.[1] They supplied useful and otherwise costly administrative information to the center about production, participated actively in problems of supplies procurement and planning, and mobilized the labor force and the local population to work for national goals. Most important, the local party organs served as regional coordinators, regulating "the relationships of the specialized development institutions [read: planning organs, ministries and enterprises] with each other and with the community," hence the analogy with the French prefect.[2]

The SED's regional (*Bezirksleitung* or BL) and district (*Kreisleitung* or KL) organizations also performed these functions. The prefect model thus seems generally applicable to the GDR. However, in East Germany, the impression one gleans from evidence on the local party secretary is less that of a development administrator or a French prefect, and more that of a crisis manager struggling to stave off industrial decay and social unrest. As I argue in this chapter, Hough's image of the party secretary gathering economic information, procuring supplies for local enterprises, participating in production scheduling and planning, executing and initiating economic campaigns, and the like must be supplemented with a second image. Into the tapestry of party secretaries rationally following the incentives of the center and their locality is woven a complex administrative culture, involving symbolic displays of power and bureaucratic infighting, with its statuses and rewards only partially coinciding with economically rational behavior.

Economic Information

Like their Soviet counterparts, the local SED organs provided the center with a source of information separate from the more elaborate network of economic ministries and state statistical offices.[3] Directors of important enterprises regularly presented reports on the state of plan fulfillment before a meeting of the entire BL or KL secretariat (a local version of the Politburo). Such meetings were taken very seriously and could, at times, become quite uncomfortable for the director of the plant in question. As one observer notes, when faced with difficult questions about plan shortfalls, management had little choice but to sit "in silence, like school boys before an examination board."[4]

This kind of reporting went on at every level. Party secretaries who exuded confidence before their subordinates were noticeably anxious days before going to the Bezirk capital for "supervision" at the hands of the BL first secretary.[5] Similarly BL first secretaries, ministers, and general directors of major enterprises often reported directly to the Politburo on projects under "party supervision" (*Parteikontrolle*). Reports to the party apparatus were normally delivered at regular intervals. However, if an enterprise was having difficulty meeting its production quota for a particularly important product, visits to headquarters increased in frequency.[6]

Apart from the participation of economic officials in secretariat meetings, BL and KL secretariats possessed several information sources of their own. Through the highly developed network of "party information"—the written reports of enterprise party organizations—and visits of professional party "instructors" to the enterprises, the secretariat could generally acquire a rough sense of the effectiveness of enterprises in its region.[7] The secretariat also had access to information provided by organizations outside the party apparatus altogether. First, the Workers' and Peasants' Inspection Committee (Arbeiter und Bauerninspektion or ABI), an institutional inheritance of Lenin's Rabkrin and the Khrushchev era Party-State Control Committee, provided much useful information on economic activities.[8] Although the relationship of the ABI to the local party organs was never formally discussed in great detail, the two worked closely. The archives of the SED Bezirk organizations are filled with reports of the ABI claiming to have found hidden production reserves.[9] Despite periodic suggestions from the party apparatus that the division of labor between the SED and the ABI should be more orderly, the SED seems to have valued this alternative source of information.[10]

The Ministry for State Security (the Stasi) constituted a second source of alternative economic information. With offices in every Bezirk and Kreis and an entire division (Main Department 18) at all levels for dealing with "security matters" in the economy, the Stasi was in a perfect position to gather information. In practice, "security matters" often meant reporting on the plan fulfillment of economic sectors considered important for political stability. The evidence also suggests local level Stasi economics officers were frequently creatures of the local party apparatus. As such, they could be useful sources of relatively routine economic information by way of the economics secretary.[11] Yet such extensive information gathering did not guarantee that the "product" would be well received or acted upon by the local party organs. One former Stasi official from Leipzig notes that he did not find the economics secretary of the local BL very responsive to the information he provided.[12]

Most forms of information gathering, as could be expected, fell within the purview of ordinary bureaucratic communication. Some of this activity, however, seems to have had as much a political as an economic function, or at least consisted of a peculiar mix of the two. To illustrate this, I briefly consider the role and function of the typical enterprise visit.

The Enterprise Visit

In addition to routine types of information gathering, party secretaries often visited enterprises in their territories. Conventionally, the enterprise visit was the job of lower-level BL or KL officials called instructors. Occasionally, however, regional and district first secretaries themselves paid their respects. If the enterprise produced a valuable commodity or was having trouble in meeting its deliveries, the visits quickly multiplied.

What was the rationale for the high-level enterprise visit? One reason is certainly that such visits circumvented the cumbersome system of written reports, where fulfillment of production goals or plans for technical innovation could be hidden in a sea of manipulated statistics. The evidence is quite overwhelming that first secretaries doubted much of the written information that landed on their desks.[13]

Visits to an enterprise that were sincerely meant to gather information and check on the validity of reports were usually undertaken without advance warning to the plant management.[14] Such unplanned visits also reminded managers of the party's preparedness to check up on them at any time. One must also note, though, that visits by first secretaries often served political rather than economic ends. For one thing, the local party organs simply did not have the personnel to obtain a comprehensive picture of what was happening at every enterprise in their region.[15] For another, the top personnel of the secretariat usually did not have the expertise to determine whether the production processes of an enterprise were organized as efficiently as possible. What was usually accomplished by such a visit was a dose of moral support and, in cases where the enterprise seemed blatantly shoddy in its operation, a good deal of badgering and finger wagging.

Landolf Scherzer's reportage provides us with a good example of this genre of activity. In 1986, First Secretary Fritschler of the KL Bad Salzungen knew during his trip to the Fischbach Aluminum Works that the enterprise was once profitable but had since fallen deeply into debt. His first comment concerned not the details of production but the mess of piled up goods he found in one corner. Fritschler was told that one "garbage corner" (*Dreckecke*) is always necessary in this kind of operation. Upon finding a second such pile he launched into a lecture, "But you said that you need *one* garbage corner, comrades, *one*! . . . when the management tolerates disorder in storing materials, the workers won't respect you when you demand discipline from them."[16] From there he went on to ask a worker in the rationalization department of the factory how many industrial robots were at work in the factory. The worker responded, "six are working, the other four not yet." "But for the Kreis accounting you reported them all working," retorted Fritschler, "I'd just like to know how many dead souls we report daily."[17] Given the detailed knowledge required to make such an observation, the comment had probably been prepared for the first secretary in advance by KL instructors. It suggests that the line between actual help in organizing production or stimulating its improvement and displays of political authority "over" production were often difficult to determine. Much, of course, depended on the expertise and goodwill of the secretary concerned.

Former first secretary of the BL Berlin, Günter Schabowski, describes in his memoir, *Der Absturz*, the way he ideally conducted an enterprise visit:

After discussions with colleagues at their workplace, there was usually a discussion with 30 to 50 members of the enterprise. Younger and older employees, men and women, workers, technicians, engineers, foremen and brigade chiefs, party members and nonmembers took part. So-called accounting reports [*Rechenschaftsberichte*], chemically cleaned, rosy representations of the situation in the enterprise, together with oaths of greater performance were not permitted. I quickly gained agreement when I said: You have no time. We're also not lacking things to do; so let's not keep it at the level of empty phrases. Say where it hurts, where you're not making progress, where your reach is too short, and we from the BL will to try to help. If you have ten problems that plague you, and we can only help with two, then it was worth it for both sides.[18]

Schabowski's testimony suggests that "accounting reports," even when given on the spot, did not necessarily reveal to the local party organs a true picture of the enterprise. "Production oaths" (a theme dealt with shortly) were more a part of the political ritual of the enterprise visit than a significant part of production activity.

This is not to say that enterprise visits had no value at all. The evidence strongly indicates, however, that behind much of the personal contact between party secretaries and enterprises was a good deal of political theater, ritual, and meaning. Many enterprise visits by regional and district party secretaries, especially the first secretary, had more the flavor of an American-style election campaign stop than the lending of political assistance to serve economic goals. In an interesting aside, Schabowski critically assesses his predecessor as BL Berlin first secretary, Konrad Naumann, giving special attention to the way he conducted his relationship with enterprises in his area:

> I forbade myself early on the bad habit of ordering the workers to stand in line just because I was visiting an enterprise. When I was still a candidate member of the Politburo, twice I had experienced this in enterprises in Potsdam. I thought the fifty-meter stretch through a celebratory row was like running the gauntlet. Disconcerted and disgusted, I asked the local master of ceremonies afterward whether he did not share my opinion that the whole theater humiliated both the employees and myself. Their reaction was both shocked and confused. They didn't mean anything bad by it. But that was the point![19]

The source of "shock" and "confusion" among the workers was Schabowski's suggested violation of what had become the norm for visiting first secretaries. Maybe *he* did not expect a "theater" but the reaction of the workers betrayed the fact that most party secretaries did, and the workers had come to expect it and accept it as in some way normal. As a further sign of the ceremonial value attached to the planned visit, Schabowski notes how he was repeatedly given freshly cut flowers—an article that every worker knew to be in extremely short supply—on his enterprise visits.[20]

At least as important as the economic rationale behind the secretary's visit to the factory, then, was its celebratory and ceremonial meaning as a conspicuous display of loyalty to the person of the first secretary and the authority of the party in the economy. Such visits often received extensive attention in the Bezirk press, with published accounts of the secretary's remarks on pressing issues of the day. In short, this form of information collection and assistance provided a specific mix of the practical with the affective that typified the role of the local party organs in the economy.

Supplies Procurement and Production Scheduling

Despite the general SED principle that it should guide the work of the state and economic organs without "substituting" for them, their access to information and political clout inevitably brought the local party organs into active intervention in the economy. As Schabowski notes in his memoirs, "Emergency and disaster aid of the economic variety took up the largest part of my working time. No differently than the local council or assembly, we were occupied with the laundry division of the Charité hospital and the 'greening' of the residential areas, with the garbage and with suspicious disappearances in the liquor warehouses, with the damaged production line in a baking combine and with the rotten parquet floor in the Berlin Sports Hall, in January with drinks for the summer and in July with the Christmas parties for enterprises."[21]

Hough identifies the procurement of supplies for local enterprises as one of the crucial roles played by the local party organs in the Soviet Union—a key element in the prefect model. Although formally forbidden to go outside the chain of command, Soviet "plant managers . . . found it necessary to turn for assistance to their nongovernmental supervisors—the local party organs."[22] On the whole, Hough's model is valid for East Germany as well. The staffs of the BLs and KLs, as well as the first secretaries themselves, spent a good deal of time finding missing or undelivered supplies necessary for keeping plants running as well as securing the supply of the local population. Even when an enterprise had the money to acquire needed supplies, the "balance" as promised by the planners could often not be "confirmed." In this case, help from the BL or KL was indispensable, especially in getting those supplies for which the funds had been allocated but delivery had simply not been made.

Within their territories, local party organs enjoyed wide discretionary powers to deal with the distribution of scarce resources under their control.[23] In Erfurt, for example, the secretariat of the BL established priority lists of enterprises with access to the services of the local assembly and construction combine for renovation, modernization, and additions.[24] This was necessary, according to the deputy director of the Erfurt construction combine, because most industrial enterprises in the region put in their orders for work at the beginning of the year.[25] They did so for the simple reason that most did not wish to tie up internal reserves later in the year when they would need them in the traditional practice of "storming" to fulfill the plan.[26] Experience had shown that the construction combine could not work on all the projects simultaneously with any degree of efficiency, and the end result would be many construction projects begun and almost as many incomplete. The BL, therefore, took it upon itself to stagger the starting times (although the criteria used in ranking were not clear) as part of its more general mandate to secure continuity in production.[27]

In their role as supply coordinators and priority setters, local party secretaries confronted several obstacles. The most important was their small number despite the large demands on their time. Especially in the case of supplies procurement and the allocation of scarce resources—fields requiring great political clout to effect any change—the first secretary simply did not have the time to attend to every delivery and scheduling problem that came up. A good staff could keep the first secretary apprised of the many trouble spots but the political influence needed to speed deliveries, especially at the Kreis level, was usually the preserve of the first secretary or the economics secretary.[28]

Apart from the more obvious constraints on the secretaries' time, two additional important issues should be considered in evaluating the effectiveness of the East German "prefects." The first concerns the economic efficiency of party interventions in supplies procurement and setting priorities in production scheduling. Writing after the fall of communism, it is inappropriate to take Hough to task for arguing that the power of local Communist officials to ration scarce resources to factories in their regions or to otherwise procure hard-to-get factors of production for important factories added to the economic rationality of decision making. It is instructive, however, to show why this could not be the case.[29]

Certain prestigious enterprises, such as the computer industry in Erfurt or the brown coal combines in the southern Bezirke, or whatever the dominant industrial branch a region happened to be (shipbuilding in Rostock, oil refining in Frankfurt, and chemicals in Karl-Marx-Stadt), received the favors and energies of the local party apparatus over less politically powerful branches or enterprises. These enterprises, however, counted among the perennially largest economic losers of the GDR (the most profitable being the medium-sized formerly private enterprises, the majority of which over the years inevitably decayed due to capital starvation), and providing them with privileged access to supplies did not necessarily add up to greater economic rationality or efficiency for the economy as a whole. In the absence of a market to determine the relative merits of distributing resources, the establishment of priorities in distribution of supplies was a political decision, not an economic one. Under conditions of shortage, giving supplies to one plant was in effect to deny them to a second.

Bear in mind at this point, however, that Hough discusses *effective*, not *efficient*, development administration, and it is therefore not surprising that party interventions in the supplies realm seem to have functioned best when they were short-term, required the rapid mobilization of local resources, and the goals were limited and clear. Long-term campaigns promoting the introduction of science and technology into local industry, the incessant drives to improve materials economy in enterprises, and the effort to reduce energy use at all levels of the economy were too diffuse to have any sustained economic impact.

The second issue concerns the extent to which management actually did turn to the local party organs for supplies procurement, and the exact nature of the relationship. As is generally acknowledged, Communist enterprises engaged in a good deal of self-supply that bypassed the party apparatus altogether. Such behavior is a highly rational strategy under conditions of shortage. As noted already, starting in the 1970s the formation of vertically integrated industrial combines was undertaken with the idea that the need for constant political intervention in the supply and procurement process would be undercut by the "relatively closed" production process of each individual combine.

The combines partially solved two problems of supply procurement. First, by cutting down on the number of productive units playing the game, the combine reform appears to have streamlined the system of informal bargaining and deal making for goods that was so common throughout the socialist world. According to one East German source, the Central Committee seminars in Leipzig served as a convenient venue for much of the barter trade among general directors.[30] This system of informal bargaining created a further source for self-supply, which cut the local party apparatus out of the procurement loop altogether. Second, apart from informal bargaining, the "formal" side of the combine reform seems to have solved some of the supply problems of the enterprises that conventionally required the assistance of local party organizations. Most officials interviewed agreed: since the 1960s the activity of the BLs and especially the KLs in procurement for large enterprises had declined.

But the formal side of the reform was only a partial solution. In theory, supply problems were dealt with juridically through contracts that supplemented and reinforced the plan. Failure to deliver contracted goods or services would result in a fine to the enterprise. To adjudicate these disputes, the regime set up a network of contract courts at the Bezirk and national level. Each month the final pages of the journal *Wirtschaftsrecht* described the relevant details of cases as decided by the State Contract Court.[31] As a scholarly discipline, economic law developed a life and language of its own, with thousands of pages of journal articles and books devoted to the question of amalgamating plan and law in economic administration. Thousands of cases were heard and fines imposed with the intention of meting out the needed system of wrist slaps to keep the supplies running smoothly throughout the wholesale branch of the economy.

However, several factors limited the use of law and contracts in streamlining the supply system. First, if an enterprise could manage to have its plan reduced, it was no longer bound by the contract it had signed: in the GDR law never supplanted plan. Second, as in other socialist countries, these disputes between enterprises were often solved at levels other than the court. According to one East German jurist, a combine had to be certain that it would never again need the favors of a partner before taking it to court in a humiliating contract dispute; for even if an enterprise won, in the long run it might lose the goodwill of its sole supplier of necessary inputs.[32] A far better method was to convince the ministries or Central Committee departments to strike some sort of bargain. Even if a case did make it to court, this did not necessarily create a new incentive structure for the defendant.[33] Most managers knew that they would, in the end, probably receive as much compensation from violating enterprises as they had to pay out for their own violations, thus establishing a zero-sum, merry-go-round of contract violations.[34]

In summary then, the evidence from East Germany confirms similar observations made in the Soviet Union, that the local party organs played an active role in supplies procurement. However, their role is more complex and contradictory than the prefect model suggests. One finds little evidence proving that party intervention to secure supplies for one enterprise over another contributed to the overall rationality of the economy or to the effectiveness of industry as a whole in the regions or districts. Furthermore, the combine reform in the late 1970s and the ensuing changes in the industrial structure increasingly excluded the local party organs from the supply loop.

Soviet Production Techniques

If the impact of the local party secretaries on supplies procurement and production scheduling for local enterprises was attenuated by the growing trend toward a vertically integrated industrial structure, this did not mean that the local party organs ceased to be interested in the enterprises located in their territories. On the contrary, the perennial problems of the economy provided a steady rationale for political mobilization. Starting in the 1970s and extending into the 1980s, BLs and KLs undertook a continuous stream of campaigns intended to encourage enterprises to devote greater attention to "qualitative indicators, increases in productivity and efficiency, energy and materials economy, capital use, and other intensification factors."[35] In discussing the role of technology, Herbert Ziegenhahn, the first secretary of the BL Gera, cast it in traditional Leninist terms: "Here is the decisive battlefield of the party's economic strategy."[36]

In a milieu of ineffective vertical incentives, the local party secretaries found plenty of room to play the role of "promoter of intensification."[37] Most attempts on behalf of the local party organs to increase productivity revolved around the popularization of Soviet and East German production techniques. Usually initiated at the center with official sponsorship of both the relevant Central Committee department and ministry, production campaigns were carried out by the local party and state apparatus.[38] Some, such as the Brasov method of accident-free work and the Nina Nazarova method of machine maintenance, were implemented in enterprises with many meetings and much fanfare.[39] But the content of these methods turned out to be rather vapid—the Brasov method consisting merely of supplementing the system of workplace inspections for "order, security, and cleanliness" with a point system for rating different work stations, and the Nazarova method was primarily a promise of a brigade (the primary level of workplace organization) to complete its daily work ahead of time so that it could leave time for maintenance between shifts.

If one can momentarily withhold judgment on the dubious efficacy of such campaigns within the given systems of incentives, one may still acknowledge as admirable the goals embodied in these adapted Soviet work methods. Cleanliness and punctuality are important industrial virtues. Yet the question remains: is it really necessary to construct a political campaign to secure the care, repair, and cleanliness of the workplace? Did this not reinforce the type of interference in the details of production that the party was supposed to avoid? And even when the goals of the campaigns were noble, frequently their organizational principles and the methods of evaluation were far from clear.[40]

If, as seems reasonable, both the central and local party organs must have been aware of the limited usefulness of such campaigns (and the fact that they were the brunt of humor—even in East German cabarets—supports this assumption),[41] the question arises as to why they persisted.[42] In Berlin, production campaigns nourished the illusion that the party was actually addressing pressing economic problems. At the provincial and local level, the continuous adoption of Soviet work techniques and innovations by regional and district first secretaries (sometimes after they had been discredited in the Soviet Union itself) provided a unique opportunity to declare in public that crucial economic tasks were being addressed and, furthermore, that they were being addressed by the methods developed in the most politically important country in the world, the Soviet Union. Political careers could be built and protected by a conspicuous and symbolic display of how socialist production techniques from the East, pure artifacts of the rule of the party, had as much impact on the economy—a sphere universally regarded as decisive in legitimating the system—as any machine imported, copied, or stolen form the West. Here was the forum in which the central organs as well as the local party secretaries proved their usefulness to the SED leadership, to the sympathetic members of the community, and, most important, to themselves.

These production techniques formally promoted economic ends, which is why they took on such great political meaning and why they would be repeated over and over again. The fact that their economic contribution was modest at best, disorganizing and bothersome at worst, remained very much beside the point.[43] To get some idea of the political ethos behind these campaigns, consider a rather typical article advocating the extension of the Zlobin method (a Soviet piecework system in apartment construction, discussed in chapter 7) from a realm where, for reasons of standardization, it had a reasonable chance of working, apartment construction, into other riskier projects such as high-rise and custom industrial construction:

> The further implementation of this progressive Soviet innovator method is primarily a management problem and therefore an ideological question. Its implementation worried the party secretary of the Dresden Transportation and Excavation Combine, Comrade Poniz. The managers and the party secretaries had an argument that would have hindered the use of the Zlobin method. "We're already working according to Brasov and the principles of Scientific Organization of Labor . . . now something new? It may work in apartment construction but not in high-rise or industry." In discussions it was made clear that these methods serve the goals of intensification, and therefore can be combined. And when in high-rise there is no standardization, then this must be done in high-rise too.[44]

This was a matter of power. Party secretaries could hardly have removed themselves from the spectacle altogether and expected to stay in power. Someone as enlightened and "liberal" as BL Dresden First Secretary Hans Modrow (who became a member of the Bundestag after unification), for example, regularly published articles in the Central Committee's economics journal *Die Wirtschaft*, describing enterprise intensification conferences, economic education, and the various campaigns organized under his command to improve the efficiency of enterprises in Dresden.[45]

Production campaigns were not limited to the use of recent Soviet production methods. One common form of territorial campaign to increase productivity was known simply as the "performance comparison" (*Leistungsvergleich*), a method going back to Lenin's time and used extensively by Khrushchev as well.[46] Performance comparisons consisted of identifying two or more enterprises in a Bezirk or Kreis, and then setting up a competition for performance on certain range of production indicators. This form of production campaign received extensive political support from the center and was conducted in every region in the GDR between 1971 and 1989.[47] In Karl-Marx-Stadt during the 1970s, the BL conducted a continuous comparison between foundries.[48] In Bezirk Potsdam at the Kreis level, the KLs Neurippen and Kyritz conducted performance comparisons in agriculture.[49] The general principle was that, if two or more enterprises were compared over a range of indicators, the weaker ones could be brought up to the level of the stronger more effectively.

Two shortfalls of this campaign were serious enough to be discussed in the party press. First, the enterprises to be compared frequently had different technological starting points and political importance. In working out a system to evaluate the relative performance without market signals, the authorities faced an almost insurmountably complex task, if their intent was truly to compare.[50] Second, even when some rough comparison could be made, it was extremely difficult to transfer the good experience and methods from one setting to another. Often this transfer would involve the stronger enterprise in costly diversions of labor to the weaker enterprise, and the loss of politically important competitive advantages in the next round of comparisons.[51]

A similar campaign involved providing a chosen enterprise in a district with all the support needed to produce optimally. The idea seems to have been to demonstrate that certain types of enterprises could be made to perform well under the right conditions. In the press, this type of campaign was referred to a "leadership example" (*Führungsbeispiel*). Here, of course, the natural tendency in all production campaigns—that of political influence determining economic performance—was merely raised to a matter of principle.[52] So, for example, in 1984 the KL Schwerin decided to use one enterprise as a leadership example for science and technology, a second enterprise for sales support and export planning, and a third for the public leadership of a socialist competition.[53] In monthly plans laid down by the secretariat, enterprise directors and other representatives of public organizations and management were required to study the results and the methods employed. During 1987 in Karl-Marx-Stadt, the BL conducted a leadership example by outfitting a construction enterprise with all the best CAD/CAM equipment it could find.[54] The results of the *Führungsbeispiele* were dubious at best. By demonstrating that under the optimal administrative conditions an enterprise could prosper, managers were merely encouraged to lobby for their own enterprises to be chosen as the next leadership example.

Materials Economy and Product Quality

Apart from the use of campaigns imported from the Soviet Union and modified in the GDR, two further campaigns merit attention. Efforts to improve materials economy in production and the quality of the final product attracted continuous attention within the local party organs, although the continuity of official policy belies the notion of a campaign. Both areas were given official support from the top, and the ambitious party secretary knew that contributions (or the appearance of contributions) in either or both of these spheres brought public recognition.

Two centrally administered approaches sought to improve materials economy. During the 1970s, Mittag ushered in a series of producer price reforms increasing the wholesale costs of inputs that would ostensibly be reflected in the final financial performance of enterprises. The production indicator "cost per hundred marks of gross output" also received attention in the press and professional journals. In addition to these financial incentives, on the organizational level the management of every enterprise included an entire division devoted to the full-time regulation of material inputs.[55]

Such tinkering with incentive structures and the organization of management, however, did not fundamentally alter the microeconomic and political relationships at work. Notwithstanding production costs, a firm's financial performance remained a function of the political decisions on its credit line and access to raw materials and labor. The true constraint on production therefore continued to be supply, not cost. The new types of production indicators, for their part, never displaced gross output (and indeed could not in a physically planned economy), and the wise manager knew not to sacrifice the former to the latter.

In the absence of effective centrally determined incentives, the BLs and KLs instituted a series of campaigns designed to achieve more output with less input. The process was encouraged by regular articles in *Die Wirtschaft* and *Neuer Weg* written by party secretaries and instructors under the rubric "Materialökonomie." The campaign for materials economy did not alter production profiles or change content in order to streamline resource use, but was aimed simply at a better use of the given inputs. In typical party style, the campaigns were pitched in terms of a problem of overcoming rigid technocratic thinking. In the Eberwalde Crane Works, the party secretary reported that "In the past many comrades . . . were of the opinion that they and their colleagues could have no influence on the process."[56] During the materials economy drive in the Furstenwalde Tire Combine, the party secretary noted in typical fashion: "At first there were many who considered the goals for material economy to be unrealistic. They were of the opinion that wastage is technologically conditioned and could not be lowered without changing the technology. . . . The party leadership and the union in the enterprise as well as the combine management organized a round-table discussion in order to develop the personal initiative of the workers into a mass initiative. . . . The employees promised to have cord wastage not exceed 2.5 percent while increasing output by 500 tires."[57] In energy-intensive regions working groups under the direction of the BL secretariats were deployed to reduce energy use in the enterprises located in their territories.[58] In several Bezirke, party organizations received information from the head bookkeeper of large enterprises and formed teams of roving cost controllers.[59] In Gera, on the initiative of the BL, enterprises were encouraged to conduct cost-benefit analyses of materials use and to work out technically based material use norms.[60] In 1981, the BL Halle supported the introduction of computer-guided production processes to reduce the use of materials.[61]

The press identified a number of successes. In the case of the Eberswalde Crane Works, the party secretary reported that a 50 percent materials savings had been achieved in some areas, and that 80 to 90 percent of cost lowering was due to the influence of local party initiatives.[62] Wilfried Deumer, the economics secretary of the BL Halle, claimed spectacular success for the campaign in his region, the most astounding of which was the Chemical Combine Bitterfeld where one department declared that it had reconditioned its equipment for 10 percent of the projected materials cost.[63]

The Bitterfeld example indicates some obvious inconsistencies in the entire materials campaign. Ordinarily a project can be completed for 10 percent of its projected cost only with extremely distorted original cost estimates. This seems to have been the case in Bitterfeld. Success in other enterprises was invariably accompanied by a deluge of statistical indicators, which under most circumstances do not tell very much. One suspects the opacity was intentional. Party officials must have faced a high degree of uncertainty in evaluating the successes of their particular materials programs—how much their campaigns contributed as opposed to other factors—or even in getting them started. Most managers and workers believed that material shortages resulted from faulty planning and transport breakdowns rather than inefficient use. For this reason, the local party organs constantly warned enterprise party organizations that "discussions of materials economy should not turn into discussions of supply problems."[64]

It is worth bearing in mind that the campaign in materials economy was directed at a more efficient use of the existing distribution of materials, not at changing the distribution to reflect economic needs. Although using less materials more efficiently is generally a good idea, this need not always be the case. In production, the generous or overgenerous use of one input can frequently lead to savings of a second or third highly valued input. Making the transition to intensive production is not simply producing more from less, but of putting resources in the proper amount, in the right hands, at the needed time. Above all, it is not simply the saving of material or production using minimal materials but, rather, a matter of creating greater value per unit of used resources.[65] A campaign designed to encourage miserliness in the use of all inputs may have the opposite effect, that of squandering the valuable ones. In the absence of accurate economic information, the decisions on where to apply pressure for savings could only be political and administrative.[66]

The GDR's economic and political managers understood this quite well. Yet, long after such campaigns became ineffective, they continued to be initiated with much fanfare. The political carnival surrounding the campaigns apparently more than compensated for their limited usefulness. As one typical press article in the campaign for materials economy put it: "The chief task . . . is not simply technical-economic, but to let everyone know how important the task is for the GDR. The employees of the enterprise have obligated themselves to contribute to savings of materials worth 1.2 million marks. By the time of the eighth party congress they had already saved 600,000 marks."[67] The numbers here are meaningless. However, the party found one more outlet for its activities and seemed to be satisfied with the progress made in the campaign. Awards for low material use, such as "collective of model material and energy use" and "best heating technician," were incorporated into the complex of socialist production honors and titles.[68] Clearly, the economic environment had made campaigns and experiments necessary. But from a political point of view, the party did not need (nor could it fashion) experiments that worked or made economic sense.[69]

Much the same can be said for the steady flow of campaigns to improve the quality of products. The question of quality is, of course, intimately connected to that of materials economy. The higher the quality of the product, the lower the number of defective articles and those needing repair, which in and of itself is the largest source of waste in most production processes.

Soviet-type economies suffered from poor quality goods for a number of reasons. The most important, of course, was the emphasis on gross output above all else. Added to this, machines designed for production generally received priority over those designed for testing. Furthermore, planners' preferences for quantity over quality also found expression in differing wage structures. Employees involved in production were normally paid piece rates and on average earned significantly more than quality controllers who worked with hourly wages. Those workers specially trained for quality work usually tried to transfer into production work as soon as possible. Quality control thus became the realm of elderly or infirm workers. Not until the end of the 1950s was this system altered at all, and its main features remained in place into the 1980s.[70]

The primary method for ensuring product quality in the GDR was an administrative designation "Q" for products of superior quality, as developed by the Central Office for Standardization, Measures, and Testing of Goods. An enterprise producing a higher percentage of its goods above the "Q" standard received a higher price for its product.[71] The percentage of production receiving the "Q" varied, but the figure given by the BL Dresden economics secretary in 1982, 33 percent, was quite common, although in Gera in 1976 it was put at 21.6 percent, and many enterprises never made it above the 15 percent level.[72]

Party campaigns to improve quality, therefore, generally entailed a good deal of political agitation to increase the percentage of "Q" production. In 1976, for example, the BL Gera reported that it regularly measured the quality of the work of enterprises in its territory on the basis of proportion of gross production receiving a "Q," the number of defects and repairs, costs, valuta income, and the results of investigations by the ABI, and banking and finance organs.[73] Enterprises in the area were obliged to increase their percentage of gross output designated to receive the "Q" by 2 to 3 percent above the plan. As in the campaigns for materials economy, (nonmonetary) awards were given for high-quality work, such as the title "enterprise of outstanding quality."[74]

Once again, however, one encounters a widespread pattern of behavior that suggests not only serious flaws in the evaluation process, but also indicates that such political campaigns had their own logic largely unconnected to the actual quality of articles produced.[75] The first sign of political flimflammery is the inflation over time in the percentage of "Q" products.[76] The rising numbers stand in blatant contradiction to the decreasing quality of GDR goods (relative to world standards and in absolute terms) after the nationalization of the semiprivate firms in 1972.

A reasonable explanation for this "Q" inflation (and for the ineffectiveness of the program) runs as follows: local officials learned that the only way to stand out from the pack was to show a faster increase in "Q" production than the surrounding localities without making their results seem absurd, thus bringing down upon themselves a formal investigation as a reward for hubris. During the 1970s and 1980s therefore the norm for "Q" production gradually rose, even though as an actual reflection of production quality it had ceased to have any meaning.

The evidence on SED campaigns in materials economy and quality control offered here suggests that both were subject to the same general political logic as other campaigns in the economy. Into an otherwise well-intentioned tapestry of formal incentives was woven a complex bureaucratic culture, whose actual rewards and sanctions coincided only partially with economic rationality.

Campaigns in the Planning Process

Local party organizations spent a great deal of time in production planning and investment. The participation of the local party secretaries in planning is difficult to characterize, however, not only because the archival evidence is contradictory but also because their influence seems to have been so varied. In relation to locally subordinated enterprises, the KLs and the BLs seemed to have almost unlimited power in ordering plan changes, hence their frequent activity in the construction sector.[77] But since the scale of the operations was generally smaller at the local level and the information on the performance of the plant more secure (since the managers were creatures of the BL or KL), there was little reason for political power plays around changes in the plan.

Power plays were more common in the relationship of local party secretaries to plants and managers subordinated to a higher instance. Party secretaries were constantly told to discover new "reserves" in enterprises, which the center knew managers hoarded for the day they might be needed for production or barter trade. But when dealing with general directors of combines subordinated to Berlin, KL first secretaries, for example, lacked the immediate authority to change the plan, although with enough memos and telephone calls to the top they could (if so suicidally inclined) encourage the plan to be increased.[78]

One widespread, centrally initiated campaign used frequently during the 1970s and less so in the 1980s was "counterplanning."[79] Its principles of operation were quite straightforward.[80] A plant received its plan assignments and, under political pressure from the BL or KL, the management and workers pledged to uncover "hidden reserves" and overfulfill the plan by a set amount. In effect, therefore, the counterplan was a planned overfulfillment of the plan. There were, of course, quite obvious problems with such a campaign. Not only did planned overfulfillment take the punch out of the already moribund system of year-end bonuses, but clever plant directors very quickly grew wise to this strategy designed to uncover their emergency supplies. Their rational response was to continue to lobby for low plan targets, always reserving a small portion of capacity to comfortably meet the counterplan.[81]

Since BL and KL first secretaries were aware that counterplans and other periodic production commitments connected with party congresses or national holidays constituted a normal part of economic life, they adapted to the rhythms of counterplannning relatively quickly. Like their managerial counterparts, regional and district party secretaries had no wish to make their lives uncomfortable with unexpected and unfulfillable new tasks. It is hardly surprising, then, that the BL Dresden Secretariat regularly planned well in advance exactly how much production from each combine should be kept in reserve to be "used for special occasions,"[82] or when in 1986 KL Bad Salzungen First Secretary Fritschler warned the party secretaries in the enterprises in his area that they had better hold "something in reserve" for the next party congress.[83]

While the local party organs usually did not try to increase the plan for enterprises in their areas, enterprises themselves were subject to arbitrary plan raises from the center. Politically unprotected and locally subordinated small and medium-sized enterprises were especially vulnerable. First secretaries thus spent a good deal of time trying to get enterprise plans reduced in the face of increases coming from above, and, with a good deal of effort, this could be done. Such practice had a long pedigree in East Germany, as Fritz Schenk reminds us from his days in the State Planning Commission in the 1950s, when directors, party secretaries, and even ministers commonly waited for hours for an audience to plead their case for a plan reduction.[84] Time spent reducing the plan could be just as strategically wise for the party secretary as actually finding additional resources to facilitate fulfillment. The rationale for such behavior was quite straightforward: a reduced plan meant a better chance of fulfillment and overfulfillment, an easier life, and all the more praise when successful results could be shown.

Illustrative of this pattern is the situation faced by the Immelborn Metalworks in 1987. Its export plan had suddenly been raised by 150 percent. The choice was simple. Either move to a six-day workweek (which threatened to undermine the sociopolitical pact) or keep things as they were and threaten to fall behind in the export plan. Immelborn was the only enterprise in the GDR to make certain kinds of heavy machinery. As things stood, Immelborn barely covered domestic demand. Increasing its export obligations may have earned several hundred thousand valuta marks for the GDR's coffers, but because the exported machines were needed for domestic production, the net loss to the economy would have amounted to over 9.5 million marks.

Bad Salzungen First Secretary Fritschler stepped in and placed a call to the combine director in Berlin, with the intention of recalling a promise made by the minister and the combine director several months before that there would be no increase in the export plan. When this failed, he decided to "pull in a marker." At the eleventh party congress in 1986, he had met and talked with the minister for construction of machine tools and processing machinery, Rudi Georgi, a powerful minister who had been at his post since 1965. Georgi had said to the first secretary, "If you need my help, call me." In the end Fritschler succeeded, but it was clear that in order to roll back the export plan he needed the help of the minister.[85]

Battles over plan increases and reductions involving the local party secretaries did not always play themselves out so collegially, but were part of the elaborate power struggles that extended to the top of the SED hierarchy. Berlin First Secretary Schabowski reports that in the last years of SED rule, due to shortages of hard currency, materials, new investment, and replacement parts and excessive demand for labor, several days before the beginning of the plan period there were up to 400 million marks of shortages in his Bezirk.[86] The BL Berlin had the time and resources to take an active interest in a dozen enterprises. One was a large clothing combine. As an export-oriented enterprise, it was subject to arbitrary plan increases, although it had little of the political clout enjoyed by the heavy industrial combines that would have allowed it to manipulate its supply situation or make it one of the recipients of the latest technologies. In clothing enterprises the primary problem was a shortage of workers. In one instance, Schabowski reports, the BL Berlin sought help from the Academy of Science on ways to substitute for needed workers but the academy concluded that it was simply not possible to do certain types of sewing without human hands, which meant more workers—a useless recommendation as well as a hopeless request. Only by completely shutting down the line and rebuilding it (and thereby endangering plan fulfillment) could the technology be made to produce more with the existing work force.[87]

The general director of the enterprise decided he could no longer meet the plan and formally refused to accept his production assignments.[88] Such a move was highly risky and unusual. It would have been wiser simply to accept the plan as it was and only later attempt to have the plan reduced. The minister, himself under pressure from Mittag to increase output, decided to come to the enterprise to give the general director a good dressing down. The general director defended himself before the minister. "How do you expect us to do what you set out for us? . . . You can't just lay down the plan numbers and then forbid us to talk about the requirements to fill them. You know that technically we have no more air to breathe. There is no more labor for hire. You demand that from two times two I get not five, but nine. This is a mathematics that rules only in the ministry." For Schabowski, who had come to the meeting, the situation had become too absurd for patience. The minister sat in silence, insisting on the given plan figures until Schabowski exploded. "I've sat here for half an hour listening to your dispute. The director has explained simply and clearly why the plan cannot be fulfilled. You have not even engaged the facts. Maybe you expect him to rent a medicine man from the Navajos—for hard currency—and go with him to the works in order to ask for inspiration or a heavenly solution. Please try to explain to me, an interested layman, how with the given conditions or nonconditions the plan-miracle can be fulfilled."[89] Schabowski was certain that without his presence the director would have been forced to accept a plan that the minister himself knew was unrealistic. But he too was under pressure to show results. "The plan had to look on paper as they wanted it and formally be confirmed." Normally during the year, the plan would be reduced by various bureaucratic maneuvers, but this time the director would not play along.

With Schabowski's help, the enterprise received supplementary workers from Vietnam. (Here, of course, the line between plan-reduction and supplies-procurement strategies is blurred.) Having obtained the extra workers, however, the plant still had to play the roundabout game of contracting out part of its production to Yugoslav enterprises for hard currency, and, in order to cover the costs of producing abroad, goods had to be sold in the West at prices below what had been paid to the Yugoslavs.

But the affair did not end here. When Mittag found out about Schabowski's interference in the matter, he managed to have the operation of the enterprise put on the agenda for discussion in the Secretariat of the Central Committee. The Berlin BL assured the management that it should present the matter simply and, in turn, it would receive the backing of the first secretary. Honecker, who usually followed Mittag's advice, when confronted with the management team wanted to come off on the side of the little man, and ordered Mittag to help the enterprise. But Mittag, ever the bureaucratic intriguer, ensured that at the next conference of general directors, held during the Leipzig Trade Fair, the management of the plant received hefty criticism and it became common knowledge that at the first possible moment its general director would be fired.[90]

This last, less than congenial, example of the local secretaries' activity in the economy leads to the question, If the first secretaries understood that their activities in the economy were at best a rearguard action to stave off decay and ultimately collapse, why did they not move against Honecker, Mittag, and the rest of the SED elite? Why did they continue to perform the increasingly empty rituals of the campaign economy? What explains their inaction? Part of the explanation undoubtedly has to do with the barriers to collective action inherent in a totalitarian polity. The chances of success if one acted alone were minuscule at best. Who would be so foolish to risk his career with criticism that would never see the light of day and probably be forgotten tomorrow, while the other "free rider" first secretaries continued to move up the ladder? Had history not shown that change under socialism was exceedingly difficult, not to mention risky? Under Honecker, even top secret monthly BL reports judged too honest in their portrayal of economic conditions were likely to land the offending first secretary in hot water. Such was the fate of BL Dresden's first secretary Hans Modrow who, in 1985, became the object of a series of official investigations from the center. Although Modrow kept his job, he was forced to write a humiliating letter of self-criticism and thereafter was kept on a very short leash and remained subject to frequent investigations from the center. Such petty harassments served as a warning to the other provincial barons that obedience to the center remained the highest command.[91] The optimal survival strategy for the idealistic midlevel party secretary was to continue to perform the rituals of the campaign economy in the hope that at the margins such activity would improve the lives of ordinary people.

The evidence presented in this chapter, however, suggests a supplementary explanation to the logic of collective action. First secretaries did not rebel or even resist. More important, however, they did not want to rebel—not merely because they understood that change would have cost them their jobs, but because most had made their political homes within the confines of the campaign economy. The campaign economy is a good example of what Schattschneider has termed the "mobilization of bias."[92] While appearing to address pressing economic problems, the campaign economy as an institution organized some issues into politics and organized others out. The public rituals and political theater surrounding the endless cycles of ever new "methods" helped to prevent alternative ways of conceiving the GDR's economic problems from coming to the fore by nourishing the illusion (at least among the central and provincial elites) that the economic challenges of the 1970s and 1980s were being addressed in a specifically Communist manner that had always worked. In the campaign economy the party secretaries were the big men, the men who appeared to get things done, when nothing else worked. The contradictions of central planning justified and gave meaning to their existence. What use was economic success if it was not their success?

Of course, it is worth asking whether politicians in any institutional setting look favorably upon economic successes for which they can take no credit. The answer is, probably not. Or at least they prefer successes for which they can plausibly claim credit. And this logic may account for one of the reasons why politicians do not like technocracy. Technocracy dreams of removing most important issues from the political agenda and placing them in the hands of those most competent to deal with them. But, in such a polity, no political harvest could be reaped because policies would not be openly and publicly value-laden. Power would be secured by mere rank and competence, and not by public affirmation and celebration. I have yet to encounter a human society with political leaders so confident and secure as to resist all power-affirming public ritual. In this respect, the East German provincial and central elites were no different from any American president or governor in recent memory.

The difference, of course, was that in East Germany the necessary values and culture to be transmitted by economic action—that the party was the economic savior—could only be reproduced in an economy of severe disproportions. Indeed, it is ironic that the only way the party's authority could continually be reproduced was if the difficulties in fulfilling mundane tasks of production remained as severe as they were. Otherwise, one could have easily imagined a world without party secretaries running to and fro, playing the role of the "chaser and fixer."[93] In short, their authority relied on a kind of economic crisis and the need for campaigns that can only be sustained in a centrally planned economy, an economy unique in its inability to achieve something within the range of even the most primitive economies, the satisfaction of solvent economic demand.[94] Here we have one more clue to the puzzle of political stability amid economic decay.

Chapter 6 The Party in the Factory

Labor Motivation

in the Twilight

of Communism

Bertold Brecht's sarcastic suggestion, made originally in 1953, that since the SED had lost confidence in the people, it might like to elect a new people, undoubtedly found bitter resonance in the minds of the regional, district, and shop floor party elites. After thirty-five years of Communist rule, the SED still lacked the power to shape industrial relations as it saw fit. A report to the Dresden party organization in 1980 complained, for example, that even on legal workdays, some factories stood idle because up to 80 percent of the work force took legally mandated "housekeeping" holidays. Much to the consternation of the party organization, the plant closures, which really amounted to legalized work slow downs and strikes, had been arranged between management and labor in factories throughout the Bezirk.[1] This chapter examines the attempts of the regional and shop floor elites to improve labor motivation and streamline deployment during the 1970s and 1980s. After framing the environment in which the party operated, I discuss two types of SED labor policies and activities: socialist competitions and a program to deploy labor more effectively, known as the Schwedt initiative. Despite the SED's repeated efforts to increase labor productivity through political campaigns, some of which required a good deal of administrative imagination, the regime's capacity to squeeze more out of its working class was remarkably limited by the context in which it operated.

Understanding this context will perhaps be made easier by comparing it to the situation described by Walder in his study of authority in Chinese factories.[2] Although the differences in scale and scope of Chinese industrial administration from the East German case are obvious, one is unavoidably struck by their similarities, which lends credence to the idea of a generic form of Communist industrial authority. Walder demonstrates that the post-Mao Chinese state enterprise is not simply a place where products are made but is the primary point of contact between the state and the worker. The workplace is the locus of political identity and, in some sense of the word, citizenship. Furthermore, the enterprise provides an array of social services, such as housing, consumer goods, low-cost vacations, health care, and day care for children, usually associated in the West with the market or the sphere of state authority.

Much of this was true for East Germany as well. Walder also notes that a special feature of the Communist factory is the extraordinary degree of job security enjoyed by its employees. Workers cannot be fired or laid off. Since Communist workers do not confront the same intensity of internal enterprise competition for jobs as their non-Communist counterparts, party and management face special kinds of problems in organizing the workplace for the maximization of productivity. Historically, three approaches have simultaneously been used to deal with this problem: segmenting the work force with differential rewards for political-ideological loyalty; segmenting the work force with differential rewards for superior performance; and altering the organization of labor or the technology used in production. The party-state, according to Walder, manipulates the admixture of these three elements in pursuit of greater productivity and political control.

Again, this description fits the situation in East Germany quite well. Several differences between the cases, however, are worth noting. Whereas in China, the development of a labor market was hindered by a number of administrative measures and the oversupply of applicants willing to take up industrial careers, in East Germany starting in the 1950s workers changed jobs relatively freely. By the 1970s, the leadership had succeeded in employing virtually every able bodied adult in the country. Up to 93 percent of adults had full-time jobs and the percentage of female employment was among the highest in the world. Furthermore, the number of agricultural workers left to be mobilized into industry was small.[3] Labor thus remained scarce.

Whereas Walder's description of China indicates a buyers market for labor, East Germany was dominated by a strong sellers market. Workers could not be fired but they could vacate their positions and easily find new jobs. Emigration, legal or illegal, also remained an option. Low labor productivity and steady emigration ensured that labor continued to be in short supply and jobs plentiful. In an attempt to retain their work force, most

Table 6-1. Worker Absenteeism in East Germany and West Germany, 1980s (in percentages)

Industry	East Germany	West Germany
Food	7	7
Engineering	5	4
Clothing	25	6
Furniture	7	4
Miscellanous	7	4
Total	10	6

Source: D. M. W. N. Hitchens et al., *East German Productivity and the Transition to the Market Economy* (Aldershot: Avebury, 1993), 63.

industrial combines responded to the labor market by offering a fairly similar and generous range of social services.

Such market conditions gave the working class a power of sorts. It was not the power to strike, organize, or bargain collectively, but as the rates of absenteeism in table 6-1 illustrate, it did entail the power to withhold services.[4] The SED tried to combat the workers' tacit power with a number of administrative measures. Resignation from work required an employee to justify in writing his or her reasons and usually entailed a discussion with management. Party members could be barred altogether from changing jobs if it contradicted the enterprise party organization's wishes. Such administrative measures helped, but the continuous official concern with *Fluktuation* (job switching) in the 1970s and 1980s indicates that the center could not successfully control the labor market with the tools of decades past.

A second feature of the GDR's labor market set it apart from China. The SED came to power facing an already existing and highly skilled labor force working in industries that were among the most advanced in the world for their time. Chinese planners, conversely, created their industries largely from scratch and had a much better opportunity to influence the development of formal as well as informal organization among the work force. The high skill level of many East German workers made it difficult to replace them with workers mobilized from agriculture. And the experience among older workers of a pre-Communist social order gave those in industries such as printing and machine building a further advantage over their Chinese counterparts. These two traits, the sellers market for labor and a highly skilled and mature labor force, gave the East German worker significant, if tacit, bargaining power with respect to party and management that could not easily be taken away.

Wages and Productivity

This power is best illustrated by the continuing concern with wages and work norms. By 1974, the State Planning Commission noted that officially set wages had lost whatever stimulative function they might have had. In many industries, wages had not changed in fifteen years; in metallurgy and machine building, twenty years. Workers increased their incomes not by working hard during normal hours but by "overtime." Given the chronic supply shortages and irregularities in production, management welcomed the flexibility offered by overtime wages because it provided the means to satisfy a work force that had no choice but to "hurry up and wait." Piece-workers increased their wages through easily overfulfilling weak piece rates. With the specter of the workers uprising in June 1953 still haunting the SED twenty years after the event, party and management refused to touch the issue. In consequence, piece rates became hopelessly outdated. In VEB Mikromat, for example, an electronics enterprise in Dresden, piece rates had not changed at all since 1956 and, by the 1970s, were usually met at a rate of 160 percent.[5]

Ignoring the center, management set wages informally as it saw fit. In 1974 a mere one-quarter of wages fell within the centrally determined guidelines, and in industry and construction only one-tenth. Notwithstanding official guidelines requiring significant wage differentials within an eight-tiered scheme, in practice wage differentials remained small. According to one report, 21 percent of unskilled workers, 40 percent of skilled workers, and 47 percent of highly qualified specialists earned between 3.5 and 4.5 marks per hour. The average aggregate figures can be seen in table 6-2. As illustrative as these undifferentiated figures are, they nevertheless conceal some especially egregious cases of wage leveling in certain branches of the economy. In a number of enterprises, combines, and even entire industries, it was quite common for the average worker to make more than a foreman. In the machine tools and heavy machine industries, for example, an average worker took home 63 and 50 marks respectively more per month than his immediate superior. Under these conditions, most workers had little reason to improve their skills or aspire to a position of greater responsibility on the shop floor.[6]

Less than three years into Honecker's rule, the economic elite started to

Table 6-2. Monthly Average Gross and Net Wages in Industry, 1988
(in GDR marks)

Wage Earner	Gross Wage	Difference from Worker	Net Wage	Difference from Worker
Worker	1,014		899	
Foreman	1,312	+298	1,017	+118
White-collar				
with degree	1,467	+453	1,137	+238
without degree	893	−121	688	−211

Source: Günter Kusch et al., *Schlußbilanz–DDR: Fazit einer verfehlten Wirtschafts- und Sozialpolitik* (Berlin: Duncker & Humblot, 1991), 109.

think through some of the implications of the GDR's wage structure. As long as centrally set wages remained low and the main route to higher pay was "overfulfillment" and "overtime," workers had little interest in adjusting output norms. In a 1974 letter to Mittag, planning chief Schürer maintained that, with an effective hourly wage of 3.5 marks, the set time portion of which was 1.5 marks, an average worker had to overfulfill existing norms by 7 percent simply to earn 10 pfennigs more per hour. Since extra wages and bonuses comprised such a large part of workers' pay packets, Schürer argued that workers would only become interested in changing norms if the centrally set wages were increased and the bonus portion of the wage package decreased.[7]

This logic inspired the wage reform of 1976, which introduced new *Grundlöhne* (base wages). The reform envisioned no wage decrease for any class of workers but a significant increase for workers in the middle salary range. The key task of the reform was to reclassify workers according to the functions they performed. At the enterprise level, "scientific labor organization" (*wissenschaftliche Arbeitsorganisation* or WAO) working groups were to carry out this task according to guidelines established in Berlin. Norms and piece rates would change for production workers only after they received new classifications. In every case the result would be higher base pay.

As in many other well-intentioned programs, the difficulty came at the implementation stage. When carried out honestly, workers resented and resisted the introduction of new wage structures. The logic of industrial relations, as they had evolved over the past quarter century in the GDR, shaped the dominant working-class interpretation of the wage reform:

whatever the SED might claim, the only genuine reason for a new wage structure was, once again, to make a not very well hidden run at the norm question.

Management's initial response (in collaboration with other economic officials) was to delay implementing the reform and thus avoid antagonizing the work force. In 1982, five years after the reform had been announced, reports from Dresden to Berlin complained that several important enterprises had yet to reclassify workers and introduce new wages.[8] One year later, a report of the Research Institute for Labor, a body attached to the State Secretary for Labor and Wages, found that powerful officials such as the chairman of the Dresden regional economic council, whose own ideas had gone into the design for introducing the reform, had allowed it to languish in administrative limbo. According to the report, the deputy chairman of the regional council, whose working group had been assigned the job of implementing the new wage system, "did not take it seriously."[9] Most important, managers of various enterprises sabotaged the work of the rationalization collectives that were supposed to recategorize workers according to their qualifications and function. In order to ensure labor peace and continued cooperation, management preferred to place workers into artificially higher wage categories, well above where their productive contribution or qualifications justified.[10] As in the 1940s, socialist managers transformed central wage policies at the enterprise level in a way that shored up their disadvantaged position in a very tight labor market.

The irony in much of this is that the cat-and-mouse game between the regime and the working class continued to be conducted on the old, familiar Taylorist and Fordist terrain precisely at the moment when mass production was being phased out in much of the West in favor of flexible, specialized production.[11] That is, had the SED succeeded in transforming the culture of authority on the shop floor and instituting a rigorous system of piece rates, it would have been perfectly positioned to produce long runs of relatively low-quality goods at competitive prices. But, in doing so, it would have been competing not with the West, but with the third world, which was just about to embark on its own mass-production phase.

But even this battle could not be won. In an important sense, therefore, the GDR was a weak state, not only relative to the West, but also compared with many of the third world; unlike Chile and Indonesia, for example, it could not win its "early twentieth-century" Taylorist battles. Despite rising wages (which increased 162 percent between 1971 and 1988), East German labor productivity stagnated.[12] Whereas in 1967 East Germany's GDP per employed person was 67 percent of the West German GDP, this proportion steadily declined to 40 percent by the time GDR collapsed.[13] It might not have appeared to be the case to most East Germans, but when one considers the development of labor productivity in the last two decades of the SED regime and the overall performance of the GDR's economy, East German workers were increasingly overpaid.

Socialist Competition in the Computer Age

Trapped in this structural deadlock, the SED returned time and again to the theme of political and ideological commitments to higher production goals. Its inability to increase labor productivity with administrative wage tinkering continued to lend the older mobilizational methods a type of appeal they might otherwise have lost. Whereas most production campaigns came and went with the ebb and flow of official interest, socialist competitions remained a constitutive feature of the campaign economy.

Perhaps this continuity of interest had to do with the deep roots of socialist competition in Marxism-Leninism. In its labor doctrine, Marxism-Leninism draws a distinction between capitalist competition (*Konkurrenz*) and socialist competition (*Wettbewerb*). The former conjures up images of the most destructive aspects of the anarchic marketplace, whereas the later is linked to Marx's ideas on competition in *Kapital*. Here, Marx characterizes competition as a natural activity that stimulates production so that it is done in the shortest period of time and with the utmost care; but nature is deformed by capitalist production relations.[14] For purposes of domestic legitimation, East German theorists attempted to anchor the idea of socialist competition in Marx's comments on the subject in *Kapital*. It is worth noting, however, that Marx himself rarely used the term *Wettbewerb*, preferring the related concept of *Wetteifern*, which can be translated not only as "competition," but also as "emulation": in a society of free producers, workers naturally *emulate* each other. They do not *compete* in the same sense that capitalists might compete. The East German use of the term *sozialistischer Wettbewerb* (socialist competition) is easily traceable to the Russian word *sorevnovanie*. Only after its translation into the Russian *sorevnovanie* by Soviet theorists and its subsequent retranslation into German by occupation authorities did the term *Wettbewerb* appear.

At every level of the SED, from Central Committee organizers to the first secretaries of the Bezirksleitung (BL) and the Kreisleitung (KL), party officials were ordered to make the most of socialist competitions. Enterprise party organizations that set competition goals too low invited official reprimands.[15] During the 1970s and 1980s, the SED employed a number of different forms of socialist competition. Among the more popular and frequently employed were:

1. Awards given to *Aktivisten*. These direct successors to the original Hennecke activists received monetary prizes for their achievements. In 1982, 45 "heroes of labor," 4,097 "activists," and 281,405 "activists of socialist labor" received prizes.

2. Rewards, usually nominal amounts of money, given for cooperation between workers and scientific intelligentsia.

3. The *Neuererbewegung* (innovators movement), the modern incarnation of the Soviet *novatori*. Participation meant suggesting rational solutions to everyday production problems or taking on extra assignments so that new ideas came to fruition. Workers were strongly encouraged to participate and party secretaries were under pressure to show that at least a third of the inhabitants of their territories and half of the industrial workers were "innovators." According to the GDR Labor Code, the minimum prize for a production innovation was 30 marks and the maximum 30,000 marks.

4. Other intermittently employed competition schemes, such as "personal creative plans" and "collective creative plans," which purported to set up individually and collectively accountable tasks. A further program was the *Notizen zum Plan* (Notes for the Plan) begun in 1975 in the Furstenwalde Tire Combine. In this campaign every worker had to put in writing his weak points and where he had unused reserves in his work area. In 1977–78, 800,000 East Germans were said to have been writing up *Notizen zum Plan*.[16]

Assessing the productive contribution of the various competitions is almost impossible due to the influence that variables in production have upon each other. In 1982, for example, the SED leadership put the total productive contribution of the *Neuererbewegung* at 4.9 billion marks, and in 1983 it had risen to 5.3 billion marks, or 2.5 percent of GDP. Whether these claims corresponded to the reality on the shop floor is, of course, a separate question.

Several factors indicate that they did not. Apart from the various difficulties in calculation and the opportunity for statistical manipulation, studies from the shop floor reveal widespread disinterest and ignorance of socialist competitions among the work force. Many workers interviewed were not aware of the range of production indicators included in competitions or even the times at which they participated. Survey data by one East German language specialist show that the larger portion of a group of managers in 1978 did not know the difference between a "competition program" and a "competition obligation." Only 12.2 percent knew that the document in which the competition assignments were written down was called the "competition obligation." Only 7.1 percent knew the contents of the competition program of their own enterprise. The vast majority of those polled thought that innovation suggestions were accepted only in written form, when by law they could be given orally as well. Although 98 percent of questioned managers claimed to be able to explain what a Neuererbrigade was, only 34.1 percent actually could. Similarly, 80 percent of workers thought they knew what a Neuererbrigade was, but only 28.4 percent actually did.[17]

Evidence on the motivational force of the competitions shows that the large monetary rewards attached to the individual "Aktivist" prizes were somewhat effective but those attached to the collective awards, such as "Collective of Socialist Labor," much less so. In a survey of engineers during the 1980s, one GDR sociologist found that, among the effectiveness of different kinds of recognition for good work, almost all considered a salary increase to be effective, about three-quarters considered bonuses effective, 71 percent thought the award "Activist of Socialist Labor" (carrying a moderate monetary reward) effective, 43 percent considered public praise as stimulative of good work, while only 38 percent considered the award "Collective of Socialist Labor" to be effective.[18]

A 1988 booklet, designed to help trade-union officials run the competitions, points to a number of problems that plagued their execution. Enterprise party organizations and trade unions often used such a large number of production indicators (sometimes twenty or thirty) in setting up competitions, that they became almost impossible to evaluate. "Such a competition," complained the manual, "is no longer possible to supervise and makes difficult a goal-oriented evaluation."[19] To make matters more complicated, planners encouraged enterprises to include "net profit" as an indicator in competitions, but they also advised them that this indicator was often inappropriate for competitions within enterprises because some parts of the production process were inherently more productive than others.[20]

Much of the SED's attention in the later years focused on the problem of making competitions meaningful for the production indicators associated with intensification, such as energy use, quality, and capital productivity.[21] The archival evidence clearly shows resistance to such competitions from a ministerial hierarchy that remained fixed on gross output. The previously cited trade-union pamphlet, for example, admonishes enterprises to display more "courage" and reduce the number of indicators in their competitions. Such a plea was necessary because managers and trade-union officials often included as many indicators as possible in the competition in order to water down results and reduce the odds of being politically embarrassed by poor performance on indicators, which, if fulfilled, would endanger other parts of the plan.[22]

Apart from the problems in execution, it was far from clear how to evaluate results. Here the question of political manipulation remained ever present, if somewhat ill-defined. Enterprise party organizations were advised as late as 1988 that "The final choice of the competition winners is always a political task. In determining the place in the competition, nonquantifiable positive aspects or nonblameworthy existing performance lags are to be taken into account if a true evaluation of performance of individuals is to be undertaken. . . . In the VEB Kombinat IFA-Nutzkraftwagen great value is placed on the political basis of choosing the competition victors."[23] The advice here is ambiguous. Party secretaries are neither clearly advised to employ "objective" criteria, nor are they pushed in an unambiguously "ideological" direction. After all, "nonquantifiable positive aspects" may be understood simply to mean a positive contribution to production in a way that genuinely defies conventional measurement. And "a political task" may merely indicate that the leadership wanted the enterprise party and union organizations to take the matter seriously. One suspects, however, that the ambiguity was intentional and secured for enterprise party organizations the power to manipulate rewards as they saw fit.

The litany of troubles with planning, execution, and evaluation of socialist competition from a purely economic perspective was apparent to party leaders at every level, but especially to those at the local level and in the factory party organizations responsible for their operation. The same kinds of complaints about the usefulness of competitions could be heard in 1985 as in 1955. Nonetheless, socialist competitions retained their appeal for the leadership because, as much as any other kind of party activity in the economy, they provided an opportunity for party secretaries to demonstrate and build their authority and, above all, take action. Party secretaries continued to conduct socialist competition and invent ever new variations on the competition theme because competitions were a specific mix of the political and economic that promoted their own careers and provided an endless source of publicity and theater in a social realm that was of concern to all.

The appeal of competitions, however, went beyond the career concerns of the party secretaries. They were indispensable political rituals of public affirmation. Socialist competitions were usually run in the form of workers "obligating" themselves to achieve something extra, over and above what they would normally do. But to whom were the workers obligating themselves? The answer is the party and its production goals. When activists as well as ordinary workers offered, even symbolically, to do something that they normally would not have done, they publicly displayed their support for the party-led management in the most forceful way that workers can, by agreeing in effect to work for free or very little. What the East German elections were to politics, socialist competitions were to economics. Just as socialist "elections" represented for the SED an important exercise in public devotion, even if everyone knew they did not determine who actually ran the country, socialist competitions were a ritual and theater of working-class political affirmation in the sphere of production relations with which the party could not easily dispense, even though it was clearly understood that their net effect on production was minimal.

The political theater had by the 1980s become political farce. Had the economy been performing well, the SED could have claimed credit. Whether or not socialist competitions actually made a difference would not have mattered—the proof, of course, being that the SED claimed full credit for success even as the economy faltered. But economic stagnation rendered daily reports of success using the latest form of competition a cruel joke, proof that the party apparatus itself was steering the economy onto the rocks.

Labor Deployment

Sagging worker motivation and labor productivity brought about in part by a stagnating sellers labor market could only be weakly countered by political mobilizational methods. Apart from labor motivation, the SED also spent an extraordinary amount of time and energy on labor deployment. And for good reason; the GDR had long suffered from an acute shortage of labor. The only solution to this shortage, apart from technological innovation (a matter discussed in the next chapter), was to rationalize the work process by redeploying workers. Notwithstanding some important national variations, labor deployment is addressed more or less automatically in a capitalist economy (if not without a good deal of pain and politics), as workers are fired or laid off from sectors with low capital productivity and later retrained and hired by sectors with higher productivity.

The GDR leadership took the position (and used it as one of the central elements of its political formula) that, in a socialist society, rationalization of the workplace should not entail the kind of existential fears experienced by the industrial working class under capitalism during times of economic adjustment. Yet the absence of a capital market meant that in practice there was no mechanism to close down inefficient enterprises and the existing incentive structure did not ensure that labor would necessarily flow to where it was needed most urgently. Consequently, job switching or *Fluktuation* was largely viewed with official displeasure because it was understood that this was not a matter of workers following market efficiency signals but, rather, workers following the signals of an extremely distorted and inefficient labor market.

The prevailing shortage of labor made increasing capital productivity (one of the main goals of intensification) dependent on a more efficient deployment of labor. Under the rubric of *Grundfondsökonomie* (capital economy), the journal *Die Wirtschaft* ran a regular feature in the 1970s on the relationship between labor use and capital productivity, and the party construction journal *Neuer Weg* followed suit. The articles discussed accepted ways for improving the use of the existing capital stock and expensive imported machinery.[24] The most common suggestion, and one taken up by the BLs and KLs, was to organize a transfer of day workers to shift and night work. In this way, expensive equipment could be employed at the recommended minimum of fifteen hours per day. The BL Rostock, in cooperation with several enterprise organizations, for example, organized a study of the use of capital in the different shipbuilding yards along the Baltic coast and came up with a plan for changing the shifts of the work force.[25] Enterprises with higher shift rates were to given preferential access to new capital investment.[26]

This SED campaign to promote shift work intensified in the 1980s. The party commissioned a number of studies to assess the social as well as medical consequences of shift work. They showed that, despite the significant social problems to be solved if shift work was to become an important part of GDR life, the challenges could largely be met. East German physicians denied that from a medical standpoint there were any long-term adverse effects in store for those who took up shift work, despite the fact that in other countries it had been shown that shift work was associated with several bothersome, if not fatal, health problems. And the regional party leadership spent a considerable amount of time and effort trying to convince the working class that shift work was "normal."[27]

The SED faced a good deal of social resistance to the introduction of shift work, especially for the night shift. Several GDR researchers discovered that the higher the qualification of the worker, the more reluctance there was to switch over to shift work.[28] However, with considerable political effort the percentage of the industrial work force engaged in shift work had grown from 38.6 percent in 1970 to 41 percent in 1981. Such figures meant that one in every eight workers in the country worked in shifts.[29] Intensifying capital use in this way, however, had its limits. When taken to the extreme, shift

Table 6-3. Skilled Labor on the Shop Floor in East Germany and West Germany (in percentages)

Industry	East Germany	West Germany
Engineering	88	68
Clothing	97	48
Food	76	23
Miscellanous	90	22
Total	88	42

Source: D. M. W. N. Hitchens, *East German Productivity and the Transition to a Market Economy* (Aldershot: Avebury, 1993), 59.

work could actually draw workers away from necessary day tasks, not to mention the social strain associated with high rates of night shift work.

An internal report written for the State Planning Commission in 1979 demonstrated quite plainly the need for a new plan to "create" workers. Not only were the possibilities of increasing the size of the labor pool through shift work quickly diminishing, but, as table 6-3 indicates, very little additional output could be expected from increasing the skills of an already well trained work force.[30] The bottom line of the report was especially distressing in that it demonstrated that each mark of new investment actually worsened the situation on the labor market. That is, between 1970 and 1978, new investment had freed up 51,000 workers for other assignments in the economy, but at the same time the very same investment had required 190,000 new workers to absorb it, a quantity of surplus manpower simply not present in the GDR. The report concluded that not only had the number of industrial workers been sinking since 1975, but that in the period 1985–90 if production grew it would have to do so without growth in the size of the labor force. The report mentioned in passing the connection between the GDR's sagging labor productivity, its constant labor shortage, and the pattern of inefficient, politically directed and motivated capital investment. Such a diagnosis, while true, could not be expressed very forcefully and in any case did not make much of an impact. The SED was not likely to give up its control over capital simply because a few middle-level bureaucrats at the State Planning Commission pointed to inefficiencies in the economy. Instead, the leadership chose to respond to the need for more workers in the way it had always done, with one last campaign.[31]

The Schwedt Initiative

The Schwedt Petrochemical Combine became the sight of the last great production experiment in GDR history. The plant had been built at the end of the 1950s in the sleepy town of Schwedt near the border with Poland on the river Oder, a traditionally backward area of the GDR. The choice of location was determined by the proximity to water, oil from the Soviet pipeline, and a potentially large supply of workers from unproductive farms, whose laborers were largely exiles from the areas lost by Germany after the war. The employees of the new group of enterprises in Schwedt were mostly young and uprooted, had not established an intricate network of informal shop floor relations, and were thus far more amenable to the political initiatives of the center than the workers in the tradition-steeped machine building industry.[32]

Notwithstanding Schwedt's relatively favorable initial conditions, throughout the 1960s productivity remained miserably low. As a West German study notes, "if the workers were not in a position to develop informal bargaining structures, their veto position was strong enough to obtain some room for maneuver in the area of work norms and to subvert any campaign to increase performance."[33] The situation of the combine changed in the 1970s when it apparently became the subject of political attention in Berlin. The old director was replaced by Werner Frohn, who, after the eighth party congress in 1971, was chosen as a member of the Central Committee and was generally acknowledged to have high-level party connections. The secretary of the enterprise party organization and the chairman of the union organization were replaced as well, setting the stage for deeper changes.[34]

New management and political leadership set the combine on a course of experimentation. The first attempts to experiment with the organization of labor came in 1973 and were based fairly closely on the experience of the Soviet chemical combine Shchekino. The idea at Shchekino was simple. Maintenance departments gave up several workers for redeployment in other parts of the enterprise. Savings from the planned wage bill were then distributed in part among the workers in the form of higher premiums.[35] Of the wages saved, 50 percent remained with the collective affected by the reorganization and 50 percent was given over to the main enterprise of the combine. The maximum any worker received as a bonus could not exceed 30 percent of the total wage package, which, by any standard, was still a sizable bonus.[36] According to the official Schwedt enterprise history, between 1973 and 1975, 226 workers were made available for new kinds of work within the combine through the use of the Shchekino method.[37] Other enterprises in the country picked up on the method, and, from this time forward, the method of "saving" on labor deployment became a fundamental part of the political campaigns.[38]

In late 1978, the Schwedt combine was scheduled to put several new production complexes into operation. The new equipment required an additional staff of approximately 1,700 new workers, engineers, and foremen. Such a large number of extra bodies, however, could be found neither in Schwedt nor in other parts of the country. A series of job advertisements in Frankfurt on the Oder had failed to come up with the personnel, at which point the BL Frankfurt/Oder ordered the combine to cover its labor needs from its own work force under the slogan "produce more with less!" as part of a competition initiative.[39] Once again management followed a Soviet example, this time of the chemical combine Polymir in Novopolotsk, which had been the sight of a visit by a working group of the BL Frankfurt/Oder in 1977.[40] Stimulated by the Soviet experience, between 1978 and 1981, the Schwedt combine succeeded in covering demand for 2,400 employees from its own personnel. So successful was the program that between 1983 and 1985 a further 820 workers were to be freed for other work on part of a new oil refinery.[41]

The principles of the Schwedt initiative remained similar to the Shchekino method, but now the proportions were much higher. In the 1970s, for example, worker "rationalization"—that is, the release of workers for new assignments—had averaged approximately 2 percent per year. Now the number rose to 5.5 percent per year.[42] And, in some parts of the enterprise, cuts were to exceed 20 percent per year for several years. The percentage of required cuts came on the orders of the BL Frankfurt/Oder in consultation with management. Rationalization committees made up of workers and management determined the exact number and location of the reductions. Approximately 25 percent of the newly available personnel were encouraged to take up shift work. Each worker taking up new work was included in extensive personal and political conversations with his departmental party organization and union division. Other workers destined for new kinds of work were delegated to special after-hours retraining courses, run by the local Schwedt council and coordinated by the regional and district SED organizations.

The Schwedt initiative and other similar campaigns were moderately successful. Given the distorted labor market, such administrative and political actions contributed to utilizing capital and labor more efficiently than if nothing had been done. As an effective substitute for a capitalist labor market, however, the Schwedt initiative was plagued with many of the difficulties of administrative measures in a centrally planned economy.

First, the evidence suggests that workers did not respond very well to the Schwedt initiative, especially when employed in enterprises with a fairly cohesive work force. Leaving a workplace in which one has been employed for many years is always difficult. In the GDR, where official propaganda on the importance of the "collective" had succeeded in creating a warm, Gemeinschaft-like atmosphere, supplemented by important informal relations that take years to establish, the stress associated with moving to a new collective, or perhaps a new enterprise, was especially acute.[43]

Furthermore, workers feared that this campaign might be a form of crypto–norm breaking.[44] The Schwedt measures of reducing the enterprise work force were supposed to bring gains through a more rational organization of the workplace, and not through a manipulation of the norms that would require harder work. But, as one engineer noted, "in conversations we find again and again that reservations regarding the method have as their main cause the assumption that it will require greater intensity in work."[45] This impression could only be reinforced by the fact that along with the Schwedt initiative a whole series of competition initiatives were undertaken to assist in the transition to a smaller work force.

Managers also resisted the initiative in order not to reveal that they actually had surplus labor. They continued to hoard labor in the face of pressure not only from the local party organs but from the center as well. After 1980, a new "production indicator" had been introduced in the planning order, "workers to be released." According to most reports, the expected number of workers to be released hovered around 3 percent per year. In fact, however, the definition of what constituted a "released worker" became a matter of debate, as well as a point around which management could continue to hoard labor.[46]

Additional evidence that the initiatives of the local party organs modeled on the Schwedt example had limited usefulness came in 1983 when the center chose to act again. On this occasion, the Council of Ministers issued a new ordinance designed to strengthen the new production indicator "released workers," since it did not seem to be having the desired effect on the behavior of managers. The new law required all enterprises to pay 70 percent of the total value of their wage bill as a tax, referred to as a "contribution for social funds."[47] Such a reference to the role played by the state in securing the welfare of workers simply masked the fact that this tax was an attempt by the state to force enterprises to consider more carefully their use of labor, and offered a large tax break for enterprises that could shed.

Before embarking on the Schwedt initiative, enterprises had to receive the go-ahead from their ministry. Ministries, however, had just as little interest in this latest input savings program, the last in a very long line, as they had in socialist competitions or materials economy. Not only did it increase the wage bill, it also diminished the labor reserves of enterprises. The BL Frankfurt/Oder, for example, complained that many of the enterprises in its territory were hiding behind ambiguous orders from above in order to delay releasing workers.[48]

As with all SED-directed campaigns, the Schwedt initiative took on a life of its own, and grew from a very specific task to a generalized and vague approach to the more efficient use of labor. Throughout the republic, from the largest combines to the smallest communal service enterprises, from local administration to the school system, the initiative came to be seen as a panacea for the chronic labor shortage.[49] Such a loss of focus was characteristic of the campaign economy. Local party organs felt constrained to introduce the initiative even in areas where it was not appropriate. Responding to the Schwedt's ubiquitous use as a general label, the state secretary for labor and wages, Wolfgang Beyreuther, warned in 1982 that not all enterprises were appropriate locations for the Schwedt initiative, hinting that some enterprises had few workers to spare.[50]

In the early stages, many large enterprises could be badgered into coming up with a sizable number of extra workers, if only to meet the wishes of political authorities. However, high-level officials, including Werner Frohn the director of the Schwedt combine, saw that it would be much more difficult to find extra employees after the first round of Schwedt rationalizations was over. Instead of a reorganization of the labor process based on the work of the rationalization collectives, continuation of the campaign would increasingly depend on the ability of enterprises to replace workers with technologically advanced equipment—a far different and more demanding task.[51]

Extending the campaign gave rise to additional difficulties. Some enterprises simply did not have workers to spare. Here we confront the same issue as in the campaign for materials economy. To repeat: in some instances it makes sense to use certain factors of production, of which labor is one, generously, even overgenerously in order to save on more expensive ones. The Schwedt initiative was never able to operate in a subtle enough manner to be useful in all contexts, and it is likely that it starved several enterprises of excess labor necessary for efficiency, all in the name of creating greater efficiency. Perhaps at some level the leadership understood this as well; for by the mid-1980s discussion and promotion of the Schwedt initiative had greatly subsided.

Explaining the relative success of the Schwedt initiative in the Bezirk where it was founded, two German sociologists fall back on the peculiarities of the Schwedt and Frankfurt/Oder environment. I find their explanation convincing.

> In the 1970s, a young and newly gathered work force encountered an effective management, which was able to transform a certain amount of enthusiasm into a willingness to rationalize. Through wage incentives and qualification measures, internal mobility was intensified. A relatively closed regional labor market and, by GDR standards, an acceptable communal and enterprise infrastructure created the willingness of the workers to remain at Schwedt. On this basis, there developed a specific relationship between pressure from the party and participation that characterized the Schwedt initiative.[52]

The specific local conditions that allowed the initiative to work with a modicum of efficiency in Schwedt were absent in other parts of the country. In Magdeburg, for example, employees of the machine-building industry put up stiff resistance to reassignment. Much, of course, depended on the capacity of the local party organs to coordinate their territorial institutions (such as training centers, day care clinics, and shopping hours), and the supply of quality consumer goods that might have made it attractive to leave a comfortable day job for a night job that paid more but required further training for middle-aged men and women and carried high "start-up" costs. The vexing problem of local and regional coordination is the topic to which we turn next.

Chapter 7 Local Politics

Housing and

Consumer Goods

The well-known aphorism that "all politics is local" may be too strong a statement for the GDR. But here too, one finds a fascinating politics of central versus local authority. Regional and district party organizations found themselves caught between two conflicting imperatives. On the one hand, they were expected to provide support and assistance to enterprises subordinated to ministries in the capital but located in the industrial provinces. In theory at least, they were held accountable for the performance of these industries. On the other hand, the Politburo also issued incessant reminders to the Bezirk and Kreis secretaries that they constituted the primary point of contact between the people and the party, and it was therefore their responsibility to ensure that the basic needs of the local population were met, that specific complaints were noted and addressed, and that any dissatisfaction did not translate into political mobilization against the regime. Often, local party secretaries were unsure of which constituency to serve, the ministries in Berlin or the people among whom they lived.

This three-player game, between branch industries, local authorities, and the population was perhaps the most important cleavage in Communist society. In his *Soviet Prefects*, Hough characterized the mediation of this conflict as "regional coordination," hence his use of the prefect analogy.[1] This chapter reexamines this analogy and assesses its relevance for East Germany in the 1970s and 1980s. During the last twenty years of its history, the SED spent the lion's share of its time on two politically sensitive problems of regional coordination, housing and the supply of consumer goods, which will be the substantive focus here.

Housing is an especially interesting field of regional politics, for although investment funds were allocated from Berlin, construction itself was primarily an operation directed from the regional and district levels and was strongly dependent on the participation of industrial enterprises subordinated to ministries in Berlin. As we shall see, the record of the Bezirksleitungen (BLs) and Kreisleitungen (KLs) in solving housing shortages was mixed. Although nearly two million new suburban apartments were built between 1971 and 1989, this feat could be accomplished only by starving the urban centers and small towns of investment. Starved of capital, the older housing stock and the prewar commercial centers decayed substantially. In the end, new apartments could barely be built fast enough to replace increasingly uninhabitable older ones. Despite some noteworthy successes, then, the GDR never solved "the housing problem as a social question," as Honecker promised would be the case by 1990. Instead, local party secretaries continued to confront widespread dissatisfaction with the housing supply as well as a growing sense of threat to an important part Germany's national patrimony, its city centers.

If the population remained less than enamored with the SED's housing policy, it was downright enraged with the supply of consumer goods. After a notable upswing at the outset of the 1970s, consumption levels stagnated at the start of the politically crucial 1980s. After more than thirty years of socialism, most East Germans considered intermittent shortages of basic goods as well as an unsatisfactory assortment of luxury goods to be unacceptable. Long queues for small packets of facial tissues or decades-long waiting periods for second-rate automobiles could not easily be explained away, even by the most fertile of dialectical imaginations. Acutely aware of the explosiveness of the issue, the Politburo ordered the local party organs to keep careful watch on retail supplies and ensure that their enterprises produced enough consumer goods to stave off social unrest. In the end, however, the GDR's was not an economy designed for the satisfaction of consumers; no matter how insistent the pleas of the center, local party elites could not hope to satisfy the demands of their constituents.

In short, the performance of the SED at the local level suggests that if the regional and district party secretaries were prefects in any sense of the word, the environment in which they operated did not permit them to be good prefects. Nowhere was the disparity greater between what was needed and what could actually be done. As in other spheres of the economy, unable to accomplish what had been assigned from the center, the local SED elites retreated into the campaign economy.

Historical Background

East German leaders usually expressed their understanding of the role of the local party and state officials in terms of the "territorial conditions for the carrying out of the primary task," which was production.[2] Accordingly, the SED viewed attempts to represent local interests with some suspicion. They had good reason for doing so. Historically, Germany had come together as a nation-state rather late, at the end of the nineteenth century. Until Hitler's seizure of power, its constituent parts had retained much of their own cultural distinctiveness and political autonomy. Culturally this distinctiveness was expressed in the concept of regional identity or *Heimat*, and politically through a tradition of administrative fragmentation in which the constituent parts of the country retained significant decision-making powers. It was only natural, then, that in the German context, Communists would be concerned with localism.

The evidence suggests that the Communists need not have worried as much as they might have about, say, an independent Mecklenburg-Vorpommern or Saxony heading off in its own direction. In East Germany, by 1946, the *Heimat* feeling had been significantly attenuated by the large proportion of the population (between one-quarter and one-third) that had moved into the Soviet Occupation Zone from farther east only at the end of the war.[3] Notwithstanding what should have been reassuring circumstances, by the end of the 1940s Stalin was arguing (somewhat disingenuously) that American attempts to revive German federalism in the West were meant to weaken Germany rather than democratize it, and the Soviet Zone would not head down this route. Stalin feared federalism in his zone of Germany because it threatened to diminish the capacity of the SED to influence events in the provinces. Already during the late 1940s Ulbricht had noticed with some concern that *Land* Communist Party organizations were developing a style of their own that often clashed with the tone of their superiors in Berlin.[4]

Whatever the source of their concern, in 1952 the traditional German notion of local politics or *Kommunalpolitik*, understood as an independent field of politics in which localities enjoy the rights of self-administration (*Selbstverwaltung*) and communal freedom (*Gemeindefreiheit*), was abandoned when the SED declared that the construction of socialism required an administrative reform.[5] The reality of this "reform" was a reorganization of the administrative structure in which five states were replaced by fourteen smaller Bezirke as the provincial administrative unit. By creating a larger number of weaker units, Ulbricht hoped to prevent the formation of other loci of political power.

Beyond these changes, the local level of administration was generally neglected during the 1950s, as Ulbricht and the SED elite fended off challenges to their authority from outside the country. The first full-blown law on local administration was not passed until 1957. The law merely established juridically what existed in fact: the obedience of the lower state organs to the will of the higher. Ordinances passed by local assemblies were to contribute to national economic goals. Any interpretation of the role of the local assemblies and councils not in harmony with the notion of a unified hierarchy received a hostile reception in Berlin. In 1970 the State Council issued a decree giving wider horizontal powers to communities.[6] Apparently, though, this new decree did not satisfy the leadership, for in 1973 a second law was passed along with a number of Central Committee decrees, with the intention of finding the proper place for, and in some ways widening, the powers of the local organs in the administrative hierarchy.[7] The discussion of "socialist communal policy" (*sozialistische Kommunalpolitik*) began in earnest in the early 1980s.[8] Although East German officials and academics vehemently denied the possibility of conflict between central and local powers under socialism, they acknowledged that the local organs represented an important and untapped reserve for economic growth.[9] In 1985 a third law on the local state organs appeared, not very different from the 1973 law, but which firmly declared the SED's intention to raise the contribution of local authorities to meeting national economic plans.[10] It was followed up with a number of articles, pronouncements, and even an entire series of pamphlets, entitled *Kommunalpolitik aktuell*, devoted to important questions of local politics.

What was the meaning of the continual stream of laws and decrees on the local state organs? Why did the leadership regularly feel the need to qualify and reemphasize what it had said only several years earlier? Here the SED had to confront head on its ambivalence with the entire notion of local administration. On the one hand, the supremacy of branch planning over territorial planning clearly indicated the preferred role for the territorial organs—ensuring the fulfillment of central demands. On the other hand, to do so the local leadership had to have the necessary powers, as well as the support of the local population.

When asked if local authorities were "representatives" of the center or of the locality, East German experts did not usually give a straight answer. The reason was that they were a bit of both. While BL first secretaries might lobby the center for more apartment construction or a new investment project, there was no confusing these officials with the *Ministerpräsident* of a West German *Land*. The latter is elected expressly to represent particular geographic—that is, the *Land*'s—interests, whereas the former was appointed from above to implement plans devised at the center. First secretaries of Bezirksleitungen were not only local politicians and administrators, but national politicians and administrators. Several held seats on the Politburo and all were members of the Central Committee. Kreisleitung first secretaries were more provincial, but they too enjoyed membership in the nomenklatura of the Central Committee and their apparatus was largely chosen at the Bezirk level.

One important indicator of relative local power was the capacity to influence investment decisions made in Berlin. Given the resources attached to large industrial projects, decisions about where and when to invest influenced just about every aspect of daily life in a region or district. Here the evidence is clear: local party and state officials had very little influence over the big decisions, although they might successfully lobby in the case of smaller ones.[11] And while the regional leaders had little power to attract investment, they had even less to resist it. Thus, even in the face of considerable out-migration from the industrial southern Bezirke to the north between 1971 and 1988 (an indicator that the quality of life in the south was deteriorating), the southern BLs could (or would) do little to resist new industrial investment. A further indicator of their inability to channel investment optimally for local conditions was the paradoxical situation of apartment construction, the service sector, and the health system being the most weakly developed, relative to local needs, in the most heavily populated southern industrial Bezirke. In sum, there is little evidence that the local party or state organs could effectively play the "representational role" assigned to them in Hough's prefect model.

Regional Duties

What were the regional duties of the local party apparatus? Being political officials, the BL and KL secretaries spent a fair amount of time dealing with a wide array of issues that had nothing to do with the economy. The operation of the local press and propaganda machine, the recruitment of officers into the army, and the supervision of the organs of law, order, and security all fell into the lap of the first secretary. Such activities must be placed under the heading of regional coordination as well, although it is difficult to extend to the GDR Peter Rutland's observation from the Soviet Union that "these politically-focused activities represent the core of the party organs' regional role, and not its tasks in the economic arena."[12] Even if this were true for the apparatus as a whole, there is too much personal testimony on behalf of first secretaries to the effect that the bulk of their activities were indeed economic.[13]

The problem for regional coordination in the Leninist world reflected the dominance of the vertical branch planning over territorial planning.[14] In East Germany, the eleven industrial ministries, the State Planning Commission, and the relevant Central Committee departments constituted a vast empire that ran over 90 percent of the country's industrial capacity and economic agencies, all from Berlin. Local party and state organs were in no position to match the potential and actual ministerial control over resources.

Accordingly, local governments tended to be at the mercy of enterprises located on their territory that were subordinate to combines and ministries located either in other Bezirke or in Berlin.[15] In setting up a system of vertically integrated autarkic units, the combine reform exacerbated the problem because enterprises were now more independent of their environments than ever. Within the combine itself, a shadow combine party organization, interregional in scope, undercut many of the coordinative functions of the territorial organizations. Its head, the secretary of the main enterprise of the combine, was a nomenklatura cadre of the Central Committee and ran the periodic meetings of the combine-specific "council of party secretaries."[16] Territorial bodies, such as the local councils (Räte), assemblies, regional planning agencies (Bezirk and Kreis planning commissions and commissions on territorial rationalization), and local party secretaries often found themselves supplicants to large enterprises in getting territorial projects off the ground.

The dominance of the combines had the effect of raising the "company town" phenomenon, so common in all East European countries, to a matter of principle. In Jena during the 1980s, for example, it was widely known that no major decision on local construction, retail supplies, or housing could be made without the assent of Wolfgang Biermann, the general director of the powerful Zeiss Optics Combine. The situation was the same in other municipalities. On taking up his post in the Thuringian mining town of Merkurs next to the potash mine in Werra, the new mayor was informed by the enterprise employees, only half-jokingly, that he might as well take down the sign "Town Council of Merkurs" and put up "Communal Political Department: Potash Enterprise Werra."[17] Most first secretaries, not to mention chairmen of town councils, treated the directors of large enterprises located on their territories with a great deal of respect, as equals in a complex game of give-and-take to secure the conditions of production.

The main sore point of regional coordination concerned the relations between centrally subordinated combines and enterprises on the one hand, and Bezirk or Kreis councils on the other. Under the rubric of territorial rationalization, the two sides came together in pursuit of goals that would benefit each other. If the relationship became stable or permanent, it might become juridicized in the form of a "communal contract."[18] The themes most commonly appearing in communal contracts were housing, the service sector, and day care. In the 1970s, the city of Dresden established a form of cooperation between a number of enterprises located on its territory to train skilled workers. In Freital the local council promoted a spare-parts cooperative among a number of centrally subordinated enterprises. And in Meissen a communal heating plant was built with the resources of twelve enterprises, along with two day care centers, two schools, a kindergarten, an old-age home, and a physical therapy center.[19]

Notwithstanding reports of success, there were also some serious problems. For one thing, the strength of enterprises relative to the local state organs often led them to ignore the latter's wishes.[20] In the case of non-fulfillment of communal contracts, local councils had the right to take enterprises to court, but financial restitution did not help as it might have in a capitalist economy. What the local councils really needed, and what could only be supplied by the combines, was capacity and control over resources. Souring relations with an enterprise might endanger future relations of mutual benefit. Managers understood that BLs and KLs still wanted enterprises on their territories to perform well, for industrial performance was reflected in territorial gross output figures that worked their way up the chain of command. This gave the managers a degree of leverage unavailable to the local SED organizations.[21] Such a situation rendered contracts mostly into statements of good intentions. Throughout the 1970s and 1980s, reports from the provinces complained of combine managers ignoring the orders of local organs.[22] Perhaps in order to bolster the power of local councils, managers received constant reminders that they need not wait for permission from above for every small joint project with local authorities.[23]

Managers were, in fact, responding quite rationally. If the planners did not include the resources necessary to carry out a local project in the enterprise plan, cooperation with local authorities contained only costs and very few payoffs. Local projects of such a seemingly innocuous nature as allowing municipalities to make use of excess capacity in transportation or unused machine time inevitably came up against stiff resistance. By revealing their excess capacity to local organs, managers risked being swamped by local demands with little prospect of reward.

One way of putting off local authorities was to demand long lead times for cooperative projects. In Karl-Marx-Stadt (Chemnitz) the Bezirk council reported that cooperation with most large enterprises required agreements six to nine months before the beginning of the following plan year and that they be formally included in enterprise plans.[24] Even then, enterprises subordinated to the ministry for general machine building conceived of the whole process not as territorial rationalization but, according to the Bezirk council, as a "territorial burden."[25]

Many plans for territorial rationalization never made it past the planning stage. Others found homes in specialized commissions or bureaucracies with even less power than local councils. East German territorial specialists warned, for example, that territorial rationalization should not become the duty of the Bezirk or Kreis planning commissions or deputy chairmen of the local councils, for this would doom it to ineffectuality.[26] Cues such as these provided the party with the impetus to get deeply involved in territorial coordination and rationalization. Naturally, the party was never far from the action, even in the activities of the local councils. Party organizations in councils regularly reported to the first secretaries, and the first secretary himself took part in (and, in most cases, dominated) council meetings.

As in other spheres, many of the SED secretaries' activities in small towns and cities were intended as much to focus public attention on themselves as "charismatic centers" as they were exercises in regional coordination. The distinction between "the trappings of rule and its substance" was, in any case, often difficult to distinguish.[27] Roving the city streets and the collective farms of his territory, the first secretary felt and radiated the ethos of the "master of the house" (*Herr im Haus*). In his book on the first secretary of KL Bad Salzungen, Scherzer draws the analogy between the first secretary and the former noble rulers of the region quite explicitly. During one walk on an "inspection" through the city with the first secretary, Scherzer remarks: "It felt good to walk with him through the city, and I had to think of the *Meininger Theaterherzog* Georg II who, in his time, was ruler of Salzungen."[28] The power of the party secretary in the locality was limited not by law but by the power of other bureaucracies (the main ones being the ministries and Central Committee apparatus) that controlled resources in his territory. His power was not regulated but it *was* limited. Having limited powers, the secretary relied heavily on symbolic displays for the establishment of his own authority, and the economy provided the most visible and important field of action where the concrete and practical could be mixed with the symbolic and the affective.

In typical SED fashion, regional coordination quickly became a continuous source of political campaigning. Yearly conferences on territorial rationalization took place from 1973 to 1989 in every Kreis in the republic. As early as June 6, 1973, the Secretariat of the Central Committee laid the groundwork for the conferences with a decree propagating the "positive experience" of Kreis Strassfurt.[29] At the conferences, delegates who represented local party, state, union, and economic institutions were brought together to confirm programs prepared in advance by the KL.[30] Thereafter, local authorities established a special section of the local yearly economic plans called "territorial rationalization."[31]

As in other campaigns, territorial rationalization was pitched in terms of overcoming the technocratic idea that coordination and rationalization are "the task of experts."[32] Those workers who also served in local legislatures were called upon to pressure their managers to work with the local authorities.[33] Local party organizations along with the National Front, a public service arm of the party, organized territorial "pitch in!" (*Mach-Mit!*) competitions that mobilized local enterprise and communal resources to take care of such minutiae as painting, street cleaning, grass cutting, and park construction.[34]

Notwithstanding the various campaigns, the BLs and KLs seem to have had very little success in their struggles with enterprises in the provinces. But failure did not induce "learning," nor did it redirect behavior in an economically beneficial direction. Although the SED secretaries do not appear to have been particularly effective regional coordinators, the campaigns devoted to this end took on a meaning that exceeded their practical value. Their activities were designed more to serve as political ritual, to show the first secretary as the "big man" helping out the weaker "small boys" of the Bezirk and Kreis councils, than as elements of an effective development administration or any type of economic activity at all. Once again, as in other campaigns, this was not simply a matter of pure politics or economic administration but a particular amalgam of the two, one that is particular to the Communist political economy.

Housing

The local party organs' tasks in the housing sector provide a good case study of their precarious position between the central authorities and the population. One can identify two main stages of housing policy in the GDR's

Table 7-1. Condition of Apartments in East Germany and West Germany

Condition	GDR, 1971	GDR, 1989	FRG, 1988–1989
Apartments per 1,000 population	353	424	429
Square meters per inhabitant	20	27	35
Square meters per apartment	58	65	85
Percentage with bathroom	39	72	94
Percentage with bath or shower	39	79	93

Source: Günter Kusch et al., *Schlußbilanz—DDR: Fazit einer verfehlten Wirtschafts- und Sozialpolitik* (Berlin: Duncker & Humblot, 1991), 66.

history. From 1948 until 1970, the GDR concentrated investment in areas other than apartment construction. Housing construction that did take place focused on repair of the existing stock. The second stage began with Honecker's social program, the centerpiece of which was housing construction, which picked up steam after 1973. In a era of declining investment in almost every other sector of the economy, housing investment increased every year until 1989. As in other Soviet bloc countries, the overwhelming proportion of new housing was built outside of city centers in large socialist housing estates. Though notoriously ugly and of poor quality, these estates had the virtue of being built from standardized modules and could thus be ready for habitation relatively quickly. As tables 7-1 and 7-2 indicate, from a purely quantitative standpoint, the GDR scored some noteworthy successes in this period, especially in closing the gap with West Germany. However, apart from the poor quality of construction not reflected in the tables, a closer analysis of the numbers themselves reveals some disturbing trends. Whereas throughout the 1950s and 1960s lower levels of housing construction added to the overall housing stock, during the 1970s and 1980s the marginal return on this investment declined precipitously. That is, despite larger numbers of new apartments each year, the overall housing stock was rising at a decreasing rate. How could this happen? The answer is quite simple: new suburban apartment construction took place at the cost of urban decay. Had the trend continued into the 1990s, soon more apartments would have become uninhabitable than could be built anew, even with increasing levels of investment. This was already occurring in Rostock, Leipzig, Weimar, Brandenburg, Wismar, and countless small towns throughout East Germany. Thus, despite negative population growth, by the time of the

Table 7-2. GDR Housing Stock, 1950–1989

Year	Housing Stock: Apartments	New Construction Time Period	Apartments	Difference between New Construction and Growth of Housing Stock
1950	4,970,000	1950–57	290,000	—
		1958–60	209,000	—
1961	5,506,980	1961–70	780,000	—
1971	6,057,032	1971–81	1,020,000	−230,600
1981	6,562,467	1982–89	790,000	−514,570
1989	7,002,539	1990	65,000	−305,000

Source: "Wohnen in der DDR," in *WZB Mitteilungen,* no. 57 (September 1992): 38.

1989 revolution the regime still had 800,000 unfulfilled applications for apartments.

In retrospect, the rational housing strategy would have been to allocate investment more evenly among new construction and restoration. But within the SED elite, the idea of building thousands of apartments each year relatively cheaply, and in this way solving the housing problem with one great push forward, appealed to a venerable tradition in the culture of Communist planning. Not only could hundreds of apartment buildings be built in more or less standardized fashion, but the entire program could be controlled and mobilized by the center. The various large housing projects undertaken throughout the GDR during the 1970s thus quickly assumed the proportions of a 1930s Stalinist steel drive, which explains in part why the housing program continued even when it no longer made economic sense.

But the housing program did make ideological and especially organizational sense to the SED elite. It provided a vehicle of organizational integrity to the regional and district party organizations by way of the campaign economy. The BLs and KLs thus focused their energies on building as many large apartment estates as they possibly could. In doing so, they relied on a campaign imported from housing construction in the Soviet Union, the "Zlobin method." Although its organizational principles were never fully and clearly articulated in the press, when working with the Zlobin method, instead of the entire construction combine of a Bezirk taking responsibility for completion of a building, the responsibility was shifted down to the level of the brigade for a specific part of the building or a number of brigades for the entire building. On completion of the project, each brigade received bonuses according to "the supplementary economized profit." According to one source, "The amount [was] also dependent on the length of the construction time, the quality of the work, the careful use of construction materials, and a series of other factors."[35] In effect this amounted to brigade-level piecework.

In 1975 the BL Rostock kicked off the campaign in the local press, encouraging the use of the Soviet Zlobin method in apartment construction. The newspaper campaign portrayed workers chomping at the bit to use the much-heralded construction method of the famous, two-time Soviet Hero of Socialist Labor.[36] But according to GDR economists and other experts, the Zlobin method suffered from similar problems plaguing all such campaigns.[37] The success of a typical construction brigade depended not simply on its will to work carefully and quickly, but on the supply of the necessary materials so that it could work continuously. A primary problem at construction sites was downtime due to shortages of several key elements in construction, the main one being concrete blocks. In 1976, for example, the economics secretary in Erfurt reported that in his Bezirk only a few brigades had started working with the Zlobin method due to difficulties in supply and resulting difficulties in comparing responses.[38] The Erfurt experience shows that notwithstanding priority in investment, planning in housing construction remained so taut that shortages could not be overcome. A brigade's positive performance therefore more often reflected the local director's preferred access to concrete and other raw materials, than it did the diligence of construction workers.[39] Even when poor performance could be documented, however, construction managers were hesitant to punish workers for substandard performance because of labor shortages in the construction sector. As a result, the evaluation of work was subject to a good deal of leveling by brigade chiefs and managers.

It appears from the example of housing that local party secretaries did not have the kind of control over resources that might have allowed them to be good regional coordinators of production despite the fact that housing was, by and large, a regionally directed affair. The campaign economy could not cure the shortages induced by the command economy; in fact, the necessity and importance of the former depended on the continuity of the latter. Campaigns would have taken on neither the meaning nor urgency they did had there been no shortages of construction materials and apartments. Ironically, then, the housing program of the 1970s provided a compelling organizational task to the SED at the regional and district levels, even though it did not solve the housing shortage in the GDR and, indeed, probably exacerbated it during the 1980s.

Apart from the organizationally functional aspects of the shortage economy, administering the housing shortages became an irresistible realm of "rent seeking" and power accretion for party secretaries. That is, where they may not have been able to do much on the production side (hence the retreat into the campaign economy), on the distribution side BLs and KLs enjoyed a good deal of discretion in adjudicating housing disputes for already completed apartments. Much of the contact of the KL first secretaries with ordinary people concerned the subject of apartment size and location. East German citizens, at any rate, believed that the KL secretaries had a decisive voice in solving difficult apartment problems and the authority to raise their priority on the allocation lists, whether for repairs or for new apartments. Such popular wisdom probably had a good basis in fact. It had obviously worked for enough people on a sufficient number of occasions, so that bringing one's housing problems to the first secretary was a matter of common sense.

During the 1980s official policy began to reflect the need for the restoration of the existing stock, but did not move away vigorously enough from new apartment construction to forestall urban decay. As a result, by the end of the decade the downtown areas of countless East German small cities, which constituted the genuine cultural core of eighteenth- and nineteenth-century Germany, were reaching the point of collapse. Hard-line Communists might have secretly felt that the loss of the architectural symbols of bourgeois Germany was really no loss at all, but official policy declared otherwise, and at the local level party secretaries encountered popular resentment that an important piece of German history was endangered.

Of course, as all good bureaucrats, clever KL secretaries knew how to manipulate the rules to undertake projects that were formally prohibited by the center, but they did not have the power to reverse completely the effects of central policy. During 1986 in Bad Salzungen, for example, construction engineers informed the first secretary that the downtown desperately needed reconstruction. According to the yearly plans, however, only apartments, and not townhouses, could be built from scratch. While "renovations" could be included in the Kreis economic plan, other "new" construction or reconstruction could not. The policy not only threatened to destroy the old downtown but would also deprive the residents of Salzungen of the quickly crumbling market and the main eating establishments. The local construction experts suggested the following: start "renovating" from the rear (since it could not be seen from the street) and rebuild the area piece by piece. Finally, when the whole interior is redone, quickly strip the old facade off the front of the new building, without ever having to put it into the plan as "new." The KL first secretary declared he had nothing against pulling a fast one on his superiors in Suhl, in principle, but "so many months of fear that someone would look behind the facade" finally turned him against the proposal.[40] As in other localities, the restoration of Bad Salzungen had to wait until the collapse of the East German regime.

Consumer Goods

Other regional issues confronting the local party organizations did not pack the same kind of emotional and political punch as housing, with one exception: consumer goods. The evidence from the archives on this point is truly overwhelming. Nothing attracted the attention of the center faster than reports from the provinces indicating supply shortages or politically threatening consumer dissatisfaction.[41] The SED, in this instance, understood the importance of the issue. In his interviews with older workers in the industrial provinces of East Germany, Lutz Niethammer found that the most frequently heard complaint concerned the miserable situation in supplies of food and desirable consumer durables.[42] As in other countries of Eastern Europe, since the 1960s the GDR had been able to guarantee almost all members of its society a minimal standard of living that consisted of housing, moderately priced essentials, and as much basic food products as one cared to buy. But living next to West Germany gave the average East German a daily smorgasbord (via television) of products largely unavailable for purchase in the GDR. Table 7-3 illustrates the disparity between the two countries in 1970. In addition to the demoralizing political impact of the poor consumer goods supply, there was an economic dimension that tended to feed back into already flagging labor productivity. The shortage of consumer goods rendered a strategy of wage differentials for stimulating productivity inoperative by devaluing the currency. The problem for the East German consumer was generally not a lack of marks but a lack of products on which to spend them.

To remedy this problem, the SED leadership pursued two main centrally guided policy directions. First, starting in the 1970s, GDR citizens had the opportunity to buy high-value food and textile items in special retail shops, *Delikat* and *Exquisit,* whose prices were usually three to four times those in normal shops. In addition to these outlets, starting in 1973, those with access to hard currency could buy an impressive range of items otherwise unavail-

Table 7-3. Comparative East and West German Consumption, 1970

Area of Comparison	East German/West German (%)
Endowment/100 households	
Television	93
Color television (1973)	7
Refrigerator	66
Freezer (1973)	14
Washing machine	89
Automatic washing machine (1973)	3
Food and beverage consumption	
Meat	86
Milk	105
Cheese	46
Potatoes	149
Vegetables	134
Fruit	44
Tea	59
Coffee	51
Wine, champagne	29
Beer	68

Source: Jonas Kornai, *The Socialist System: The Political Economy of Communism* (Princeton, N.J.: Princeton University Press, 1992), 306.

able to their fellow countrymen through the chain of *Intershops*. But while such pricy retail outlets enabled financial authorities to "soak up" a good deal of pent-up demand (in the form of excess savings) and provided a conduit for hard-currency transfers from West to East, they also engendered a good deal of popular resentment. Officially, the argument in favor of a two-tiered retail system was that under socialism people are genuinely paid according to their productive contribution ("to each according to his work"). People who worked harder or at more important jobs, so the argument ran, were supposed to have higher incomes and more frequent access to highly prized consumer goods. Hence the special stores. Such logic might have partially held true for the *Delikat* and *Exquisit* shops, but, since those who could most easily take advantage of hard-currency outlets were foreigners, the entire range of Interhotels, Intershops, Intergas stations, Interrestaurants, and Interbars reinforced the impression among East Germans that they were really second-class citizens in their own country. To make matters worse, those East Germans who did have Deutsche marks generally received them from contact with relatives or friends in West Germany. This arrangement not only disadvantaged middle- and lower-level officials who were forbidden sustained contact with West Germans, but it also contradicted official policy in favoring those who cultivated contacts in the capitalist world over those who did not. Not surprisingly, by the late 1970s, the socialist dictum "to each according to his work" had been revised in the popular mind to the more ironic "to each according to where his aunt lives." Regardless of the official explanations, it was widely understood that *Delikat*, *Exquisit*, and especially *Intershops* had very little to do with socialism.

Given the limits of this strategy for satisfying consumers, the regime tried a second approach: throughout its latter years the SED attempted to make the combines produce more and better-quality consumer goods. Combines were required by central decree to devote at least 5 percent of their production to consumer products. Even enterprises not normally producing consumer goods had to contribute their share.[43] In order to sweeten the deal, enterprises that went beyond mere compliance and produced some sort of technical or stylistic innovation in their products received significantly higher prices from state buyers. The former measure (East Germany's "5 percent rule"), although mildly successful in increasing supply, was not terribly efficient. Having enterprises manufacture consumer goods when they possessed no experience in the field, had done little if any market research, and most likely lacked the proper equipment constituted a violation of the most basic principles of the division of labor. Furthermore, managers of enterprises involved in manufacturing or processing mostly producer goods understood quite well on which side their bread was buttered. Consumer goods divisions within these enterprises inevitably became the stepdaughters of the main operation.[44]

The latter policy, that of encouraging technical innovation by rewarding it with higher prices, had a rather curious yet predictable effect. Most GDR industries had innovation rates at the beginning of the 1980s of between 3 and 5 percent annually, making for a renewal rate of the production profile every fourteen to twenty-three years. This rate put the GDR's industries significantly behind successful (though by no means the most innovative) firms in the West, such as IBM, Siemens, and Phillips, all of whom enjoyed innovation rates of 9 to 10 percent per year.[45] As a response to the galloping pace of technical innovation and product change, in 1986 the SED leadership declared at the eleventh party congress that "products are to be renewed at a rate of 30 to 40 percent per year."[46] Naturally, these rates could not be met. In fact, between 1970 and 1985, the number of East German patents registered in West Germany sank by 33 percent in machine building, 31 percent in electrical technologies, 14 percent in the chemical industry, and 22 percent in applied physics—strong indicators that during the Honecker era, the GDR's economy was actually becoming less rather than more innovative.[47]

Declarations such as the one made at the eleventh party congress, which amounted to a campaign to catch up with western rates of innovation in two years, merely forced enterprises to fulfill their obligations by behavior bordering on deception.[48] So, for example, in 1985 the leather bag industry reported an innovation rate of 69 percent, innovations consisting primarily of petty alterations in design.[49]

These pseudo-innovations in product assortment and quality did more harm to the East German political economy than good. Higher wholesale prices for products that could still not be sold in the West had to be met either with higher consumer prices to cover costs or higher state subsidies to keep prices down. With the budget already overburdened by subsidies for staples, the SED leadership chose the former strategy on a number of items. Prices for selected consumer goods were often much higher in the GDR than West Germany. In the example of leather handbags, prices rose 30 to 50 percent in one year. In the 1980s, for clothing of comparable or worse quality, East Germans had to pay four to seven times the price, and for technical consumer durables, eight to fifteen times the price of their West German counterparts.[50]

The regional and district party organizations stepped into the structural breach with programs of their own to address the consumer goods situation. Since most enterprises that processed food, manufactured clothing, and other consumer products (with the exception of heavy consumer durables) operated under Bezirk guidance, it made sense for the BLs and KLs to get involved. Much of their energy was concentrated on ensuring that retail enterprises and manufacturers shared information on what needed to be produced. The economics secretary from BL Suhl, Eberhard Denner, reports that it was especially difficult to induce retail enterprises to participate in the design of new products, even though their managers had daily contact with customers. His task was not made any easier by the fact that the center had placed the BL under a great deal of pressure to increase consumer goods production while at the same time cutting back on any imports from the nonsocialist world that might be necessary for their manufacture.[51]

The BL Dresden confronted similar difficulties when the secretariat worked out a program to reduce the accumulation in warehouses of presumably stylish clothes that could not be sold. Faced with a rather dull selection and a "buying" plan to fulfill, buyers would simply order what was available without regard for what might sell. As an antidote, the BL required large department stores to share their market research with clothing enterprises, collaborate with the clothing combines in the design of new men's fashions one year in advance of their appearance, and work with the enterprises in planning large-scale knitwear runs. Even when this rather modest arrangement could be worked out in Dresden, the BL noted that "what has been formulated here as an assignment or even an obligation, is at the present time in other Bezirke, such as Berlin, an unfulfillable demand."[52]

The image of regional party officials (men and women not known for their aesthetic acuity) actively involved in determining the prevailing men's fashions borders on the laughable. The BL Dresden seems to have been aware of the situation but, as the following quotation from the party press on the proper division between stylish and conservative clothing illustrates, it could not resist getting in its opinion. "Willy-nilly one always hits up against the question: what actually is fashionable? During the last meeting between stores and manufacturers in Dresden, some of the retail outlets were of the opinion that the selection was too stylish and there was a lack of standard wares. Is this opinion right or is it subjective? Of course, we can not answer this question definitively. . . . [But] the relation between stylish and standard wares should be about 50/50."[53]

Apart from the supervision of consumer goods production, local party organs were intimately involved in the local distribution system. Their purview ran from television and car repairs to the supply of meat in the stores. Their most important task in this regard was securing continuity in food supply. The former BL Berlin first secretary Schabowski, for example, reports that during the Christmas season it was his task to ensure that the supply of politically sensitive goods, such as oranges and other fresh fruit, were released to the stores at the right time and, above all else, not too early.[54] To appreciate the weight carried by food questions, up to the highest levels of power, consider the following extended quotation from Schabowski's memoirs:

> Every year Günter Mittag, the economics secretary of the Central Committee, called me three weeks before Christmas: "The orange supply for the holiday is about to be delivered. I ask of you to make sure that they do not appear too soon in the stores, so that the supply will last until Christmas and, if possible, longer." I reminded him that the *government* had long understood how to deal with goods and how to sell them. It happens, after all, every year. Mittag reacted crossly. "I am speaking from the office of the general secretary. He requests that you make sure that nothing

goes wrong with supplies." After this pointer, and with big brother standing in the background, I saw no reason to continue the conversation. I called *Oberbürgermeister* Krack and informed him of my conversation. He got upset: "We do the same thing every year according to a proven model. Does he not have anything better to do?" I told Krack that he shouldn't lose his head over it. . . .

Several days later the secure telephone rang again. Alas, it was Mittag. It wasn't only microelectronics that seemingly had him going. He was still working on a solution to the "orange question." This time he left absolutely no doubt from where the wind was coming: "Erich has noticed that on Klement-Gottwald-Allee there is a line at the vegetable store, presumably for oranges." The Allee is a part of the so-called protocol stretch that was used by the [Politburo-controlled] Wandlitz inhabitants on their way to downtown Berlin. "We don't need any lines in the capital right now," continued Mittag.

I sensed that my patience was growing thin: "We have to sell the oranges where the people live and where the vegetable stores are located, whether it be in a main street or a side street. . . ." Mittag quickly told me that the lines had to disappear. End of conversation. I called the *Bürgermeister* again. We quickly agreed that the sale would continue as it was. How could one explain to the salespeople and the buyers that their oranges could no longer be sold in the usual stores because the lines were embarrassing for someone?[55]

Despite my skepticism of Schabowski's Captain Queeg–like caricature of Günter Mittag and his regular defiance of Mittag's orders, archival evidence confirms that the party apparatus faced an almost unquenchable demand for oranges. A November 1988 report of the BL Dresden confirmed that "the sale of oranges is running according to centrally established guidelines. [But] regarding the further growth in purchasing power, the quantities put on sale are sold immediately, so that no 'predictable' supply can be guaranteed."[56] The same bureaucratic to-and-fro took place at Easter. Mittag's regular interference in local affairs reveals simply that he knew the local party organs faced an almost insurmountable task in carrying out the workaday routine of food supplies.

The point here is neither trivial nor anecdotal. The SED had great hopes that *Kommunalpolitik* would improve the quality of life of ordinary East Germans and thus bind them more strongly to the regime. In the absence of the right to choose their own leaders, East Germans understood their own citizenship rights largely in economic terms, which in the 1980s had come to mean a middle-class life-style. The eighth party congress in 1971 with its emphasis on "social policy" had, in fact, encouraged such an understanding of citizenship. For years, the SED had desperately fought Western conceptions of political rights with an image of a package of economic rights, present only in a socialist society. The failure of the regime to deliver on significant portions of its own political promises, promises of an economic nature, accounts for the speed with which it lost power in 1989.

In one of the final crisis meetings of Honecker's Politburo in 1989, Gerhard Schürer put the question of consumer goods directly on the table. "There are poorer countries than the GDR with a much richer offering of goods in the stores. One has to admit that the people have a lot of money in their hands. When people have a lot of money and can't buy the goods they want, they curse socialism."[57] Schürer's words suggest that, if so inclined, one can raise the issue of consumer goods to the level of social theory. The revolutions of autumn 1989, seen from this point of view, were largely political actions of dissatisfied consumers, not, as Marxian social theory might have us expect, of dissatisfied producers. One measure of East Germans' pent-up demand is their rate of savings. As table 7-4 indicates, the rate of savings, which in a socialist economy amounts to a state debt, had been rising steadily since 1980. Cast in absolute numbers, whereas in 1966 the savings of the East German population amounted to 35 billion marks, by 1988 it had grown to 152 billion. The interest payments alone on this latter sum came to 4.8 billion marks per year, approximately the value of 400,000 Trabants.[58]

In 1989 the West German left tried to trivialize consumer dissatisfaction by dismissing it as a type of false consciousness on behalf of the East German working class. The back page of a compendium of articles on the East German revolution issued by the left-wing West German daily *tageszeitung*, for example, states: "Everybody is talking about bananas. We're not."[59] But was not the absence of bananas from the internal East German market a symbol of great political weight—a symbol of the impotence of the East German political economy? In fact, it was. Everybody was talking about bananas because they signified a system in which you could buy as much bread as you wanted but had to wait ten years or more to buy a car, fifteen years for the installation of a telephone, and could only dream of taking a trip to Paris, London, or even West Berlin.

In the local elections of May 1989, which were slated to be typical Communist exercises in public acclamation, the voters of the GDR vented their frustration with the supplies situation and with the general absence of basic

Table 7-4. Yearly Increase in Savings and Cash Holdings in Relation to Personal Income (in percentages)

Year	Savings
1980	2.2
1981	2.6
1982	3.8
1983	4.7
1984	4.2
1985	4.4
1986	5.6
1987	6.5
1988	6.4

Source: Kusch et al., *Schlußbilanz—DDR*, 21.

freedoms. Record numbers of East Germans risked their careers and futures by voting against the "unity" list at the polls. They were telling the leadership that they expected something better and that the regime would be held, if only in the minds of the people, to some kind of performance standards. The SED responded by falsifying the voting results in the national press. Church organizations, however, had monitored the voting and came up with final numbers at odds with those in the press. This exercise in vote fraud marked the beginning of the final crisis for the SED, foreshadowing the events to come a few months later.

Lest one doubt the impact of the local supplies and consumer shortages on the popular mind, consider the role played by pent-up consumer demand in the vote for unification in March 1990, which was at the same time a referendum on the rule of the SED.[60] Using a correlation analysis of the voting results of the fifteen Bezirke with a panoply of social indicators, savings per capita as a measure of pent-up consumer demand consistently comes out as the most significant explanatory factor.[61] In Bezirke with higher per capita savings, the vote went strongly against the left, and in Bezirke where savings were lower, the left fared better.

When we combine this analysis with one further correlation, namely that of the housing infrastructure of a Bezirk, as measured by the number of employees working in the construction sector, with the final vote, a picture emerges of the failure of the two main tasks of regional coordination: housing and consumer goods. The weaker the construction sector and other elements of urban infrastructure, the weaker was the performance of the Party of Democratic Socialism (the successor party of the SED) and the Social Democratic Party, and the stronger the performance of the right. The rapid collapse of the GDR is thus explainable, in part, by the failure of the SED in provinces. For the SED, too, politics was ultimately a local affair.

Two generations of scholars have studied the relationship between communism and modernity. One group has maintained that communism was uniquely modern.[1] Its use of mass politics, bureaucratic terror, and impersonal norms, its construction of cities and industry, and its espousal of a secular ideology that above all else valorized instrumental rationality characterize an institutional order that could only have existed in modernity. A second group of theorists have argued that communism may have been modern in some ideal-typical sense of the word, but it was a failure as far as "modernization" *cum* sustained economic advancement is concerned.[2] This study, while acknowledging the contribution of the first group, reinforces the insights of the second: the gap between modernity and modernization proved fatal for communism. Who, after all, really needs or wants a society run on merit, bureaucracy, and the devaluation of tradition, if these traits do not in some way assist in the creation of relative prosperity? Economic modernization may be one thing that makes the other elements of modernity appealing or even tolerable.

The moral of the story is that industrial society and scarcity do not mix well. Governments in industrial societies that do not successfully address the issue of scarcity have difficulty retaining the affections and loyalties of their citizens. One may ask, however, has this not always been the case, even before the age of industry? Have not ruling groups always been elevated to and swept from power in the wake of famines, droughts, and the internal hardships of war? Perhaps. The difference today is that, for most people living in the industrialized world, scarcity is no longer experienced as the denial of basic needs, but rather as unfulfilled desires.[3] The transformation of luxuries into necessities within national societies, a process so vividly described by Veblen almost a century ago, has become truly global.[4] Driven by the force of information technologies, new needs and desires spread across political borders with breathtaking speed. To appreciate this fact, one need only consider how many of us in different countries watch the same television broadcasts and purchase the same goods. On top of this, with the collapse of status-based orders, permanent structural disparities within or among countries are no longer perceived as legitimate, even though they are more keenly felt than ever.[5] As Ernest Gellner has so eloquently phrased it, universal affluence is the *Danegeld* of modernity that governments pay their peoples as the price for political stability.[6]

This change in the meaning of scarcity, luxury, need, and desire since the eighteenth century has greatly complicated the task of governing elites all over the world. In the West it has led to a general crisis in governability, as states fend off demands on their resources from interests, all of which appear equally legitimate. In the third world, elites face the dual pressures (largely imposed on them from the West) of maintaining a stable democracy in the face of a never-ending tide of socially and politically articulated demands, without sabotaging the market or otherwise cannibalizing the economy to shore up political support. Hence, the continual swing of the pendulum between democratization and authoritarian closure.

Communists faced a different set of problems, for they sought to fashion an alternative to liberal modernity. A small minority, such as Pol Pot's Cambodia, Mao's China, and, temporarily, Enver Hoxha's Albania, took the route of a Rousseauian cultural revolution, which refused economic development and attempted instead to redefine human needs. Most Communist regimes, however, and here I include those of the former Soviet bloc, did not attempt to redefine human needs but rather promised to meet them in the future. The official ideology, Marxism-Leninism, called for personal sacrifice and delayed gratification. The underlying hope was that somewhere down the road Communist economies would catch up with and overtake the West in productive output, leisure time, and consumption. Such an ambitious goal (or dream) was perhaps communism's most fatal act of hubris. In setting up capitalist modernity as the yardstick against which it measured itself, rather than defining a "yardstick" of its own, communism was doomed to live in capitalism's shadow. Communism lived not only under the influence of a capitalist standard of material success but also under the influence of political liberalism. Just as Communist parties could not dispense with elections, parliaments, law, courts, a formal separation between party and state, and the other trappings of political liberalism, they could not escape from capitalist modernity. If the people increasingly understood that their political institutions, such as elections, parliaments, courts, and the law, were mere facades of the real item, they understood with even greater clarity that Communist industry, roads, housing, shopping centers, and supermarkets were not very authentic imitations of what industries, roads, housing, shopping centers, and supermarkets were supposed to look like.

Marxism-Leninism's incapacity to develop its own unique understanding of modernity, its own vocabulary for it, its own discourse that would have enabled people to experience scarcity in a qualitatively different way, ensured that its version of modernity would be less appealing than liberal capitalism. The doctrine of delayed gratification could not prevent Western conceptions of scarcity from seeping into the popular culture and, in the long run, it could not be sustained. Instead, the regimes of East Europe scrambled to meet the consumer demands of their populations within the confines of the old structures. The history of communism therefore was not so much a genuine search for a unique path to a new socialist modernity as it was a series of responses to crises brought on by its failure to escape from capitalist modernity. These responses, however, cast as they were in terms of competing with the West, merely intensified the daily experience of second-rate citizenship in a capitalist world.

Arguably no country in the Communist world faced this dilemma more squarely than the GDR. The preceding chapters have sought to account for East Germany's pattern of responses to increasing relative economic backwardness within the framework of Marxist-Leninist institutions over a period of forty years. As noted at the outset of this study, most students of communism predicted that the challenges of Western capitalism and subsequent adaptive responses would induce a gradual change in the structure of authority to allow for more rational and technical criteria in economic policy and administration. To some extent this did occur in East Germany. At critical junctures in its history, however, the SED's adaptive choices imposed constraints on its options in subsequent periods that prevented economic renewal. In very distinct ways the GDR's developmental history was path-dependent. Having lost its battles with the working class during the 1950s, the SED elite was severely restricted in its choices of economic reform in the 1960s. Having abandoned serious reform and outlawed reformist thought in the 1970s, the SED was ill-prepared to confront the challenges of the international political economy in the 1980s. Seen in this way, the immobility of the latter years was largely determined by the choices of the early years.

None of these policy standoffs and failures, of course, in any way diminished the need for viable substitutes for the efficiency-producing mechanisms in market economies. They merely intensified it. The response was what I have called the campaign economy, a set of programs undertaken by the local party organs that only partially addressed the problems they were intended to rectify. Notwithstanding its limited economic rationality, however, the campaign economy had a political rationality of its own that sustained it far longer than was economically justifiable. By promoting

Table C-1. Per Capita Income of East European Countries as Percentage of Advanced European Countries

Country	1926–34: Europe = 100	1980 Method I: Europe = 100	1980 Method II: Europe = 100
East Germany	81.8	44.9	65
Czechoslovakia	56.9	36.4	54.7
Hungary	44.8	33.4	40.8
Poland	35.1	28.4	39.1
Yugoslavia	40.8	19.8	31.1
Bulgaria	32.3	27	39.9
Romania	29.7	20.4	24.1
Average of six	36.9	27.6	38.3

Note: East German (future GDR) per capita income: 103 percent of total German income per capita. Figures (100) in columns 1, 2, 3 represent averages of six advanced industrial countries: Germany, France, Sweden, Belgium, Holland, Switzerland. Source: Andrew Janos, "Continuity and Change in Eastern Europe: Strategies of Post-Communist Politics." *East European Politics and Societies* 8, no. 1 (1994): 4.

and protecting the careers of central and regional officials, and supplying a source of political rituals and theater, the campaign economy became a realm of authority building and cultural continuity rather than production.

Given the constraints under which the leadership operated and the administrative culture that developed in the intersticies of these constraints, it becomes easier to account for a remarkable record of continuity amid economic and political decay. The paradox of Communist political economy is that it provided the necessary administrative tasks and political rituals to reproduce the organizational integrity of the party; it prevented market-oriented, capitalist modes of thought from penetrating the elite; and it secured for Communist Europe a modicum of economic development—all the while dooming these countries to fall farther behind the West each year with no hope of making up the difference in the future. The net effect of the Communist experience is illustrated in table C-1. By the 1980s, never had East Europe been so backward in relation to the West. And never had East Germany been so backward relative to its West German counterpart. Whichever method of statistical comparison one uses, whether it be purchasing power parities (method I) or physical indicators and dollar equivalents of reported gross domestic product (method II), East Europe did not improve its relative economic position on the European continent under communism, and East Germany emerges as the real loser.[7]

Modernity and German Identity

But if East Germany was an economic failure, it was certainly not a failure compared with the third world or even compared with its own living standards of previous decades. Had the GDR been a country of dire poverty, it would have been psychologically easy for the individual party secretary and eventually groups of officials from Berlin and the provinces to lose their nerve, to lose their confidence that history had intended them to rule for the good of the German people, to convince themselves that something had to be done. But no one starved in East Germany and there was no genuine poverty, with the possible exception of a small number of senior citizens. And although environmental conditions had adversely affected the quality of life, basic medical care was universal and free. Furthermore, most East Germans received a first-rate education, albeit tainted with the daily catechism of Marxism-Leninism, as well as a world-class selection of sports, culture, and the arts.

Seen purely from the point of view of economic performance, the revolution of 1989 and the demise of the GDR were in no way inevitable. Such determinism defeats the point of historical inquiry and offers us very little in the way of understanding. Why could the GDR not have become a second Austria? Whereas only a minority of Austrians considered their own republic as viable before World War II, today an even smaller minority would be willing to give up national sovereignty altogether. As one sociologist has cleverly speculated, one could picture an alternative course of events for the two Germanys: the year is 1996, Social Democratic Chancellor Oskar Lafontaine, after his second election victory, meets with GDR State Council Chairman Egon Krenz and signs a deal on freedom to travel and a unified German citizenship, as well as a Volkswagen joint venture in Zwickau to produce a new cheap car for domestic consumption and Europe-wide export on the basis of low East German wages.[8] With political and economic assistance from the outside, East Germany might have survived.

Such a counterfactual thought experiment brings us back to the conditions under which East Germans might have been persuaded or convinced to retain rather than shed their East German identity in 1989 and 1990. These conditions must be understood in economic terms. For at the heart of East Germany's failure to construct an appealing, alternative, "socialist" German identity was its perennially disappointing economic performance compared with that of West Germany. Put bluntly, had East Germany been a more appealing place to live, more East Germans would have found it reasonable to adopt a new, East German identity. If East Germany's economic performance had been as robust as that of the West, might not the leadership have permitted the people to travel, certain that most would return? Taking the counterfactual to its extreme, had economic performance and the standard of living outpaced that of West Germany, how many East Germans would have risked their lives by calling for the overthrow of the SED and a unification with the West, all in the name of an abstract political freedom? I suspect depressingly few.

Am I proposing a materialist explanation of identity? Not really. I do not believe, for example, that either Hungary or Poland would give up its national institutions and symbols to join Germany. Any Hungarian or Pole so foolish as to suggest this as an option for his country would be quickly dismissed as a kook or a criminal no matter what the economic situation or however much money the Germans offered. By definition, strong identities are not for sale.

Apparently, in 1990 East Germany's identity was for sale. Am I proposing, then, a materialist explanation of German identity? I would hardly be the first writer to note the importance of economic performance in maintaining German political stability and constructing German national identity. The latest and most obvious case of this is the election strategy of West Germany's Christian Democratic Union (CDU) in the first and last free national election in the GDR's history in March 1990. In throwing his political weight behind the East German CDU's promise of rapid unification with the West, it was not enough for Helmut Kohl simply to say that unification was good because Germans belong together. This, had it stood on its own, would have been the strong "identity" argument. Instead, Kohl felt constrained to lure the East Germans with promises that no one would be materially hurt; to trick the West Germans into believing that it could all be done without raising taxes; and to fool the entire world that the East could be brought up to the level of the West in five years.

Having unified under such an illusion, the same forces that caused the collapse of communism and the desire for rapid unification—the absence of a strong, nonmaterialist German identity—continue to plague a unified Germany. The hope that Germany united could simply be a bigger and better version of the old Federal Republic, based on values no more controversial than a tested model of economic prosperity, has faded. In the short run at least, rapid unification has been very costly, painful and, some have argued, irrational. While by the end of 1994, due to the vigorous efforts of the German privatization agency, the Treuhand, only 350 of 13,781 formerly socialist enterprises remained on the books, such wide-scale change could only be accomplished at very great cost. Privatization of the combines and a currency union carried out at a rate of one to one brought on a deep recession in the East, the dimensions of which surpassed all expectations. Unemployment, a phenomenon virtually unknown in East Germany before unification, rose quickly, climbing to 15.8 percent in 1992 and falling only slightly by the end of 1995. But this number does not come close to representing the genuine idle capacity in the East German labor force. According to one author, by 1995 open and hidden unemployment in East Germany reached 30 percent.[9] Regionally, however, it is much higher, with Mecklenburg-Vorpommern being the hardest hit. If one subtracts the number of "make work" positions from the East German employment totals, the number of jobs in the East German economy decreased between 1989 and 1992 by approximately 46 percent of the pretransition level, and by 1994 the region had lost 80 percent of its industrial work force, which numbered 3.2 million in 1989. The governmental transfers of money from West to East Germany to cover unemployment, "make work," and industrial restructuring has exceeded all original estimates, surpassing one trillion marks by the end of 1995, and these transfers are expected to continue well into the future. With a mounting debt, rising taxes, and upward pressure on interest rates, for the first time Germans have begun discussing whether their future is that of an American-style *Defizitstaat*.[10]

Economic problems have coincided with new social tensions in the first half of the 1990s in both eastern and western Germany. The most dramatic manifestations of these tensions were the activities of right-wing youth gangs. The televised spectacle of attacks on foreigners in Rostock and Hoyerswerda, the burning of the living quarters of asylum seekers, the defacing of synagogues and other Jewish cultural institutions have embarrassed and shocked the German public.

Even if eastern Germany does not drag the rest of Germany down with it, there is no gainsaying that unification has changed everything. The way back to the old Federal Republic appears to have been closed off. Most Germans, East and West, regardless of political orientation, have an uneasy feeling of being on terra incognita. Limited resources suggest that many postunification issues cannot simply be "bought off." Apart from the economic difficulties and social tensions resulting from unification, Germany's evolving international role continues to nourish the sentiment that national identity and public discourse must be based on values more substantial than the belief in economic prosperity.

German identity is once again on the table. Questions about its most fundamental national values, its national mission, its national heroes, and its national villains have been taken up in earnest. Unlike other nations in Europe, Germans experienced the cold war in a unique way. From the zonal period to the founding of two separate German states in 1949, from the construction of the Berlin Wall in 1961 to its destruction in 1989, it was the fate of divided Germany, the national question, that provided the backdrop to the political conflict between capitalism and communism. Behind every vitriolic public exchange between Ulbricht and Adenauer, behind every diplomatic initiative and counterinitiative, behind every threat and counterthreat, lay the issue of who truly had the right to represent the interests of the entire nation—West Germany or East Germany.

Fortunately for humanity, the national question was never settled militarily. Instead, political competition between the two states boiled down to an evaluation of which system could ensure a better quality of life for its citizens. Notwithstanding the high drama of the postwar years, the proposals and counterproposals for unification, the disputes over national boundaries, and the spectacles of spy trades, kidnapping, and midnight escapes, the decisive, identity-defining battle of the cold war was fought on the economic front. Both countries defined themselves in economic terms—East Germany as the first workers' and peasants' state in German history. Likewise, the material basis of West German identity is supported by survey evidence from various periods and, perhaps more important, by the repeated critique of this identity and its resonance in popular culture.[11] The patriotism that ultimately appealed to the East Germans was not the *Verfassungspatriotismus* (constitutional patriotism) of Jürgen Habermas but the *Wirtschaftspatriotismus* (economic patriotism) of the Bonn republic.

It is in this light that I understand the recent debate on the German nation taking place in Germany itself.[12] Although the terms of the debate are not always clear and readers of the popular press often dismiss it as overly intellectual and marginal to the quotidian concerns of real people, it has exceeded the bounds of journalistic or academic interest.[13] In any case, debates about such fundamental questions as identity tend to evolve slowly, as the different sides define their positions more clearly and learn to understand each other's arguments, and as the terms of the debate filter their way into popular discourse. Whatever the outcome of the debate, whether it be a victory for the proponents of constitutional patriotism or for those favoring a renewed emphasis on the *Germanness* of Germany, or some new synthesis between the civic and ethnic principles, I believe that the dialogue is important. For if the public sphere in Germany remains preoccupied exclusively with scarcity or what Arendt has called the social question, the more fundamental issues of national identity and public values will inevitably be left unresolved—or, worse, the fringe will fill in the void.

Abbreviations

BAP SPK	Bundesarchiv Abteilungen Potsdam, Staatliche Plankommission (Archive of the GDR's State Planning Commission)
BPA SED, Dresden	Bezirksparteiorganisation Parteiarchiv SED, Dresden (Archive of the SED's Dresden regional party organization)
SAMPO-BA	Stiftung Archiv der Parteien und Massenorganisationen der DDR im Bundesarchiv (SED Central Party Archive)

Introduction

1. Telegram BPA SED, Dresden, unsorted.

2. See for example the interview given by Horst Sindermann just before his death in *Der Spiegel*, no. 19 (1990): 58.

3. Günter Mittag, *Um jeden Preis* (Berlin: Aufbau Verlag, 1991).

4. Barrington Moore, *Social Origins of Dictatorship and Democracy* (Boston: Beacon Press, 1967), 12.

5. Janos Kornai, *The Socialist System: The Political Economy of Communism* (Princeton: Princeton University Press, 1992); Jan Winiecki, *The Distorted World of Soviet-Type Economies* (Pittsburgh: University of Pittsburgh Press, 1988); Peter Rutland, *The Myth of the Plan* (London: Hutchinson, 1985).

6. Formally, Walter Ulbricht became general secretary of the SED only in 1950. However, from notes prepared for Stalin and Molotov by Mikhail Suslov in 1947 before a visit to Moscow of the two party chairmen, Wilhelm Pieck and Otto Grotewohl, along with Walter Ulbricht, it was already clear that the Soviets regarded Ulbricht as more powerful and politically reliable than his two "superiors" in the SED: more powerful than Wilhelm Pieck, the gray eminence from the prewar KPD ("In devising and implementing the political line of the SED, he does not always play a leading role"), and more reliable than Otto Grotewohl, the social democrat co-opted into the SED in 1946, who, according to Suslov, "tends toward vacillation and inconsistency. . . . Denies the responsibility of the German people for the war, does not consider the decision on the eastern border of Germany as settled once and for all." Bernd Bonwetsch and Gennadij Bordjugov, "Stalin und die SBZ. Ein Besuch der SED-Führung in Moskau vom 30.Januar–7.Februar 1947," *Vierteljahrshefte für Zeitgeschichte* 42, no. 2 (1994): 287–89.

7. A word of explanation is necessary for figure I-1. Economists have estimated the degree of decay (*Verschleissgrad*) of East Germany's industrial equipment in 1988 at 55 percent. This proportion, however, only makes sense in a comparative context. Internationally the rate of decay of industrial equipment for an economy structurally similar to the GDR's should be approximately 45 percent, a difference of 10 percent. Even so,

this number does not fully capture the extent of industrial decay, because the normative use time for equipment in the GDR, as in other socialist countries, was considerably longer than in the West. In part this was offset by higher rates of investment; but such investment could not, according to one source, prevent the rate of fully worn-out equipment in use in GDR industries from increasing to 20 percent of all industrial equipment in 1988 from a level of 14 percent in 1980. Günter Kusch et al., *Schlußbilanz—DDR: Fazit einer verfehlten Wirtschafts- und Sozialpolitik* (Berlin: Duncker & Humblot, 1991), 55.

8. See, for example, Thomas Baylis, "Explaining the GDR's Economic Strategy," *International Organization* 40, no. 2 (1986): 381–420, "The GDR's success casts some doubt upon the fond belief of many Western commentators that a centralized system of economic direction . . . is hopelessly clumsy and an inefficient way of organizing a technologically sophisticated economy."

9. Forced to rely on official figures, Western scholars and governmental agencies came to unrealistically optimistic and often bizarre conclusions about East Germany's economic performance. In 1986, for example, the CIA calculated East German income per capita at $10,440, placing it ahead of West Germany. *Handbook of Economic Statistics* (Washington, D.C.: Central Intelligence Agency, 1986), 24–25. Since 1989, several analysts have commented on the poor quality of GDR statistics, especially when compared with those of other, reforming centrally planned economies. For early reports of statistical falsification at the Council of Ministers level, see *Neue Zeit*, November 16, 1989, 1.

10. "Czech's Velvet Revolution Snags," *Boston Globe*, November 17, 1990, 8.

11. Gabriel Almond and Sidney Verba, *The Civic Culture* (Boston: Little Brown, 1965). For an extended criticism of this element of the German national character, see Heinrich Böll, *Billiard um Halb Zehn* (Cologne: Kiepenhauer und Witsch, 1966).

12. David P. Conradt, "West Germany: A Remade Political Culture," *Comparative Political Studies* 7, no. 2 (1975): 222–38.

13. Andrew Janos, *Politics and Paradigms* (Stanford, Calif.: Stanford University Press, 1986).

14. Chalmers Johnson, "Comparing Communist Nations," in Johnson, ed., *Change in Communist Systems* (Stanford, Calif.: Stanford University Press, 1970), 1–33. T. Anthony Jones, "Modernization Theory and Socialist Development," in Mark G. Field, ed., *Social Consequences of Modernization in Communist Societies* (Baltimore: Johns Hopkins University Press, 1976), 19–49. Zygmunt Bauman, "The Party in the Systems Manaagement Phase," in Andrew C. Janos, ed., *Authoritarian Politics in Communist Europe*, Research Series, no. 28 (Berkeley: Institute of International Studies, 1976), 81–109.

15. See the various contributions in H. G. Skilling and Franklyn Griffiths, eds., *Interest Groups in Soviet Politics* (Princeton: Princeton University Press, 1971); Peter H. Solomon, *Soviet Criminologists and Criminal Policy* (New York: Columbia University Press, 1978).

16. Jerry Hough, *The Soviet Prefects: The Local Party Organs in Industrial Decision Making* (Cambridge, Mass.: Harvard University Press, 1969); and *Soviet Leadership in Transition* (Washington, D.C.: Brookings, 1979).

17. Alexander Yanov, *The Drama of the Soviet 1960's: A Lost Reform* (Berkeley: Institute of International Studies, 1984).

18. Peter Rutland, *The Politics of Economic Stagnation in the Soviet Union* (Cambridge: Cambridge University Press, 1993); Stephen Fortescue, *The Communist Party and Soviet Science* (Baltimore: Johns Hopkins University Press, 1986).

19. In American sovietology the prediction of a "retraditionalization" of Soviet-style polities can be traced back to Barrington Moore's *Terror and Progress USSR* (Cambridge, Mass.: Harvard University Press, 1954); but the most influential study on this theme remains Ken Jowitt, "Soviet Neotraditionalism: The Political Corruption of a Leninist Regime," *Soviet Studies* 35, no. 3 (1983): 275–97.

20. One scholar to criticize this trend was Norman Naimark, "Is it True What They're Saying about East Germany?" *Orbis* 23, no. 3 (1979): 549–77.

21. Peter Ludz, *Parteielite im Wandel* (Opladen: Westdeutscher Verlag, 1969); Thomas Baylis, *The East German Elite and the Technocratic Intelligentsia* (Berkeley: University of California Press, 1974).

22. Gert Joachim Glaeßner, *Herrschaft durch Kader* (Opladen: Westdeutscher Verlag, 1977); Gero Neugebauer, *Partei und Staatsapparat in der DDR* (Opladen: Westdeutscher Verlag, 1978). Ursula Hoffmann's work on the personnel structure of the GDR's Council of Ministers is typical of the entire genre: "The requirements of industry usher in a trend toward convergence in the economic policies of modern industrial states. . . . Since the success of economic organization overwhelmingly depends on the extent to which the adaptation to changed environmental conditions is made through the use of experts and new methods of organizing work, one can pose the hypothesis that the two variables 'economic success' and 'greater employment of experts' correlate with each other, and the presence of the one is an indicative factor for the presence of the other." *Die Veränderung in der Sozialstruktur des Ministerrats der DDR 1949–1969* (Düsseldorf: Droste, 1971), 14–15.

23. It should also be noted that most of these scholars placed themselves on the political left. As such, they were inclined to judge the SED on its own terms—namely, the claim to be building a better, more just society than existed in the West—rather than subject it directly to the standards of liberal-capitalist democracy.

24. Fred Klinger considered this problem in "Die Transformation der DDR" and "Das Scheitern des real-existierenden Sozialismus in der DDR. Ein Gespräch," *Deutsche Studien* 28, no. 109 (March 1990).

25. It can either be construed as a "least likely" (least likely to fail) or "most likely" (most likely to succeed) case. On the logic of the crucial case, see Harry Eckstein, "Case Study and Theory in Political Science," in Fred I. Greenstein and Nelson W. Polsby, eds., *Handbook of Political Science*, vol. 7: *Strategies of Inquiry* (Reading, Mass.: Addison-Wesley, 1976), 118–19.

26. The essentials of the developmental state were first put forward by Johann Gottlieb Fichte in his *Der geschlossene Handelsstaat*, in Fichte, *Ausgewählte Werke*, vol. 3 (Darmstadt: Wissenschaftliche Buchgesellschaft, 1964), 417–544. In this work, meant as a model for Germany in the post-Napoleonic era, "the closed trading state" suppresses consumption, monopolizes foreign trade, and otherwise controls production and penetrates civil society in order to catch up with the economies of more advanced states. The Asian model is simply a moderate or "liberal" version of Fichte's original scheme. The standard work remains Chalmers Johnson, *Miti and the Japanese Economic Miracle* (Stanford, Calif.: Stanford University Press, 1986); see also Stephan Haggard, *Pathways from the Periphery: The Politics of Growth in the Newly Industrializing States* (Ithaca, N.Y.: Cornell University Press, 1990). For a study that challenges Johnson's model, see Frances McCall Rosenbluth, *Financial Politics in Contemporary Japan* (Ithaca, N.Y.: Cornell University Press, 1989).

27. Laurence McFalls, "Une Allemagne, deux Sociétés distinctes: Les causes et conséquences culturelles de la reunification," *Canadian Journal of Political Science* 26, no. 4 (1993): 721–43. See also the articles in *German Politics and Society*, no. 26 (summer 1992), especially Laurence McFalls, "The Modest Germans: Towards an Understanding of the East German Revolution," 1–20, and Henry Krisch, "Explaining the Wende: Five Early Efforts," 109–16. For a view emphasizing changing value orientations, see Christiane Lemke, *Die Ursachen des Umbruchs 1989: Politische Sozialisation in der ehemaligen DDR* (Opladen: Westdeutscher Verlag, 1991).

28. Susanne Lohmann, "Dynamics of Informational Cascades: The Monday Demonstrations in Leipzig, East Germany, 1989–1991," *World Politics* 47, no. 1 (1994): 42–101.

29. Moore, *Social Origins*; Theda Skocpol, *States and Social Revolutions* (Cambridge: Cambridge University Press, 1979).

Chapter 1

1. In a recent contribution to the controversy, Wilfried Loth, *Stalins ungeliebtes Kind: Warum Moskau die DDR nicht wollte* (Berlin: Rowohlt-Berlin, 1994), has argued that not only did Stalin not want a separate East German state (a point many historians concede), but that he was more than willing to permit a Western-style democracy in postwar Germany. This second, far more controversial thesis, based on interpretations of notes taken by the GDR's first president, Wilhelm Pieck, during conversations with Soviet officials, has been roundly criticized by Heinrich August Winkler, "Im Zickzackkurs zum Sozialismus," in *Die Zeit*, no. 25 (June 17, 1994): 40 (German edition).

2. The best reevaluation of reparations to date is Rainer Karlsch, *Allein bezahlt? Reparationsleistungen der SBZ-DDR 1945–53* (Berlin: Ch. Links Verlag, 1993). On the average growth rates and pride in achievement, see BAP SPK, E-1 51764.

3. The phrasing here indicates that my thinking on these questions has been influenced by the new institutional economics. Douglass R. North, *Institutions, Institutional Change, and Economic Performance* (Cambridge: Cambridge University Press, 1990); Jack Knight, *Institutions and Social Conflict* (Cambridge: Cambridge University Press, 1992).

4. Peter J. Katzenstein, *Small States in World Markets: Industrial Policy in Europe* (Ithaca, N.Y.: Cornell University Press); Adam Przeworski, *Capitalism and Social Democracy* (Cambridge: Cambridge University Press, 1985).

5. Milovan Djilas, *Conversations with Stalin* (New York: Harcourt Brace Jovanovich, 1972), 114.

6. Wolfgang Zank, *Wirtschaft und Arbeit in Ostdeutschland 1945–1949* (Munich: R. Oldenbourg Verlag, 1987), 113.

7. This image is drawn from R. H. Tawney, *Land and Labor in China* (Boston: Beacon Press, 1966), 77, cited in James C. Scott, *The Moral Economy of the Peasant: Rebellion and Subsistence in Southeast Asia* (New Haven: Yale University Press, 1976), 1.

8. For an especially moving article, see *Tribüne*, March 3, 1947: "We demanded that the enterprises conduct a medical investigation of its younger workers. We came to the conclusion that the enterprise youth is not gaining but losing weight and that the overwhelming portion of youths is considerably underweight. One of the most blatant cases recently is that of Liselotte W., sixteen and a half years old, who works in Tempelhof. She is 1.5 meters tall and weighs 26 kilos. Another youth from the same district is

1.69 meters tall and weighs 40 kilos. A fifteen-year-old is 1.38 meters tall and weighs 32 kilos." In Dietrich Staritz, *Die Gründung der DDR* (Munich: DTV, 1987), 206–7.

9. Klaus Ewers, "Der Konflikt um Lohn und Leistung in den Volkseigenen Betrieben der SBZ/DDR" (Ph.D. diss., University of Osnabrück, 1985), 24; Waltraud Falk, *Kleine Geschichte einer großen Bewegung* (Berlin: Dietz, 1966), 46, where he notes that in 1947 Saxony had an absentee rate of 19.3 percent.

10. Siegfried Suckut, *Die Betriebsrätebewegung in der sowjetisch besetzten Zone Deutschlands (1945–1948)* (Frankfurt: Haag and Herchen Verlag, 1982); Dietrich Staritz, *Sozialismus in einem halben Lande* (Berlin: Verlag Klaus Wagenbach, 1978), 104–6.

11. Zank, *Wirtschaft und Arbeit*, 53–54.

12. Gregory Sanford, *From Hitler to Ulbricht* (Cambridge: Cambridge University Press, 1983).

13. "Aus einem SED-Referentmaterial zum sächsischen Volksentscheid," in Hermann Weber, ed., *DDR: Dokumente zur Geschichte der Deutschen Demokratischen Republik 1945–1985* (Munich: DTV, 1986), 73. On the creation of the SED and the GDR, see Henry Krisch, *German Politics under Soviet Occupation* (New York: Columbia University Press, 1974). On the creation of the security police, see Norman Naimark, " 'To Know Everything and to Report Everything Worth Knowing': Building the East German Police State, 1945–1949," Cold War International History Project, Woodrow Wilson International Center for Scholars, Washington, D.C., August 1994.

14. Ewers, "Der Konflikt," 23.

15. On SED lobbying for the creation of a central coordinating authority, see Andre Steiner, "Zwischen Länderpartikularismus und Zentralismus: Zur Wirtschaftslenkung in der SBZ bis zur Bildung der Deutschen Wirtschaftskommission im Juni 1947," *Aus Politik und Zeitgeschichte*, B49–50 (1993): 32–33.

16. John Gimbel, *The Origins of the Marshall Plan* (Stanford, Calif.: Stanford University Press, 1976); on Soviet reactions, see Woodford McClellan, "Molotov Remembers," *Cold War International History Project Bulletin*, no. 1 (Spring 1992): 20.

17. SAMPO-BA, SED IV 2/602/85.

18. The term *Leistungslohn* was used to denote piecework or other types of wages with bonuses for extra output.

19. Heidurn Homburg, "The 'Human Factor' and the Limits of Rationalization: Personnel-Management Strategies and the Rationalization Movement in German Industry between the Wars," in Steven Tolliday and Jonathan Zeitlin, eds., *The Power to Manage: Employers and Industrial Relations in Comparative Historical Perspective* (London: Routledge, 1992).

20. SAMPO-BA, SED IV 2/602/85.

21. Letter from Paul Merker to Walter Ulbricht February 26, 1948, SAMPO-BA, SED IV 2/2027/22.

22. Ibid.

23. Report written for SMAD Karlshorst, February 19, 1948, by the special commission for Brandenburg. Trade-union chief Herbert Warnke launched a similar complaint on July 5, 1948; see SAMPO-BA, SED 2/602/85.

24. See, for example, the report from the Gera district textile industries in SAMPO-BA, SED IV 2/2027/22.

25. Minister for Social Affairs Schwab in report to SMAD, February 19, 1948. "Minis-

ter Schwab declares himself against the People's Control Commissions in their present form. He believes that organization and tasks of the committees must be regulated through ordinances. He especially criticizes the present composition of the PCCs, which are often made up of criminals and ex-convicts." SAMPO-BA, SED IV 2/602/86. See also reports in SAMPO-BA, SED 2/2027/22.

26. SAMPO-BA, SED IV 2/602/85. In the case of the post in Wismar, however, corruption was endemic. In January, the 234 committee visiting the region reported that the administration had already been changed four times. SAMPO-BA, SED IV 2/602/86.

27. James Scott, *Weapons of the Weak* (New Haven: Yale University Press, 1985).

28. SAMPO-BA, SED IV 2/2027/22.

29. State Department Decimal Files, XR862b.555/6-1053.

30. SAMPO-BA, SED IV 2/2027/22.

31. Suckut, *Betriebsrätebewegung*, 196.

32. Ewers, "Der Konflikt," 45. A report from Mecklenburg-Vorpommern of February 20, 1948, prepared for the SMAD, complained that, since the implementation of Order 234 was primarily in the hands of the Department for Labor and Welfare, all the emphasis was on the social rather than on the production side.

33. SAMPO-BA, SED IV 2/2027/22; see also Jörg Roesler, "Vom Akkordlohn zum Leistungslohn: Zu den Traditionen des Kampfes der deutschen Arbeiterklasse und zur Einführung des Leistungslohnes in der volkseigenen Wirtschaft der DDR 1948 bis 1950," *Zeitschrift für Geschichte* 32 (1984): 778–95.

34. SAMPO-BA, SED 2/2027/22.

35. On promise of Sokolovski, see Horst Barthel, *Zur Wirtschaftspolitik der SED* (Berlin: Dietz, 1984), 1:27. On the complaint, see Rainer Karlsch, " 'Das Selbmann Memorandum' vom Mai 1947. Fritz Selbmann und die Reparationslasten der sächsichen Industrie," in *Beiträge zur Geschichte der Arbeiterbewegung* 35, no. 2 (1993): 88–125.

36. SAMPO-BA, SED IV 2/602/85.

37. SAMPO-BA, SED IV 2/2027/22.

38. SAMPO-BA, SED IV 2/5/232.

39. See the half-year report on Order 234 of SED Economics Department, SAMPO-BA, SED IV 2/602/85. The Louis Blumer Chemical Works in Zwickau reported that its employees "strongly reject the bonus system because it is too reminiscent of the Nazi era."

40. Ewers, "Der Konflikt," 48.

41. *Arbeit und Sozialfürsorge*, no. 3 (1952): 494. On falling wages in the first months after Order 234, see reference to letter of Heinrich Rau to Ulbricht in a report for Ulbricht, dated Februrary 4, 1948, in SAMPO-BA, SED IV 2/602/85.

42. Jörg Roesler, *Die Herausbildung der sozialistischen Industrie der DDR* (Berlin: Akademie Verlag 1985), 82.

43. As Zank notes, labor was scarce, not because of any shortage of warm bodies, but because of other factors, such as poor bureaucratic deployment and other labor market inefficiencies, as well as the expansion of uranium mining in Wismut. Zank, *Wirtschaft und Arbeit*.

44. This source of managerial motivation became more pressing after 1948, when the numbers of people leaving the Soviet Zone for the West shot up dramatically. Ewers, "Der Konflikt," 75–77.

45. On the Soviet experience with Taylorism, see Mark Beissinger, *Scientific Manage-*

ment, Socialist Discipline, and Soviet Power (Cambridge, Mass.: Harvard University Press, 1988).

46. Homburg, "The Human Factor," 236.

47. SAMPO-BA, SED IV 2/2027/27.

48. *Tribüne*, May 8, 1948, quoted in Ewers, "Der Konflikt," 52.

49. Exactly who came up with this idea remains unclear. Some discussion of it occurred among experts in the DWK in early February 1948. Letter of Dr. Raphael, February 4, 1948, in SAMPO-BA, SED 2/602/85.

50. Ewers, *Der Konflikt*, 64–65.

51. SAMPO-BA, SED IV 2/2027/27.

52. SAMPO-BA, SED NL 182/922.

53. The bureaucratic battle, along with the high-level SED and SMAD adjudication, can be found in the exchange of letters in SAMPO-BA, SED 2/2027/27.

54. Letter from Perelivchenko to DWK President Rau, December 23, 1948, ibid.

55. SAMPO-BA, SED IV 2/2027/22.

56. By the end of 1948 there were 4,000 Aktivists, and by the end of October 1950, 146,000; see Roesler, *Die Herausbildung*, 85. These inflated numbers strongly suggest the dilution of what it meant to be an Aktivist.

57. SAMPO-BA, SED NL 182/977.

58. Lutz Niethammer, *Die Volkseigene Erfahrung* (Berlin: Rowohlt-Berlin, 1991), 132.

59. Reinhard Bendix, *Work and Authority in Industry: Ideologies of Management in the Course of Industrialization* (Berkeley: University of California Press, 1956), 331–50.

60. Heiner Müller, "Der Lohndrücker," in *Geschichte aus der Produktion 1* (Berlin: Rotbuch Verlag, 1974), 43. The prototype of this hero appeared for the first time in Eduard Claudius's 1950 short story "Vom schweren Anfang," which eventually became the novel, *Menschen an unserer Seite* (1951). See the discussion in Peter Zimmermann, *Industrieliteratur der DDR: Vom Helden der Arbeit zum Planer und Leiter* (Stuttgart: J. B. Metzlersche Verlagsbuchhandlung, 1984), 83–87.

61. "The one-sided orientation on high numbers created the tendency to attain higher and higher rates of norm fulfillment under unrealistic conditions—up to 1,025 percent. Unskilled workers made a sort of joke out of overfulfilling the norms, for example in mining, after thorough preparation and with correspondingly good tools so that the entire movement threatened to be reduced to farce." In one especially ridiculous instance, Otto Braun, the sixty-three-year-old director of social affairs in a coal mine, and his secretary Latta overfulfilled the average coal miners' norm by 40 percent. Suckut, *Betriebsrätebewegung*, 508–9.

62. Letter from Erich Mückenburger, April 4, 1949, SAMPO-BA, SED NL 182/977.

63. Letter from Sobottka to Ulbricht, April 19, 1949, ibid. The plan was withdrawn once the leadership understood that the remedial course in mathematics and science would take three years, followed by a further four years in specialized mining courses at the mining academy.

64. Indeed, as we shall see in the second half of the book, the campaignist orientation inherent in the Hennecke movement is paradigmatic of most Leninist economic behavior.

65. By the end of 1951, only 10 percent of norms could be classified as "technically grounded." Ewers, "Der Konflikt," 119. The sensitivity of workers to the TAN-bureaus is

revealed in one report in September 1950. In the event, a TAN official arrived at an enterprise and two days later offended almost everyone by starting time and motion studies "with watch in hand" before consulting brigade leaders. SAMPO-BA, SED IV 2/5/232.

66. The population of the Soviet Zone reached its height of 19.1 million in 1947. Thereafter it declined. Between September and December 1949, 129,000 people left; in 1950, 198,000; in 1951, 166,000; in 1952, over 182,000. Thomas Ammer, "Stichwort: Flucht aus der DDR," *Deutschland Archiv* 22, no. 11 (1989: 1207).

67. According to Roesler, in 1949 59.4 percent of directors' bonus funds was used for direct payments to employees, only 11 percent for production bonuses. Roesler, *Die Herausbildung*, 70.

68. News release of November 17, 1952, from the Agency Inter-Continent Correspondence. Noted in State Department Files 762b.00/11-2452, November 24, 1952. In January 1953, Stefan Thomas, chief of the Social Democratic Party Ostbüro told State Department officials, "At present the unrest has reached the degree where uprisings would break out if called for by the West. The unpopularity of the regime is especially evident now owing to the food shortages and to agricultural collectivization measures." Ibid.

69. SAMPO-BA, SED, NL 182/1077. Asked during a meeting with local officials in Mecklenburg on April 17, 1953, why 40 percent of the Grossbauern have left their fields, Ulbricht gave an answer highly revealing of his attitude toward private farmers: "The answer is because they have no future, because they have not met their [delivery] obligations, because of their ideological position, and where there has been a rapid growth in collective farms [LPG], it won't be long until all the criminals have left."

70. Nadija Stulz-Herrnstadt, *Das Herrnstadt Dokument* (Hamburg: Rowohlt, 1990), 82–84. Although SED slowed down collectivization, the relationship between the SED apparatus in the countryside and the more successful farmers (the so-called Grossbauern, the East German equivalent of Soviet kulaks) did not improve. A typical report filed from Schwerin in 1954 reveals just how troubled this relationship continued to be: "There are concrete indicators that hiding behind the good economic activity of the Grossbauern is not only the exploitation of working peasants but also a center of active enemy activity." SAMPO-BA, SED NL 182/1077.

71. There is evidence that the East German leadership resisted the Soviet suggestions to alter the fundamentals of the program worked out at the second party conference; see Stulz-Herrnstadt, *Das Herrnstadt Dokument*, 58. As an indication of the continued hard line on wages, a *Neues Deutschland* article appearing at the end of May 1953 made the argument that even though increased labor productivity lowers production costs, this does not mean that workers should receive higher wages, at least for the foreseeable future. It concluded by pleading with workers to discard old norms so that productivity could rise more rapidly than wages. Only after this had been achieved could the standard of living be raised. State Department Files 762b.00/5-1953 XR 962a.61 The resolution introducing the new course was published on June 11, 1953.

72. Wolfgang Eckelmann, Hans-Hermann Hertle, and Rainer Weinert, *FDGB Intern: Innenansichten einer Massenorganisation der SED* (Berlin: Treptower, 1990), 22.

73. Stulz-Herrnstadt, *Das Herrnstadt Dokument*, 82.

74. Ibid., 84.

75. Archiv für Christlich-Demokratische Politik, VII-011-1743, reprinted in Udo Wengst, "Der Aufstand am 17. Juni 1953 in der DDR: Aus den Stimmungsberichten der Kreis- und Berzirksverbände der Ost-CDU im Juni und Juli 1953," *Vierteljahrshefte für Zeitgeschichte* 41, no. 2 (1993): 277–321.

76. Ernst Wollweber, "Aus Erinnerungen. Ein Porträt Walter Ulbrichts," *Beiträge zur Geschichte der Arbeiterbewegung*, no. 3 (1990): 350–78.

77. Stulz-Herrnstadt, *Das Herrnstadt*, 132–43; A. James McAdams, *Germany Divided* (Princeton: Princeton University Press, 1993), 40.

78. Indicative of the Soviet position after Ulbricht's return from Moscow is a comment made by the Soviet high commissioner in Germany, Vladimir Semionov, a regular participant in SED Politburo meetings, to Herrnstadt, who had been arguing that Ulbricht's removal was justified by his regular violations of Leninist collectivity in the Politburo. Did not Herrnstadt believe, asked Semionov rhetorically, "that the Soviet Union was strong enough to elicit any comrade, including Walter Ulbricht, to work collectively, when it considered it necessary?" Stulz-Herrnstadt, *Das Herrnstadt Dokument*, 150.

79. See articles in *Tägliche Rundschau* and *Neues Deutschland*, June 23, 1953.

80. See, for example, Werner Mühlhausen and Richard Schmidt, *Arbeitsanalyse und Arbeitsnormung. Ein Kernstück des praktischen Unterrichts in der sozialistischen Produktion* (Berlin: Volk und Wissen Volkseigener Verlag, 1959).

81. Jörg Roesler, "Wende in der Wirtschaftsstrategie: Krisensituation und Krisenmanagement 1960–62," in Jochen Cerny, ed., *Brüche, Krisen, Wendepunkte* (Leipzig: Urania Verlag, 1990), 171–83.

82. Quoted in ibid., 176.

83. Alf Lüdtke, "Helden der Arbeit—Mühen beim Arbeiten: Zur mißmutigen Loyalität von Industriearbeitern in der DDR," in Hartmut Kaelble, Jürgen Kocka, and Hartmut Zwahr, eds., *Sozialgeschichte der DDR* (Stuttgart: Klett Cotta, 1994), p. 211.

84. On workers' egalitarianism in other Communist countries, see Gordon Skilling, *Czechoslovakia's Interrupted Revolution* (Princeton: Princeton University Press, 1976), 579–85; on Hungary, Walter Connor, "Social Consequences of Economic Reforms in Eastern Europe," in Zbigniew M. Fallenbuchl, ed., *Economic Development in the Soviet Union and Eastern Europe* (New York: Praeger, 1975), 1:65–99; and on Poland, J. M. Montias, "Economic Conditions and Political Instability in Communist Countries: Observations on Strikes, Riots and Other Disturbances," *Studies in Comparative Communism* 13, no. 4 (1980): 283–99.

85. According to a report prepared by Soviet advisors in the Ministry of Finance, during 1953 30 percent of state enterprises operated at a loss. Quoted in André Steiner, "Sowjetische Berater in den zentralen wirtschaftsleitenden Instanzen der DDR in der zweiten Hälfte der fünfziger Jahre," *Jahrbuch für Historische Kommunismusforschung* (1993): 106.

86. Ibid., 105.

87. Peter Hübner, "Balance des Ungleichgewichtes: Zum Verhältnis von Arbeiterinteressen und SED-Herrschaft," *Geschichte und Gesellschaft* 19, no. 1 (1993): 26.

88. For a good review of this literature, see Linda J. Cook, *The Soviet Social Contract and Why It Failed: Welfare Policy and Workers' Politics from Brezhnev to Yeltsin* (Cambridge, Mass.: Harvard University Press, 1994).

1. Wolfgang Schaarschmidt, "Ein Mann kam von West nach Ost," in *Wir Großge-schieben: Reportagen und Skizzen von Volkskorrespondenten* (Berlin: Aufbau Verlag, 1960), 119–57.

2. Ultimately, the Hallstein Doctrine in its pure form was too rigid to sustain, even when the "claim to sole representation" (*Alleinvertretungsanspruch*) was never abandoned. On the origins of the doctrine, Wilhelm Grewe, *Rückblenden 1951–76* (Frankfurt: Propyläen, 1979), 251–62; Timothy Garton Ash, *In Europe's Name: Germany and the Divided Continent* (New York: Vintage, 1993), 53–54; A. James McAdams, *Germany Divided: From the Wall to Reunification* (Princeton: Princeton University Press, 1993), 35–36.

3. Report written for Kurt Hager, September 29, 1957, SAMPO-BA, SED IV 2/904/46.

4. Letters cited in André Steiner, "Auf dem Weg zur Mauer? Ulbricht an Chruschtschow im November 1960," *Utopie Kreativ*, nos. 31–32 (May–June 1993): 94–111.

5. *Record of Meeting of Comrade N. S. Khrushchev with Comrade W. Ulbricht. 30 November 1960.* Russian Ministry of Foreign Affairs Archives, Fond 0742, Opis, Por 4, Papka 43, secret; translated and reprinted in Hope M. Harrison, "Ulbricht and the Concrete 'Rose': New Archival Evidence on the Dynamics of Soviet–East German Relations and the Berlin Crisis, 1958–1961," Working Paper, no. 5 (Washington, D.C.: Woodrow Wilson Center, 1993), appendix A.

6. Letter from Ulbricht to Khrushchev, January 18, 1961, SAMPO-BA, SED J IV 2/202/129; also translated in Harrison, "Ulbricht and the Concrete 'Rose,'" appendix B.

7. Ibid.

8. For a good, concise discussion of the Behrens and Benary affair, see Thomas A. Baylis, *The Technical Intelligentsia and the East German Elite: Legitimacy and Social Change in Mature Communism* (Berkeley: University of California Press, 1974), 221–25.

9. SAMPO-BA, SED IV 2/904/46.

10. Michael Keren, "The New Economic System in the GDR: An Obituary," *Soviet Studies* 24, no. 4 (1973): 554–87; Gert Leptin and Manfred Melzer, *Economic Reform in East German Industry* (New York: Oxford University Press, 1978).

11. Martin McCauley, *The German Democratic Republic since 1945* (New York: St. Martin's Press, 1983); A. James McAdams, *East Germany and Detente* (Cambridge: Cambridge University Press, 1985); Michael Sodaro, *Moscow, Germany and the West from Khrushchev to Gorbachev* (Ithaca, N.Y.: Cornell University Press, 1990); Melvin Croan, *East Germany: The Soviet Connection* (Beverly Hills, Calif.: Sage, 1976).

12. The full name for the reform is *Das neue ökonomische System der Planung und Leitung.*

13. Klaus Wiessner, "Die energetische Basis in der DDR vom Ende der 40er bis Mitte der 60er Jahre," *Jahrbuch für Wirtschaftsgeschichte*, no. 4 (1990): 52.

14. Similar discussions occurred in Czechoslovakia and Bulgaria.

15. BAP SPK, E-1 51770.

16. Ibid.

17. This thesis that political success is determined by economic success was most clearly spelled out in Ulbricht's speech to the Leipzig regional deputies conference in 1962. *Neues Deutschland*, December 15, 1962.

18. Herbert Wolf, *Hatte die DDR je eine Chance?* (Hamburg: VSA-Verlag, 1992), 25–26.

19. Interview with Herbert Wolf, February 4, 1992.

20. Interview with Klaus Steinitz, member of the executive of the Party of Democratic Socialism and former researcher at the SPK institute, October 12, 1992.

21. BAP SPK, E-1 51764.

22. Jörg Roesler, *Zwischen Plan und Markt: Die Wirtschaftsreform in der DDR zwischen 1963 und 1970* (Berlin: Haufe, 1990), 30.

23. Melzer and Leptin, *Economic Reform*; Keren, "The New Economic System."

24. Some East German reformers sought from the very outset to go well beyond Lieberman. Proposals such as the one suggested by Herbert Wolf and his staff, for a "socialist capital market," clearly went beyond anything discussed in the Soviet literature.

25. SAMPO-BA, SED NL 182/971.

26. Letter from Apel to Ulbricht, November 12, 1964, ibid.

27. A commission set up to implement the price reform made this estimate in a report to Ulbricht on April 1, 1964; ibid.

28. BAP SPK, E-1 51770.

29. Günter Mittag, *Um jeden Preis* (Berlin: Aufbau-Verlag, 1991), 42. It is interesting to compare Mittag's to Brezhnev's account of his early relationship with Ulbricht. As he told Honecker in July 1970, "You know, back then in 1964 at the Datcha—he set my delegation off to the side, pushes me into a small room and starts telling me how everything is wrong here [in the Soviet Union] and everything is exemplary in the GDR. It was hot. I was sweating. He didn't care. I noticed only that he wanted to tell me how we have to work, to rule, and didn't even let me get a word in." Quoted in Peter Przybylski, *Tatort Politbüro: Die Akte Honecker* (Berlin: Rowohlt-Berlin, 1991), 287.

30. Wolf, *Hatte die DDR*, 24.

31. SAMPO-BA, SED NL 182/972.

32. SAMPO-BA, SED NL 182/971.

33. Upon hearing of Khrushchev's fall, Herbert Wolf, by now a department head in the Planning Commission, composed poetry for the "desk drawer" that predicted "a new age of darkness" for the GDR and the socialist world. Interview with Herbert Wolf, February 4, 1992.

34. The literature is nicely summarized in Jan Winiecki, *The Distorted World of Soviet-Type Economies* (Pittsburgh: University of Pittsburgh Press, 1988).

35. On improvement, see Roesler, *Zwischen Plan und Markt*, 36.

36. André Steiner, "Die Wirtschaftsreform der sechziger Jahre in der DDR unter besonderer Berücksichtigung ihrer Endphase," unpublished manuscript (Mannheim, 1991), 19.

37. Letter from Mittag to Ulbricht, September 26, 1964, SAMPO-BA, SED NL 182/971.

38. Ibid. On May 13, 1965, Ulbricht's office sent a note to Rumpf instructing him that a recent Finance Ministry manuscript on the dynamics of industrial price reform, issued from his office, required a number of changes before publication.

39. BAP SPK, E-1 56089.

40. Herbert Wolf, who had studied with Behrens, viewed the reform this way. Interview, February 4, 1992.

41. *Deutscher Export* 28/1964.

42. SAMPO-BA, SED NL 182/972.

43. Ibid.

44. Peter Ludz, *Parteielite im Wandel* (Opladen: Westdeutscher Verlag, 1969); Gert-Joachim Glaeßner, *Herrschaft durch Kader* (Opladen: Westdeutscher Verlag, 1977); Baylis, *The East German Elite*.

45. SAMPO-BA, SED IV A 2/5/60.

46. Ibid. The report continues in an alarmed tone that the number of graduates of the PHS going back into full-time party work was decreasing every year after 1962. Whereas for the three-year course of the class of 1965, 64.5 percent of the graduates could expect to go back into full-time party work, for the class of 1967 the percentage fell drastically, to 31 percent.

47. BAP SPK, E-1 56118, in André Steiner, ". . . daß du vielmehr als bisher sogenannte 'heiße Eisen' anfassen solltest," *Utopie kreativ*, no. 6 (February 1991): 102.

48. SAMPO-BA, SED NL 182/972.

49. Information provided by two former economics officials, interviewed in March 1992, who did not wish to have their names revealed.

50. Wolf, "Hatte die DDR," 24.

51. SAMPO-BA, SED NL 182/973.

52. Werner Obst, *DDR-Wirtschaft: Modell und Wirklichkeit* (Hamburg: Hoffmann und Campe, 1973), 86, 88, 94.

53. Given Apel's past as a colleague of Wernher von Braun's, his work on Nazi rocketry, and his having joined the SED only in 1957, most of the old-line members of the Politburo viewed his prominent role from the very outset with a good deal of suspicion.

54. Letter from Mittag to Ulbricht, October, 19, 1965, SAMPO-BA, SED NL 182/973.

55. SAMPO-BA, SED, IV 2/1/191.

56. BAP SPK, E-1 51770, on Apel's extensive preparations for this meeting. He not only anticipated specific Soviet positions but also wrote out his responses.

57. *Strafsache gegen Honecker*, cited in Peter Przybylski, *Tatort Politbüro Band 2* (Berlin: Rowohlt-Berlin, 1992), 156–58.

58. The point at which Mittag made the jump from Ulbricht to Honecker remains unclear. According to the notes of a former Politburo member, Werner Krolikowski: "The close connection between Honecker and Mittag came in the last stage of Ulbricht's career as first secretary, as Honecker turned to every means to force Ulbricht's ouster. . . . In Willi Stoph's presence, at his hunting lodge Honecker had a talk with Mittag, and gave him a choice: either break with Ulbricht or be tossed out of the Politburo. Mittag decided for Honecker but, in the last period of Ulbricht's first secretaryship, still seemed to stick by Ulbricht's side." Cited in Przybylski, *Tatort 2*, 46, 356.

59. See the closing speech by Ulbricht in *Kahlschlag: Das 11.Plenum des ZK der SED 1965: Studien und Dokumente* (Berlin: Aufbau Taschenbuch Verlag, 1991), 344–58.

60. It is worth noting that 1965 saw an explicit retreat from reform in the USSR, a trend that undoubtedly pleased the conservatives in Berlin. On the Soviet retreat, see Karl W. Ryavec, *Implementation of Soviet Economic Reforms: Political, Organizational, and Social Processes* (New York: Praeger, 1975).

61. Interview with Herbert Wolf, February 4, 1992. The evidence of Honecker's support for Rumpf is more oblique but, nevertheless, convincing. In a meeting of the Perspektivplankommission on April 14, 1966, Rumpf once again called for tighter state

control over investment through the turnover tax rather than, as was increasingly the case, through the State Bank. When Ulbricht jumped in to argue with Rumpf, Honecker blurted out in Rumpf's defense, "Some would like to get rid of the state budget altogether!" BAP SPK, E-1 56087.

62. Roesler, *Zwischen Plan und Markt*, 38.

63. It also precluded the type of alliance cobbled together by Gorbachev after 1985 between economic reformers and the Moscow intelligentsia.

64. Interview with Rolf Kuhnert, deputy chief of the Central Committee Construction Department under Ulbricht and Honecker.

65. Obst, *DDR-Wirtschaft*, 86–91.

66. BAP SPK, E-1 56087.

67. BAP SPK, E-1 51770.

68. Letter from Willi Stoph to Walter Ulbricht, January 20, 1966, SAMPO-BA, SED NL 182/973.

69. Letter of September 12, 1966, ibid.

70. Obst, *DDR-Wirtschaft*, 94.

71. SAMPO-BA, SED IV 2/611/66, cited in Steiner, "Auf dem Weg zur Mauer," 111.

72. BAP SPK, E-1 51770. As a result of the *Produktionsaufgebot*, the buying power of the population decreased by 600 million marks in one year.

73. André Steiner, "Ökonomische und soziale Effekte von Mechanisierung und Automatisierung in der Metallverarbeitenden Industrie der DDR von den fünfziger bis in die siebziger Jahre," *Deutsche Studien*, no. 115 (1993): 305.

74. BAP SPK, E-1 56087.

75. SAMPO-BA, SED NL 182/973.

76. Letter from Berger to Ulbricht June 28, 1966, ibid.

77. Walter Ulbricht, *Die Nationale Mission der DDR und das geistige Schaffen in unserem Staat* (Berlin: Dietz, 1966), 44, cited in Martin McCauley, *Marxism-Leninism in the German Democratic Republic* (London: Macmillan, 1979), 129.

78. BAP SPK, E-1 56087.

79. Ibid.

80. Rumpf finally lost his position in November 1966.

81. The best discussion of the contradictions of this period remains the work of Michael Keren, "Concentration amid Devolution in East Germany's Reforms," in Morris Bernstein, ed., *Plan and Market: Economic Reform in Eastern Europe* (New Haven: Yale University Press, 1973), 123–37; André Steiner, "Abkehr vom NÖS," in Jochen Cerny, ed., *Brüche, Krisen, Wendepunkte: Neubefragung von DDR-Geshichte* (Leipzig, 1990).

82. Interview with Herbert Wolf, February 4, 1992.

83. Steiner, "Abkehr," p. 250. Steiner's analysis is accurate but his implicit counterfactual (the "reform" would have worked had it been given enough time without further interference from the center) is too optimistic. Had the structure-determining tasks not appeared, the GDR economy would have merely found itself in the same position of other reforming socialist economies of a later period.

84. BAP SPK, 36/1, cited in ibid., 251. A further set of structure-determining tasks revolved around a large number of "automation projects," which accounted for 15 percent of industrial investment in 1969 and 30 percent in 1970. Roesler, *Zwischen Plan und Markt*, 153. Steiner, in "Abkehr," places less emphasis on the "automation projects"

while acknowledging the general principle that the structure-determining tasks had overburdened the economy.

85. Surprisingly, of all the former officials I interviewed, very few considered the two policies as fundamentally contradictory.

86. Ulbricht understood just how taut the plans for 1968 and 1969 actually were. In a December 1968 Politburo meeting, he informed his comrades, "There has never been such a taut plan, and this means great strain in carrying it out." BAP SPK, E-1 56263.

87. SAMPO-BA, SED NL 182/973.

88. In a curious report (September 10, 1969) to Central Committee department head Carl Heinz Janson, East German economist Willi Lüchterhand, after a short trip to Hungary, wrote that he was astonished to discover that several Hungarian economists openly expressed their support for Ota Sik and their displeasure with the Soviet invasion to visiting GDR students. Lüchterhand claimed the Hungarians were doing much the same as the Czechs, only in a much less noisy fashion. The report was then passed on to Mittag, who passed it on to Honecker. SAMPO-BA, SED IV A2/2021/772.

89. SAMPO-BA, SED IV A2/2021/153.

90. A comment by Brezhnev to Honecker, critical of Ulbricht, during a meeting in July 1970 not only supports this view of Ulbricht's intentions, but also provides a tantalizing indication that our entire picture of Soviet dissatisfaction with Ulbricht needs to be revised. "It is not yet the time that the GDR can have a great influence on events in West Germany. West Germany is economically strong. It is trying to gain influence in the GDR, to swallow the GDR, and so on. We, the Soviet Union, the socialist countries, will secure the results of the victory [of World War II]. We will not permit a development that weakens or endangers our position in the GDR, or an *Anschluß* of the GDR into West Germany." Przybylski, *Tatort*, 287. Rather than hindering the normalization of relations with West Germany, this comment could be interpreted as an indication of Soviet concern that Ulbricht had plans to shape a new relationship with West Germany. Contrary to the conventional wisdom, then, it was not Ulbricht's hesitancy to establish normal relations with West Germany that upset the Soviets and caused them to back the East German proponents of his ouster, but rather his enthusiasm for a new form of economic relationship with the West based on credit and trade. However interpreted, Brezhnev's remark adds credence to the thesis that Ulbricht saw the economic superiority of East Germany as the only way of stabilizing SED rule.

91. In a meeting with Schürer in 1969, Ulbricht displayed an intricate familiarity with comparative projected differences with West Germany on a range of indicators well into the 1980s. For example, when Schürer provided several scenarios for comparative labor productivity, Ulbricht pipes in with the question: "Did you calculate the West German increase in labor productivity at 4 percent or 6 percent in your comparison." Schürer, somewhat surprised, retorts, "4–4.5 percent as a whole and for West German industry 6 percent, using progress reports from Basil." SAMPO-BA, SED NL 182/973.

92. BAP SPK, E-1 56087.

93. SAMPO-BA, SED NL 182/974.

94. BAP SPK, E-1 56128.

95. BAP SPK, E-1 50768, 56118. This last point appears to have particularly irritated Soviet Ambassador Abrassimov. BAP SPK, E-1 56253.

96. BAP SPK, E-1 56253, 56079.

97. See especially the reports written by Harry Tisch, then first secretary of the Rostock Bezirksleitung, later to become chairman of the FDGB (perhaps as reward for his persistent dissatisfaction in the *Monatsberichte*) SAMPO-BA, SED IV A2/5/14.

98. SAMPO-BA, SED IV A2/5/11.

99. Ibid.

100. SAMPO-BA, SED A2/2021/481, A2/2021/482.

101. A. James McAdams, *Germany Divided: From the Wall to Unification* (Princeton: Princeton University Press, 1993), 92. In January 1971, the SED first secretary of the Bezirk Leipzig reported lengthy discussions among workers about the strikes in Poland. To his alarm, many found the strikes directly comparable with the class struggle in capitalist countries. SAMPO-BA, SED IV A 2/5/21.

102. Steinitz notes that even at the SPK research institute many agreed that too much time was being spent on "long-range" planning, and within the institute many greeted the end of the reform with a large measure of relief. Interview, October 12, 1992. For further evidence, see BAP SPK, E-1 56126.

103. SAMPO-BA, SED IV/2/237. For a good analysis and excerpts, see Gerhard Naumann and Eckhard Trümpler, *Von Ulbricht zu Honecker: 1970 Krisenjahr* (Berlin: Dietz, 1990).

104. BAP SPK, E-1 56125.

105. The decree passed on September 8, 1970, and is referred to in the Politburo meeting of February 16, 1971. SAMPO-BA, SED J IV 2/2/1325.

106. Quoted from a meeting between Brezhnev and Honecker on July 28, 1970, in Przybylski, *Tatort*, 110, 280–96. It is interesting to note that Brezhnev's right-hand man and the well-known Soviet kingmaker, Mikhail Suslov, had twenty-three years earlier prepared a profile of Ulbricht for Stalin in which he noted, "Shows a tendency to decide all practical questions alone and to pass over the other leaders. He has never overcome this, which proves to be a considerable obstacle to collegiality in the party leadership." Bernd Bonwetsch and Gennadij Bordjugov, "Stalin und die SBZ. Ein Besuch der SED Führung in Moskau vom 30.Januar–7.Februar 1947," *Vierteljahrshefte für Zeitgeschichte* 42, no. 2 (1994): 288.

107. Przybylski, *Tatort 2*, 348–49.

108. Before a joint meeting of the Politburo and the Presidium of the Council of Ministers in April 1970, Ulbricht's argument that the economic system had now been "experimentally tested" must have shocked most of his listeners. Were the preceding seven years merely an experiment? How much longer would the SED leadership and the population have to endure such experiments? BAP SPK, E-1 56087.

109. Quoted in Naumann and Trümpler, *Ulbricht zu Honecker*, 41.

110. In October 1971, Ulbricht contacted Schürer and asked for a meeting about the upcoming five-year plan. Schürer never met Ulbricht but reported the contact to Honecker. BAP SPK, E-1 56253. On July 7, 1972, Ulbricht wrote Harry Tisch, the first secretary of Bezirk Rostock, lamenting the fact that Ulbricht would not be attending the annual *Ostseewoche* because he had not yet been invited. Tisch turned the letter over to Honecker, who, one week later, brought the matter before the Politburo. Honecker, in turn, drafted a letter to Ulbricht in which he warned the former SED chief that only the first secretary of the SED had the right to communicate directly with the Bezirk first secretaries. SAMPO-BA, SED J IV 2/2/1402.

111. That the leadership operated with precisely this orientation is supported by an interview given by Horst Sindermann just before his death. *Der Spiegel,* no. 19 (1990): 58.

Chapter 3

1. BAP SPK, E-1 56079.

2. On investment figures, see SAMPO-BA, SED IV A 2/2021/153; on raising prices, Peter Przybylski, *Tatort Politbüro Band 2* (Berlin: Rowohlt-Berlin, 1992), 29.

3. Speech of March 28, 1973, in *Reden und Aufsätze* (Berlin: Dietz, 1977), 2:234.

4. SAMPO-BA, SED IV A2/5/97.

5. See the first evaluations of the sale in the monthly reports of the *Bezirksleitung* Leipzig in November 1971. SAMPO-BA, SED IV A2/5/21.

6. On recentralization, see Ian Jeffries and Manfred Melzer, "The New Economic System of Planning and Management and Recentralization in the 1970's," in Ian Jeffries and Manfred Melzer, eds., *The East German Economy* (London: Croon Helm, 1987).

7. Interview with Klaus Steinitz, October 12, 1991.

8. SAMPO-BA, SED IV A 2/5/11.

9. *Einheit* 25, no. 11 (1971): 1215.

10. SAMPO-BA, SED J IV 2/2/1402.

11. This last hope was not always fulfilled, as large state enterprises continued to enjoy better access to scarce goods and services.

12. SAMPO-BA, SED IV A 2/5/11.

13. SAMPO-BA, SED IV A 2/5/14.

14. Ibid. November 18, 1969. In one especially outraged report, the first secretary of Potsdam noted that in private clinics operated out of hospitals in his district chief physicians would pocket an extra 50,000 marks per year through use of the old Prussian system in which young physicians pay a premium for every operation they perform under the "supervision" of their older colleagues. Such reports continue throughout 1970. SAMPO-BA, SED IV A 2/5/19.

15. BAP SPK, E-1 56076.

16. SAMPO-BA, SED IV 2/1/272.

17. Andreas Pickel, *Radical Transitions* (Boulder, Colo.: Westview Press, 1991), 65–66.

18. On the Apolda experiments, see Stoph's report to the Politburo on March 28, 1972, SAMPO-BA, SED J IV 212A/1584, where he also comments on some mild resistance among craftsmen and owners.

19. Monika Kaiser, *Dokumente 1972: Knock Out für den Mittelstand* (Berlin: Dietz Verlag, 1990), 194–95. The big exception was the LDPD luminary Kurt Wünsche, who resisted the policy and later lost his position. On this, see Manfred Gerlach, *Mitverantwortlich als Liberaler im SED-Staat* (Berlin: Morgenbuch Verlag, 1991), 130–34.

20. Ibid., 131.

21. SAMPO-BA, SED J IV 2/2/1402.

22. Ibid.

23. "Sozialpolitik," in Hartmut Zimmermann, ed., *DDR Handbuch* (Cologne: Verlag Wissenschaft und Politik, 1985), 1213.

24. *Direktive des IX. Parteitages der SED zum Fünfjahrplan für die Entwicklung der Volkswirtschaft der DDR in den Jahren 1976–1980* (Berlin: Dietz, 1976).

25. On social policy, see "Soziale Sicherheit ist nicht genug! Konzeption und Leistung der sozialistischen Sozialpolitik," in Gert-Joachim Glaeßner, ed., *Die DDR in der Ära Honecker* (Opladen: Westdeutscher Verlag, 1988), 402–21. On subsidies, see "Ich habe mich korrekt abgemeldet: Ein Zeit-Gespräch mit Alexander Schlak-Golodkowski," *Die Zeit*, no. 3 (1991): 9.

26. BAP SPK, E-1 56129.

27. Ibid.

28. *Protokoll des X. Parteitages der SED* (Berlin: Dietz Verlag, 1981), 1:65–74.

29. Jeffries and Melzer, "Planning and Management," 40.

30. Ian Jeffries and Manfred Melzer, "The Economic Strategy of the 1980's and the Limits to Possible Reforms," in Jeffries and Melzer, *The East German Economy*, 41.

31. BAP SPK, E-1 56167.

32. BAP SPK, E-1 56167, 56168.

33. Carl-Heinz Janson, *Totengräber der DDR: Wie Günter Mittag den SED-Staat ruinierte* (Düsseldorf: Econ Verlag, 1991), 65.

34. Günter Schabowski, *Das Politbüro: Ende eines Mythos* (Berlin: Rowohlt-Berlin, 1990), 20–22.

35. Peter Przybylski, *Tatort Politbüro: Die Akte Honecker* (Berlin: Rowohlt-Berlin, 1991), 322.

36. BAP SPK, E-1 56323.

37. Przybylski, *Tatort*, 323.

38. According to the CIA's 1988 dollar estimates, whereas in 1980 Poland owed western banks $14.9 million and western governments $10 million, by 1988 the Poles had reversed this proportion, so that they now owed $11.9 million to banks and $26.6 million to governments. The East Germans, on the other hand, owed $11.3 million to banks and $2.8 million to governments in 1980, but were unable to transform this proportion, so that by 1988 they owed $16.2 million to banks and $3.3 million to governments. Again, these numbers are not perfectly accurate (though they are more so than the CIA's GNP estimates) but the trend is clear enough. CIA, *Handbook of Economic Statistics* (Washington, D.C.: Government Printing Office, September 1989), 42.

39. BAP SPK, E-1 56323.

40. On Schalck, see Przybylski, *Tatort 2*, 227–325; Wolfgang Seiffert and Norbert Treutwein, *Die Schalck-Papiere* (Munich: Goldmann Verlag, 1991); Peter Ferdinand Koch, *Das Schalck Imperium* (Munich: Piper, 1992).

41. "Gespräch mit Gerhard Schürer," *Deutschland Archiv* 25, no. 2 (1992): 137.

42. BPA SED, Dresden IV B2/5/402.

43. SAMPO-BA, SED IV D-2/6-538. Similar reports can be found in BPA SED, Dresden IV B 2/5/365.

44. Letter from Honecker to the *Bezirk* first secretaries, BPA SED, Dresden IV B 2/5/400.

45. SAMPO-BA, SED 2/1/358.

46. SAMPO-BA, SED IV 2/1/357.

47. A. James McAdams, *Germany Divided: From the Wall to Unification* (Princeton: Princeton University Press, 1993), 142.

48. The meeting in Moscow took place on August 17, 1984, and was attended by Honecker, Stoph, Hermann Axen (SED chief for foreign relations), Erich Mielke (Stasi chief),

and Defense Minister Heinz Hoffmann. On the Soviet side of the table sat Chernenko, Foreign Minister Andrei Gromyko, Defense Minister Dmitri Ustinov, KGB Chief Victor Chebrikov, and CPSU Secretary Mikhail Gorbachev. Chernenko warned that the GDR had to exercise restraint in relation to the "revanchist and nationalist policy of the FRG." To put the point as sharply as he could, Chernenko noted that he had "always highly valued the trust between our two parties, the further consolidation of unity of our actions in relations, and the friendship and cooperation between the Soviet Union and the GDR. This has been and remains the central question. This relates also to you, comrade Honecker, personally." SAMPO BA, SED IV 2/2.039/280, cited in Daniel Küchenmeister, ed., *Honecker-Gorbachev: Vieraugengespräche* (Berlin: Dietz Verlag, 1993), 11.

49. Schürer reported this exchange in a letter to Honecker on March 21, 1979. BAP SPK, E-1 56243.

50. SAMPO-BA, SED J IV 2/2/A-2422, cited in Manfred Wilke, Reinhardt Gutsche, and Michael Kubina, "Die SED-Führung und die Unterdrückung der polnischen Oppositionsbewegung 1980/81," *German Studies Review* 17, no. 1 (1994): 139.

51. Jörg Roesler, "Der Einfluß der Außenwirtschaftspolitik auf die Beziehungen DDR-Bundesrepublik," *Deutschland Archiv* 26, no. 5 (1993): 562.

52. According to a department head of the Berlin KGB, the Soviet intelligence agency received a steady stream of complaints from Stoph to the effect that Honecker was both running the GDR's economy into the ground and playing a double game with the CPSU leadership and the West. Iwan Kusmin, "Die Verschwörung gegen Honecker," *Deutschland Archiv* 28, no. 3 (1995): 286–90.

53. On Honecker's promise not to incur further debt, see BAP SPK, E-1 56266.

54. Roesler, "Der Einfluß," 561.

55. BAP SPK, E-1 56266.

56. Ibid.

57. Ibid.

58. Wilke et al., "Die SED Führung und die Unterdückung," 139–40.

59. SAMPO-BA, SED 2/1/358.

60. The requests multiplied so rapidly that, by January 1983, the Politburo fired the head of the state reserve, Rudolf Tschoep. The official reason given was "because of poor health and in recent times a personality development that no longer guarantees that he will fulfill future assignments," a sure sign that Tschoep resisted what he saw as a troubling trend at his place of work. SAMPO-BA, SED J IV 2/2/1983.

61. Schalck, "Ich habe mich korrekt," 8.

62. McAdams, *Germany Divided*, 155; Timothy Garton Ash, *In Europe's Name: Germany and the Divided Continent* (New York: Vintage, 1993), 56.

63. Harry Maier, *Innovation oder Stagnation: Bedingungen der Wirtschaftsreform in sozialistischen Ländern* (Cologne: Deutscher Instituts-Verlag, 1987), 75.

64. Ibid., 76–77.

65. Although there is a good secondary literature on the combines, much of the information in this section is gathered from SAMPO-BA, SED IV D-2/6/554, 555, 556.

66. Elvira Wenda, "Zu einigen politökonomischen Fragen der Vergesellschaftung von Produktion und Arbeit im Sozialismus in den 60er und 70er Jahren," in Renate Woick and Ulrike Harms, eds., *Die Politik der SED zur Herausbildung und Entwicklung sozialistischer Industriekombinate* (Berlin: Dietz, 1984), 29.

67. The number of combines varies depending on which GDR author one chooses to read. For one of the more authoritative examples, see Claus Kroemke and Gerd Friedrich, *Kombinate: Rückgrat sozialistischer Planwirtschaft* (Berlin: Die Wirtschaft, 1987), 16.

68. Jan Wieniecki, *The Distorted World of Soviet-Type Economies* (Pittsburgh: University of Pittsburgh Press, 1988), 76–77. One example may illustrate the degree of autarky that existed in the GDR. In 1988, whereas the GDR metal industry produced internally 65 percent of the various products produced worldwide, the United States produced 50 percent internally and West Germany 17 percent. Günter Kusch et al., *Schlußbilanz—DDR: Fazit einer verfehlten Wirtschafts- und Sozial politik* (Berlin: Duncker & Hamblot, 1991), 46.

69. Interview with Harry Nick, March 15, 1992.

70. On this, see the testimony of the former (yet still loyal) Stasi officer, Reinhardt Hahn, *Ausgedient: Ein Stasi-Major erzählt* (Leipzig: Greifen, 1990).

71. Janson, *Totengräber*, p. 154.

72. Ibid., 118.

73. Kusch et al., *Schlußbilanz—DDR*, 47.

74. A 1985 report written for the Dresden party organization notes that in many enterprises the employees in rationalization divisions complained that rationalization could only be meaningfully carried out if their enterprises received more investment. BPA SED, Dresden IV E-2/6/375. Peter Boot, "Continuity and Change in the Planning System of the German Democratic Republic," *Soviet Studies* 35, no. 3 (1983): 331–42.

75. See Maier, *Innovation oder Stagnation*, 87: when Maier asks the general director of a shoe combine why he does not market his three-dimensional software program, the director replies, "And what will our combine get out of it?"

76. In fact, the case of the GDR automobiles may be slightly anomalous. During the 1980s, over 11 billion marks were poured into "upgrading" the engines of the Wartburg and Trabant from two to four strokes. Whether investing such a large sum into two obsolete models was wise in the long run remains open; the decision to do so was made, in any case, for political rather than economic reasons. East Germans wanted cars and imports from abroad were out of the question.

77. SAMPO-BA, SED IV 2/1/358.

78. Janson, *Totengräber*, 124.

79. Roesler, "Der Einfluß," 566.

80. Janson, *Der Totengräber*, 103.

81. Such was the fate of Günter Ehrensperger, the Central Committee department head of planning and finance, who in March 1985 informed the staff of his department that he fundamentally disagreed with Mittag's draft of the five-year plan for 1986–90. Ehrensperger felt that the plan was far too optimistic about the GDR's economic capacity; that it entailed too many imports from the West, which could not be covered by exports; and that it placed too much faith in Schalck's valuta empire to solve all of the GDR's problems. Ehrensperger's opinion never made it into the Politburo (only an optimistic position paper was prepared), but it did cross the desk of a Stasi colonel who had a source in the department head's staff. Przybylski, *Tatort 2*, 377.

82. Kurt Hager spoke of a "strategic course of all sided intensification" as "the key to the solution to the . . . problems of the USSR," and that the "USSR is only now at the beginning of this difficult path." It must be kept in mind that the SED leadership had

claimed that intensification had already occurred in the GDR in the 1970s. See Kurt Hager, "Eine Wende von historischer Bedeutung. Bericht über den XXVII Parteitag der KPdSU," in *Einheit* 41, nos. 4–5 (1986): 307, quoted in Walter Süß, "Die DDR und ihre Blockführungsmacht," in Glaeßner, *Die DDR in der Ära Honecker*, 202. In his March 1986 assessment of a meeting with Gorbachev at the twenty-seventh congress of the Communist Party of the Soviet Union, Honecker noted that the USSR still had to implement what had been done in the GDR since 1971 after the eighth SED congress. Küchenmeister, *Honecker-Gorbatschow*, 13.

83. Kusmin, "Verschwörung," 287.

84. SAMPO BA, SED IV 2/1/658.

85. Janson, *Totengräber*, 173.

86. Kusmin, "Verschwörung," 288.

87. BPA SED, Dresden 13200.

88. The antiperestroika campaign in the East German press is contained in the following articles: "Zur Sozialpolitik der SED," *Neues Deutschland*, January 29, 1987; Erich Hahn, "Werte des Sozialismus," ibid., February 27, 1987; Helmut Koziolek and Otto Reinhold, "Über die schöpferische theoretische Arbeit in der politischen Ökonomie bei der Gestaltung des entwickelten Sozialismus in der DDR," *Einheit* 42, no. 3 (1987): 210–15; P. H. Feist, "Sozialistischer Realismus aktuell—Positionen in der Klassenauseinandersetzung," *Neues Deutschland*, March 21–22, 1987; Honecker's speech to the first secretaries of the *Kreisleitungen*, ibid., March 7–8, 1987. For articles by Soviet general directors in the East German press, see B. I. Fomin, "Wenn das Kombinat Herr im Hause ist," ibid., January 31–February 1, 1987; W. Kowalenko, "Das Kombinat als der Verantwortliche," ibid., March 11, 1987; L. Sotnik, "Erfahrungen unserer Freunde," ibid., March 22, 1987.

89. Interestingly, it could not be hidden from the Soviet leadership. Not only were they being informed from elements in the SED, but from their own intelligence Gorbachev and Ryshkov had learned that the West German government was busy buying up East German debt in order to put greater pressure on the SED in the future. When Gorbachev warned Honecker of this in April 1986, Honecker assured the Soviet leader that the East German financial experts had the situation well in hand. SAMPO BA, SED Büro Honecker, 41666. Reprinted in Küchenmeister, *Honecker-Gorbatschow*, 90. This record of the conversation between Gorbachev and Honecker on April 20, 1986, was not, as was usually the practice, circulated among Politburo members.

90. Lignite (brown coal) and computers were the ultimate symbols of Mittag's strategy of autarky—lignite because of the GDR's dependence on foreign oil, and computers because of COCOM export restrictions. Mining lignite swallowed up approximately one-quarter of all industrial investment in the 1980s. Microelectronics used up approximately half of all funds invested in the entire electrical and electronic industries. Ulrich Voskamp and Volker Wittke, "Industrial Restructuring in the Former German Democratic Republic: Barriers to Adaptive Reform Become Downward Development Spirals," *Politics and Society* 19, no. 3 (1991): 341–71.

91. BAP SPK, E-1 56319.

92. Honecker, it appears, never gave up hope on reversing the fateful Soviet decision to cut oil deliveries. Within months of Brezhnev's death, Honecker wrote the new Soviet leader Yuri Andropov in January 1984, quoting his previous letter to Brezhnev on the

harmful effects of the cuts and pleading with the new Soviet leader to reconsider. BAP SPK, E-1 56266.

93. BAP SPK, E-1 56317.

94. Ibid.; also Janson, *Totengräber*, 105; Przybylski, *Tatort 2*, 72–73.

95. BAP SPK, E-1 56317. According to the report of May 16, 1989, prepared for the Politburo, the GDR was taking on new debt at a rate of 500 million valuta marks per month. In September, just before the GDR's fortieth anniversary, Schürer's office issued a new document in which it was noted that the GDR's yearly credit needs were between 8 and 10 billion valuta marks. This sum had to be mobilized by approximately 400 banks. The problem, as he pointed out, was that the GDR was quickly reaching its the maximum credit limit with Western banks. Przybylski, *Tatort 2*, 358.

96. BAP, SPK, E-1 56317.

Chapter 4

1. Max Weber, "Bureaucracy," in H. H. Gerth and C. Wright Mills, eds., *From Max Weber: Essays in Sociology* (New York: Oxford University Press, 1946), 232–34.

2. Rational in the sense of being able to choose the best means for achieving a desired end.

3. Daniel Bell, *The End of Ideology: On the Exhaustion of Political Ideas in the Fifties* (Glencoe, Ill.: Free Press, 1960).

4. For the implicit argument that the working class was uniquely positioned to gain social knowledge from its position in the mode of production, and that the peasants by contrast were not capable of political consciousness, see Karl Marx, *The Eighteenth Brumaire of Louis Napoleon*, in R. C. Tucker, ed., *Marx-Engels Reader* (New York: Norton, 1972), 515.

5. Lenin, *What Is to Be Done?*, in R. C. Tucker, ed., *The Lenin Anthology* (New York: Norton, 1975).

6. See especially A. J. Polan, *Lenin and the End of Politics* (Berkeley: University of California Press, 1986). Toward the end of his life Lenin started facing the problems of bureaucracy, and the sheer Babylonian complexity of running an administration in the rump of the Russian empire. See in particular his rather confused piece, "How We Should Reorganize the Workers and Peasants' Inspection," and "Better Fewer but Better," in Tucker, *The Lenin Anthology*, 729–46. At this rather late date Lenin seems to have realized that the issue was not whether there would be a bureaucracy but rather, given that there had to be one, how it could be best monitored.

7. The problem of loyalty versus competence comes up regularly in all kinds of organizations. A colleague of mine working at Radio Free Europe/Radio Liberty recalled the case of one of the commentators for the Central Asian service who had spent World War II in Nazi Germany broadcasting Nazi propaganda into the Soviet Union. As one of the only native speakers of a certain Turkic language living in the West who was qualified to work in broadcasting, he quickly made the transition to propagating the ideals of liberal democracy in the service of the Americans. The staff of RFE/RL were highly satisfied with his work. Here the issue was "brown or expert," as it were, rather than red or expert.

8. J. V. Stalin, *Fragen des Leninismus* (Berlin: Dietz, 1955), 797, quoted in Rudolf Schwarzenbach, *Kaderpolitik der DDR* (Cologne: Politik und Wissenschaft, 1976), 46.

9. Schwarzenbach, *Kaderpolitik der DDR*, 46.

10. Stalin, *Fragen des Leninismus*, 800–801.

11. L. Slepow, *Die Auslese der Kader, ihre Beförderung und Verteilung* (Berlin: Dietz, 1952); Otto Schön, *Über unsere gegenwärtigen kaderpolitischen Aufgaben* (Berlin: Dietz, 1952).

12. Richard Herber and Herbert Jung, *Kaderarbeit im System sozialistischer Führungstätigkeit* (Berlin: Dietz, 1968), 10.

13. Gert Joachim Glaeßner, *Herrschaft durch Kader* (Opladen: Westdeutscher Verlag, 1977), 223: "The old equation: cadre = party member is replaced by cadre = manager or specialist."

14. Ibid.

15. See, for example, the discussion in Schwarzenbach, *Kaderpolitik*, 47.

16. See the programs from training of cadres in SAMPO-BA, SED IV A2/5/60; for a good discussion of the East German industrial novel of the period, see Peter Zimmermann, *Industrieliteratur der DDR* (Stuttgart: Metzler, 1984), 193–299.

17. Rainer Falke and Hans Modrow, *Auswahl und Entwicklung von Führungskadern. Ermittlung, Auswahl und Entwicklung von Nachwuchskadern für Führungsfunktionen in der sozialistischen Industrie—dargestellt am Beispiel von Großbetrieben der Elektroindustrie der DDR* (Berlin: Dietz, 1967), 147.

18. This fact should come as no surprise to trained social scientists who have endeavored to make their way through the same literature.

19. Gerhard Anton, "Wir stellen vor: Die Fachschule für Staatswissenschaft 'Edwin Hörnle' Weimar," *Die Fachschule*, no. 6 (1973): 185.

20. Lothar Mertens, "Studenten in der DDR," *Deutsche Studien* 24, no. 96 (1986): 371.

21. Herbert Steininger, "Wissenschaftlichkeit und Parteilichkeit des Marxismus-Leninismus," *Einheit* 26, no. 1 (1971): 40.

22. Annelise Bräuer and Horst Conrad, *Kaderpolitik der SED—fester Bestandteil der Leitungstätigkeit* (Berlin: Dietz, 1981), 15.

23. Erich Honecker, *Die Aufgaben der Partei bei der weiteren Verwirklichung der Beschlüsse des IX. Parteitages der SED* (Berlin: Dietz, 1978), 68–69.

24. Printed in *Neuer Weg*, no. 13 (1977): supplement.

25. As early as 1971, an article by a KL first secretary, Wolfgang Enders, asserted that, "The present political qualifications of a significant part of our economic functionaries are not up to present or future demands." He went on to complain that of the fourteen cadres of the management staff in the local textile enterprise in Flöra only one had spent a year at the Bezirk party school. *Neuer Weg*, no. 8 (1971): 359–62.

26. Bräuer and Conrad, *Kaderpolitik*, 34–35.

27. *11 Tagung des ZK der SED, 13./14. Dezember 1979. Aus dem Bericht des Politbüros an die 11 Tagung des ZK der SED. Berichterstatter: Genosse Erich Honecker* (Berlin: Dietz, 1979), 68. Of this number only 37.3 percent were classified as "production workers." Bräuer and Conrad, *Kaderpolitik*, 18.

28. Bräuer and Conrad, *Kaderpolitik*, 16.

29. *Neuer Weg*, no. 17 (1982): 644–46.

30. Interview with Jörg Koch, party secretary of Wilhelm Pieck University in Rostock (now called University of Rostock), June 10, 1989.

31. Every adult in the GDR was followed (or preceded) throughout his career by a

dossier, the contents of which one had no right to see. The dossier or *Kaderakte* contained information on professional, political, and personal conduct. It could be supplemented by information from a separate dossier kept in the Ministry for State Security. Its contents often determined one's position, chances for advancement, and a host of other privileges (such as the right to travel). Dieter Voigt, "Kaderarbeit in der DDR," *Deutschland Archiv* 5, no. 2 (1972): 178–81.

32. On the involvement of Bezirk-level party economics departments in personnel recruitment, see the article by Gerhard Öcknick, economics secretary from Cottbus, in *Neuer Weg*, no. 10 (1979): 385–90.

33. This hypothetical case was constructed based on the same scenario presented to several officials and academics in the GDR.

34. *Neuer Weg*, no. 15 (1981): 606–10.

35. *Neuer Weg*, no. 12 (1972): 565–68.

36. Bräuer and Conrad, *Kaderpolitik*, 33.

37. For an example, see ibid., 35.

38. Landolf Scherzer, *Der Erste* (Rudolstadt: Greifenverlag, 1988), 166–67.

39. Jerry Hough, *The Soviet Prefects* (Cambridge, Mass.: Harvard University Press, 1969), 155–56.

40. V. I. Lenin, "Rede auf dem III. Gesamtrussischen Verbandstag der Schiffarbeiter," *Werke*, vol. 30 (Berlin: Dietz, 1961), 420.

41. Scherzer, *Der Erste*, 26.

42. Ibid., 93.

43. Ibid., 102.

44. Falke and Modrow, *Auswahl*, 62, quoted in Glaeßner, *Herrschaft*, 232.

45. Scherzer, *Der Erste*, 70.

46. Thomas Baylis, *The East German Elite and the Technocratic Intelligentsia* (Berkeley: University of California Press, 1974), 260.

47. Jerry Hough, *The Soviet Prefects: The Local Party Organs in Industrial Decision Making* (Cambridge, Mass.: Harvard University Press, 1969), chap. 4; also Jerry Hough, "The Party Apparatchiki," in H. Gordon Skilling and Franklyn Griffiths, eds., *Interest Groups in Soviet Politics* (Princeton, N.J.: Princeton University Press, 1971), 56. He makes the same argument in *Soviet Leadership in Transition* (Washington, D.C.: Brookings, 1980), 67.

48. Hough, *Prefects*, 35.

49. SAMPO-BA, SED IV A 2/5/162.

50. Career backgrounds are drawn from various sources. Newspapers (regional and national), collections such as Günter Buch's *Namen und Daten* (Berlin: J. H. W. Dietz, 1973, 1979, 1987), and *SBZ Biographie* (Bonn: Bundesministerium für Gesamtdeutsche Fragen, several years), as well as the extensive card register of the *Gesamtdeutsches Institut* in Berlin.

51. For a more extensive treatment of high politics, see Martin McCauley, *Marxism-Leninism in the GDR* (London: Macmillan, 1979), 185–89.

52. Hartmut Zimmermann, "Power Distribution and Opportunities for Participation: Aspects of the Socio-political System of the GDR," in Klaus von Beyme and Harmut Zimmermann, eds., *Policymaking in the German Democratic Republic* (Aldershot: Gower, 1984), 22.

53. Konrad Naumann, Berlin; Werner Felfe, Halle; Hans-Joachim Hertwig, Frankfurt-Oder. McCauley adds to this list Horst Schumann, although he had become first secretary of Bezirk Leipzig in November 1970. McCauley, *Marxism-Leninism*, 187.

54. Thomas Baylis, "Agit-Prop as a Vocation: The East German Ideological Elite," *Polity* 18, no. 1 (1987): 25–46.

55. Bräuer and Conrad, *Kaderpolitik*, 48.

56. I include the special economic zone of Wismut, as the SED did, as a Bezirk for the purposes of calculating the average tenure.

57. Here I include more than one secretary from Bezirke where the economics function was broken up into several sections.

58. Bräuer and Conrad, *Kaderpolitik*, 38.

59. By 1981, 62.4 percent of all general directors and 77 percent of all chairmen of Kreis councils had visited a higher party school for at least one year. Ibid.

60. Two notable examples of this phenomenon are Honecker and his temporary successor, Egon Krenz.

61. Search conducted at the Lenin State Library in Moscow, November 1989.

62. *Einheit* 25, no. 11 (1970): 1215.

Chapter 5

1. Jerry Hough, *The Soviet Prefects: The Local Party Organs in Industrial Decision Making* (Cambridge, Mass.: Harvard University Press, 1969), 296.

2. Ibid., 301.

3. Ibid., 179.

4. Landolf Scherzer, *Der Erste* (Rudolstadt: Greifenverlag, 1988), 62.

5. Ibid., 74.

6. *Neuer Weg*, no. 2 (1979): 59–61.

7. *Handmaterial für den Parteisekretär* (Berlin: Dietz, 1968), 54–69; "Information, Analyse, Leitung," *Neuer Weg*, no. 10 (1971): 457–60.

8. SAMPO-BA, SED IV A2/2021/334,335,336.

9. BPA SED, Dresden IV B2/5/365.

10. *Neuer Weg*, no. 9 (1983): 329–34, and no. 5 (1980): 173–75.

11. Evidence of the Stasi's strong local subordination can be found in the testimony of one officer gathering information on secretariat members was expressly forbidden. Ariane Riecker, Annett Schwarz, and Dirk Schneider, *Stasi intim* (Leipzig: Forum Verlag, 1990), 13. This is not to say that the surveillance of the local apparatus was not conducted by teams directly subordinate to Berlin Central.

12. "I was extremely dissatisfied that I could not conduct a reasonable discussion with the economics man from the SED-Bezirksleitung." Ibid., 20.

13. Scherzer, *Der Erste*, 35–36.

14. Ibid., 80.

15. *Neuer Weg*, no. 2 (1979): 59–61.

16. Scherzer, *Der Erste*, 89.

17. Ibid., 91.

18. Günter Schabowski, *Der Absturz* (Berlin: Rowohlt-Berlin, 1991), 139.

19. Ibid., 138.

20. Ibid.

21. Ibid., 146.

22. Hough, *Prefects*, 217.

23. Interview with former employee of the Bezirk Planning Commission of Rostock.

24. *Die Wirtschaft*, no. 16 (1976): 14.

25. Ibid., 15.

26. According to most sources, storming was common in the GDR, as it was in other Eastern Europe states. A sector chief in the BL Karl-Marx-Stadt reported that in the assembly enterprises in his Bezirk more than 50 percent of the monthly plans were completed in the last ten days of each month; see *Die Wirtschaft*, no. 13 (1976): 3. The economics secretary of BL Suhl, Eberhard Denner, in a 1975 interview lamented that at the end of the year the only thing an enterprise had in mind was plan fulfillment, which disrupted the beginning of the next planning period; see *Die Wirtschaft*, no. 8 (1975): 7.

27. *Die Wirtschaft*, no. 8 (1975): 14.

28. BPA SED, Dresden 13200.

29. Here I draw on Peter Rutland, *The Politics of Economic Stagnation in the Soviet Union* (Cambridge: Cambridge University Press, 1993).

30. Interview with director of an eyeglass enterprise in Jena.

31. These discussions might be the source of some interesting empirical studies had they not been compromised by the general absence of some important specifics, such as the names of the enterprises (revealing their size and political connections) and the amount of the awards.

32. Interview with a jurist at Friedrich Schiller University in Jena.

33. For hints at a decrease in court use over the course of the combine reform, see K. Glaess and K. Heuer, "Zur Zuständigkeit des staatlichen Vertragsgerichts," *Wirtschaftsrecht* 35 (1982), 181.

34. Interview with manager of an eyeglass enterprise in Jena.

35. *Die Wirtschaft*, no. 6 (1977): 13.

36. *Neuer Weg*, no. 19 (1985): 739.

37. Following the eighth party congress in 1971, Bezirksleitungen held a series of intensification conferences in every major enterprise in the country. The primary functions of these conferences were economic education and propaganda—to make clear to the management and the workers the nature of the tasks at hand.

38. A good example is the Zlobin method described here. It was introduced by the Central Committee Construction Department after a visit by its head to the Soviet Union, and propagated at construction conferences in tandem with the Ministry of Construction. *Die Wirtschaft*, no. 4 (1975): 11.

39. *Die Wirtschaft*, no. 21 (1976): 18. Here one might also mention the use of the Soviet quality control campaign, the Saratov method; see Heinz Uhlendorf, Guenther Winkler, and Jonny Wolf, *Theoretische und praktische Probleme des Kampfes um eine hohe Qualität der Erzeugnisse* (Berlin: Dietz, 1973), p. 31.

40. In the case of the Brasov method, for example, the evaluation of the workplace was to be carried out by the management and the trade union on a scale of 1.0 for the best and 0.1 for the worst. The lowest grade attained by a brigade determined its level, and the attained coefficient acted as the bench mark for the next round of commitments on behalf of the workers. Not clear, though, was how two different types of work, one

"cleaner" than the other, were to be fairly compared with each other, and, more important, how this whole process would affect the wage package.

41. One East German anecdote tells of a journalist coming into a factory to interview the director about the famous "Tchaikovsky" method, that has been touted in the party press for weeks. When asked by the reporter, "What exactly is the Tchaikovsky method, and how has it increased productivity in your firm?," the director answers, "How the hell should I know what it is, the important thing is that they're working with it!"

42. The word "campaign" carries a negative connotation in Leninist usage. The fact that one of the first titles of an article extolling the Zlobin method was called, "The Zlobin Method—No Flash in the Pan," indicates that the leadership was afraid that it would in fact be a typical campaign, beginning with much fanfare and gradually slipping into oblivion in the face of structural obstacles. *Ostsee-Zeitung*, February 25, 1975, 3.

43. That they were a nuisance is confirmed by the efforts of management to ignore them or feign compliance. The head of the Central Committee Construction Department warned of this tendency in *Neuer Weg*, no. 9 (1972): 385–90.

44. Ibid.

45. *Die Wirtschaft*, no. 18 (1976): 13–14; ibid., no. 6 (1977): 13–14; ibid., no. 5 (1981): 7.

46. Performance comparisons went back to Lenin's time. "How to Organize Competition," in Robert C. Tucker, ed., *The Lenin Anthology* (New York: Norton, 1975), 427–32.

47. Performance comparisons are spinoffs on the traditional socialist competitions, which are dealt with in the next chapter. However, since this involved interenterprise coordination, for taxonomical reasons I have included them in this chapter.

48. *Die Wirtschaft*, no. 2 (1975): 6.

49. *Neuer Weg*, no. 13 (1981): 493–95.

50. In the case of the Karl-Marx-Stadt comparison, the director of the steel foundry combine, Günter Tröger, warned, "What is going on here is the comparison of iron and steel foundries with significant differences in technological processes. . . . The enterprises are subordinated to different ministries. . . . These and further differences must be considered both in the formulation of the tasks and in the evaluation of the performance comparison." *Die Wirtschaft*, no. 2 (1975): 6.

51. This problem is indirectly indicated in one typical propaganda pamphlet: "Performance comparisons can only be successful when the advanced workers and collectives have the will and the capability to share the secret of their success." *Wettbewerb und Wirtschaftsstrategie* (Berlin: Verlag Tribüne, 1988), 42.

52. The criteria used in being chosen for a leadership example were very murky. On the one hand, much was made of the fact that the chosen tended to be among the best to begin with. On the other hand, equally publicized was the amount of political attention the chosen enterprises received in order to get where they were.

53. *Neuer Weg*, no. 4 (1985): 143–45.

54. *Für höhere Wirtschaftlichkeit und Qualität des Bauens* (Berlin: Dietz, 1987), 53.

55. *Die Wirtschaft*, no. 2 (1974): 6.

56. *Neuer Weg*, no. 14 (1971): 641–44.

57. Ibid., no. 17 (1982): 647–49.

58. *Die Wirtschaft*, no. 10 (1981): 6.

59. *Neuer Weg*, no. 9 (1972): 424–27.

60. *Die Wirtschaft*, no. 2 (1974): 5.

61. Ibid., no. 10 (1981): 5.

62. *Neuer Weg,* no. 14 (1971): 641–44.

63. *Die Wirtschaft,* no. 10 (1981): 5.

64. Ibid., no. 2 (1974): 6.

65. Harry Maier, *Innovation oder Stagnation: Bedingungen der Wirtschaftsreform in sozialistischen Ländern* (Cologne: Deutscher Instituts-Verlag, 1987), 81.

66. This line of analysis should not be taken to mean that the only criteria proper for the use of raw materials should be economic ones. Obviously issues such as environmental protection, occupational safety, and other social concerns have their place in economic decision making.

67. *Neuer Weg,* no. 14 (1971): 642.

68. These awards usually did not bring the winners a financial bonus, but merely a title.

69. Here, again, I agree with Rutland, *Politics of Economic Stagnation.*

70. Rainer Deppe and Dietrich Hoß, *Arbeitspolitik im Staatssozialismus: Zwei Varianten, DDR und Urgarn* (Frankfurt: Campus, 1989), 131. This last statement should not be taken to mean that the elderly are not capable of doing such work, but as an indication of the types of work preferred by the workers themselves.

71. Once again, the weakness of financial incentives for enterprises diminished the force of the program.

72. *Die Wirtschaft,* no. 1 (1982): 5; ibid., no. 20 (1976): 16.

73. Ibid., no. 20 (1976): 15–16.

74. The ineffectuality of these awards can be measured by the questionnaire that all employees of institutions of higher learning had to fill out to be considered for retention of employment after German unification. Candidates were required to indicate which medals and awards they had received, excluding those such as "collective of quality work."

75. *Neuer Weg,* no. 9 (1972): 408–10. The author complains that enterprises would prefer to make goods of inferior quality and face the consequences than fall short on their IWP.

76. By 1984, for example, the Schönow Cable Works reported that 67 percent of all its goods carried the "Q." *Neuer Weg,* no. 14 (1984): 546–48.

77. For example, in 1964 the BL Cottbus ordered the Bezirk construction system to change its entire construction program; from then on construction would be determined by the location of the large coal, energy, and chemical enterprises. "Cottbusser Erfahrung über die Anleitung der Staatsorgane durch die Partei," *Neuer Weg,* no. 2 (1964): 978, discussed in Gero Neugebauer, *Partei und Staatsapparat in der DDR* (Opladen: Westdeutscherverlag, 1978), 185.

78. Although a BL sectoral manager in Karl-Marx-Stadt complained in 1976 that the metallurgy industry in the Bezirk had goals for intensification of production that were 20 percent under the plan, he did not report that the BL could alter the plan targets—an unusual occurrence for the East German press. *Die Wirtschaft,* no. 13 (1976): 3.

79. Ibid., no. 2 (1974): 2; *Neuer Weg,* no. 16 (1972): 753–56.

80. Maier, *Innovation oder Stagnation,* 65.

81. Ibid.

82. BPA SED, Dresden IV B 2/5/401. In Dresden, the process of overfulfilling the plan

in certain production indicators before the yearly Central Committee economics seminars (run by Mittag) in Leipzig had become so routinized that each combine in the region was required to fill in a form reporting to the Bezirksleitung its rate of overfulfillment for the occasion. See also BPA SED, Dresden IV E 2/6/326.

83. Scherzer, *Der Erste*, 144. A campaign related to the counterplan, as well as to the materials economy programs, was the so-called *Fondsrückgabe*, a campaign in which enterprises promised to "give back" a certain "unused" portion of the materials and money allotted to them before the end of the planning period so that they could be used where they were urgently needed in the next period. *Die Wirtschaft*, no. 6 (1982): 12.

84. Fritz Schenk, *Im Vorzimmer der Diktatur* (Cologne: Kiepenheuer und Witsch, 1962), especially 155–66.

85. Scherzer, *Der Erste*, 58–60.

86. Schabowski, *Der Absturz*, 141.

87. Ibid.

88. In East Germany the plan had to be formally accepted by the plant management before it was made into law. Usually it was done without much trouble, and the incident here simply serves to illustrate the lines of authority and sources of conflict.

89. Schabowski, *Absturz*, 142.

90. Ibid., 143.

91. Letter to Honecker read to Politburo on September 6, 1985, in SAMPO-BA, SED JIV 2/2/2129. A second critical monthly report was sent in by Modrow on January 23, 1989. He blamed industrial production shortfalls on supply shortages, faulty planning, and decayed equipment. Mittag took offense at the report and criticized it on February 7, in a Politburo meeting. On Honecker's orders, the report was once again critically discussed during the Politburo meeting of February 28, at which the members of the Dresden Bezirksleitung were invited to hear the criticism leveled against them. Gerd-Rüdiger Stephan, ed., *Vorwärts immer, rückwärts nimmer!" Interne Dokumente zum Zerfall von SED und DDR 1988/89* (Berlin: Dietz Verlag, 1994), 63.

92. E. E. Schattschneider, *The Semi-Sovereign People* (New York, 1960), 71.

93. Alexander Yanov, *The Drama of the Soviet 1960's: A Lost Reform* (Berkeley: Institute of International Studies, 1984), 29.

94. For a good summary of primitive economies, see Karl Polanyi, Conrad M. Arensberg, and Harry W. Pearson, eds., *Trade and Market in Early Empires* (Glencoe, Ill.: Free Press, 1957).

Chapter 6

1. BPA SED, Dresden IV B 2/5/402.

2. Andrew Walder, *Communist Neo-Traditionalism* (Berkeley: University of California Press, 1986), 28–81.

3. Katharina Belwe, " 'Weniger produzieren mehr': Probleme der Freisetzung von Arbeitskräften in der DDR," *Deutschland Archiv* 17, no. 5 (1979): 497.

4. These numbers are generated from a sample of thirty-two East German enterprises before unification. D. M. W. N. Hitchens, K. Wagner, and J. E. Birnie, *East German Productivity and the Transition to the Market Economy* (Aldershot: Avebury, 1993). The West German figures exclude plants with substantial numbers of *Gastarbeiter*.

5. BAP SPK, E-1 56158.

6. Ibid. See also Günter Kusch et al., *Schlußbilanz—DDR: Fazit einer verfehlten Wirtschafts- und Sozialpolitik* (Berlin: Duncker & Humblot, 1991), 109.

7. BAP SPK, E-1 56158.

8. BPA SED, Dresden IV E-2/6/376.

9. Ibid.

10. Ibid.

11. Michael Piore and Charles Sabel, *The Second Industrial Divide: Possibilities for Prosperity* (New York: Basic Books, 1984).

12. Kusch et al., *Schlußbilanz—DDR*, 108.

13. Susanne Lohmann, "Dynamics of Informational Cascades: The Monday Demonstrations in Leipzig, East Germany, 1989–1991," *World Politics* 47, no. 1 (1994): 58.

14. Karl Marx, *Capital* (New York: Modern Library, 1906), 358.

15. The official SED history of the Schwedt Petrochemical Combine, for example, notes criticism of the enterprise party organization during the 1960s for a tendency to adopt "timid competition goals." Betriebsparteiorganisation der SED," in *Ein Werk des Sozialismus, der Freundschaft und der Jugend: Geschichte des VEB Petrochemiches Kombinat Schwedt, Stammbetrieb 1959 bis 1981* (Berlin: Dietz, 1985), 85.

16. Hartmut Zimmermann, ed., *DDR Handbuch* (Cologne: Verlag Wissenschaft und Politik, 1985), 1192–1207.

17. Helmut Schönfeld and Joachim Donath, *Sprache im sozialistischen Industriebetrieb. Untersuchung zum Wortschatz bei sozialen Gruppen* (Berlin, 1978), 151–52, 186, 192, 193, cited in K. Belwe, *Mitwirkung im Industriebetrieb der DDR* (Opladen: Westdeutscher Verlag, 1979), 298.

18. Autorenkollektiv, *Technisch rationell—sozial effektiv* (Berlin: Dietz, 1987), 106.

19. *Wettbewerb und Wirtschaftsstrategie* (Berlin: Verlag Tribüne, 1988), 40.

20. Ibid., 39.

21. Uhlendorf, Winkler, Wolf, *Theoretische und praktische Probleme des Kampfes um eine hohe Qualität der Erzeugnisse* (Berlin: Dietz Verlag, 1986), 5–15.

22. *Wettbewerb und Wirtschaftsstrategie*, 39.

23. Ibid., 40.

24. See, for example, *Die Wirtschaft*, no. 13 (1976): 3; no. 21 (1976): 13–16; no. 5 (1978): 3.

25. Ibid., no. 21 (1976): 15.

26. Ibid.

27. On the GDR's debates see, Michael Dennis, "An Objective Necessity? Shift Working in an Advanced Socialist Society," *GDR Monitor*, no. 20 (1988): 34–49; Dieter Voigt, *Schichtarbeit und Sozialsystem* (Bochum: Studienverlag Brockmeyer, 1986), 77–205.

28. This was especially true in machine building, an area of supreme importance for the GDR. See Voigt, *Schichtarbeit*, 125.

29. See unpublished report cited in Dennis, "An Objective Necessity?," 36.

30. As Hitchins et al. note, however, "the east German workers were not well trained in hydraulics, new materials or electronics. In addition their experience has been very specialised and low grade (a reflection of the fact that most companies produced long runs of relatively low quality products). They were not trained up to the required DIN standards nor in appropriate work organization or in data processing. In addition, unlike

their west German counterparts they were dependent on much detailed supervision and guidance on the shop floor." *East German Productivity,* 59.

31. BAP SPK, E-1 53092. The report drew attention to the causes of this phenomenon. First, almost no regard was given to the existing structure of the labor market before investing. Second, the insufficient removal of worthless machinery from industry diminished the capacity to absorb new investment. Both led to low capital productivity and high maintenance costs. In fact, by 1978, every sixth production worker was employed in repair and maintenance.

32. For background, see *Ein Werk,* chaps. 1 and 2.

33. Rainer Deppe and Dietrich Hoß, *Arbeitspolitik im Staatssozialismus: Zwei Varianten, DDR und Ungarn* (Frankfurt: Campus, 1989), 357.

34. Ibid., 358.

35. The GDR Council of Ministers approved the use of the Schekino method in June 1973, BAP SPK, E-1 56158.

36. *Die Wirtschaft,* no. 17 (1974): 11.

37. *Ein Werk,* 161.

38. A report on Shchekino's use of the Wolfen Film Works in *Die Wirtschaft,* no. 17 (1974): 11, is especially instructive.

39. *Schwedter Rationalisierungsstrategie und Wettbewerbsinitiative "Weniger produzieren mehr"* (Frankfurt/Oder: Tastomat, 1980), 3.

40. Deppe and Hoß, *Arbeitspolitik,* 363–64.

41. *Neuer Tag,* October 20, 1981.

42. *Schwedter Rationalisierungsstrategie,* 10.

43. On the warmth of the work collective in the GDR, see Marilyn Rueschmeyer, "Integrating Work and Personal Life: An Analysis of Three Professional Work Collectives in the German Democratic Republic," *GDR Monitor,* no. 20 (1988): 27–41; on moving to a new enterprise altogether, see *Definition für Planung, Rechnungsführung und Statistik* (Berlin: Die Wirtschaft, 1980), 67.

44. In fact, the regime had precisely this idea in mind. Additional wages were given to workers who took up extra tasks. This explains why enterprises had to get official ministerial approval before embarking on the Schwedt initiative.

45. *Die Wirtschaft,* no. 17 (1974): 11.

46. *Schwedter Rationalisierung,* 10, where the BL Frankfurt/Oder reprimands enterprises for using the general *Freisetzungseffekte* (release effect) in their reporting, rather than the strict interpretation of the production indicator.

47. "Verordnung über den Beitrag für gesellschaftliche Fonds," *Gesetzblatt der DDR,* no. 35 (1983).

48. *Schwedter Rationalisierungsstrategie,* 10.

49. For a good example of this later genre, see *Neuer Weg,* no. 13 (1984): 495–97.

50. *Die Wirtschaft,* no. 7 (1982): 9.

51. See Werner Frohn in *Die Wirtschaft,* no. 5 (1982): 7, "Whereas in the first stage of the Schwedt initiative reserves were developed overwhelmingly on the basis of organization measures, in the second stage a necessary degree of technical equipment is necessary in order to use all sources to their fullest."

52. Deppe and Hoß, *Arbeitspolitik,* 379.

Chapter 7

1. Jerry Hough, *The Soviet Prefects: The Local Party Organs in Industrial Decision Making* (Cambridge, Mass.: Harvard University Press, 1969), chap. 11.

2. Horst Sindermann, *IX. Parteitag der SED 18–22.5.1976. Direktive des IX. Parteitages der SED zum Fünfjahresplan für die Entwicklung der Volkswirtschaft der DDR in den Jahren 1976–1980* (Berlin: Dietz, 1976), 53.

3. By 1949, new settlers from the East comprised 13 percent of all *Landtag* members in the Soviet Zone, 11.9 percent of Kreistag members, 17 percent of Kreis councilmen, 12.6 percent of all mayors, and 20.1 percent of all those employed in the civil service. Alexander von Plato and Wolfgang Meinicke, *Alte Heimat neue Zeit: Flüchtlinge, Umgesiedelte, Vertriebene in der sowjetischen Besatzungszone und in der DDR* (Berlin: Verlags-Anstalt Union, 1991), 89.

4. SAMPO-BA, SED NL 182/977.

5. For good summaries of the historical background to GDR local politics, see Erika Lieser-Triebnigg, *Die Stellung der Gemeinden in der DDR* (Melle: Knoth, 1988); Gero Neugebauer, "Zur Situation der Kommunalpolitik in der DDR," in Ilse Spittmann-Ruhle and Gisele Helwig, *Veränderungen in Gesellschaft und politischem System der DDR: Ursachen, Inhalte, Grenzen* (Cologne: Verlag Wissenschaft und Politik, 1988), 117–28.

6. *Neues Deutschland*, April 17, 1970. Cited in Neugebauer, "Kommunalpolitik," 117.

7. Werner Böhme and Lothar Steglich, *Erfahrungen der politischen Führungstätigkeit bei der territorialen Rationalisierung* (Berlin: Dietz, 1975).

8. Klaus Sorgenicht, *Unser Staat in den 8oer Jahren* (Berlin: Dietz, 1982).

9. S. Petzold and O. Wendt, "Einige Aspekte der wachsenden gesamtstaatlichen Verantwortung der örtlichen Organe der Staatsmacht," *Staat und Recht*, nos. 8–9 (1982): 691.

10. For a good discussion of the details of the law, see H. Roggemann, *Kommunalrecht und Regionalverwaltung in der DDR* (Berlin: Arno Spitz Verlag, 1987).

11. There is evidence that local party secretaries could influence the amount of resources allotted to their area for housing. Landolf Scherzer, *Der Erste* (Rudolstadt: Greifenverlag), 25.

12. Peter Rutland, "The Role of the CPSU in Economic Administration" (Ph.D. diss., University of York, 1987), 154.

13. I refer once again to Schabowski's statement in chapter 5, that the majority of his time was spent in providing economic emergency aid. Günter Schabowski, *Der Absturz* (Berlin: Rowohlt-Berlin, 1991), 146.

14. Stephen Fortescue, "Regional Party Apparatus in the 'Sectional Society,' " *Studies in Comparative Communism* 21 no. 1 (1987): 12.

15. SAMPO-BA, SED IV 2/603/48, for numerous cases.

16. In creating the councils of party secretaries, the SED was very careful not to give it the power to issue decrees. *Parteiarbeit im Stammbetrieb des Kombinates* (Berlin: Dietz, 1989), 12.

17. Scherzer, *Der Erste*, 166, where the mayor of Merkurs, a particularly effective official, remarks to the party secretary of the potash mine (who happened to be a member of the Central Committee) that the special store in front of the enterprise was not being

regularly supplied: "When you whistle, everybody here jumps, but when I whistle, I hear my own echo. And if I should have time to worry about the special store, then you take care that your vice-directors work on problems in the community once in a while."

18. On the various forms of cooperations, see Kurt Schubert, *Vertragsbeziehungen zwischen örtlichen Staatsorganen und Betrieben* (Berlin: Staatsverlag der DDR, 1983).

19. Böhme and Steglich, *Erfahrungen*, 71–73.

20. Ibid., 12, where they warn against the "tendency to undervalue work with state organs or ignore their decisions."

21. KL and BL secretaries had several ways of dealing with the problem of territorial gross output figures that were too low. One way was the increased manufacture of high-value items toward the end of the plan period. The chief of the statistics office for Bad Salzungen reports that it was not uncommon to produce several million marks worth of Schnapps at the end of the plan period to top up the gross output numbers. Scherzer, *Der Erste*, p. 47. Such manipulations might give the first secretary more room to maneuver against enterprises in his area by reducing some of the overall pressure to perform.

22. *Die Wirtschaft*, no. 6 (1982): 12.

23. Böhme and Steglich, *Erfahrungen*, 70, where they write: "Waiting for 'orders from above' builds barriers to interenterprise cooperation between enterprises belonging to different economic branches."

24. *Die Wirtschaft*, no. 6 (1975): 7.

25. Ibid. In Dresden, the Bezirksleitung complained in October 1979 that enterprises in the region often demanded apartments for their workers but offered the Bezirk nothing in return. BPA SED, Dresden IV B 2/5/400.

26. Böhme and Steglich, *Erfahrungen*, 75.

27. On the party secretaries' activity as charismatic ritual, I have been influenced by Clifford Geertz, "Centers, Kings, and Charisma: Reflections on the Symbolics of Power," in *Local Knowledge* (New York: Basic Books, 1983), 121–46. The quotation is from p. 124.

28. Böhme and Steglich, *Erfahrungen*, 28.

29. Ibid., 7.

30. Ibid., 56.

31. *Die Wirtschaft*, no. 6 (1982): 12.

32. *Neuer Weg*, no. 23 (1980): 915.

33. Böhme and Steglich, *Erfahrungen*, 89.

34. In fact many of these minutiae were not performed satisfactorily, which accounted for the shabby appearance of most *Neubaugebiete* and inner cities.

35. *Die Wirtschaft*, no. 21 (1976): 20–21.

36. "Vorhaben unter Parteikontrolle," *Ostsee Zeitung*, February 25, 1975, 3, where the resistance of managers and experts to the introduction of the campaign is noted; also "Slobin Methode—Keine Eintagsfliege," ibid.; "Wir Spielen alle Trümpfe aus," ibid., April 1, 1976, 3.

37. These comments are made on the basis of discussions with two economists at the University of Rostock, and the director of the Bezirk construction combine in Rostock.

38. *Die Wirtschaft*, no. 16 (1976): 14.

39. Many of these problems were also outlined by Hans-Ulrich Gramsch, "Die besten Baustellenkollektive arbeiten nach Slobin," *Die Wirtschaft*, no. 4 (1975): 11. Gramsch points out, for example, that in the apartment construction combine the entire account-

ing system had to be changed to allow for the kind of evaluations of work foreseen in the Zlobin method.

40. Scherzer, *Der Erste*, 129–30.

41. The connection between consumer goods and political stability was drawn quite clearly on April 17, 1979, during a secretariat meeting of the Dresden party organization. Of 2,061 officially filed complaints from the Bezirk population, most concerned consumer goods and apartments, and 401 threatened not to vote in the upcoming elections if their concerns were not addressed. BPA SED, Dresden IV B 2/5/362.

42. Lutz Niethammer, *Die volkseigene Erfahrung* (Berlin: Rowohlt-Berlin, 1991), 9–73.

43. *Wettbewerb und Wirtschaftsstrategie* (Berlin: Verlag Tribüne, 1988), 20.

44. BPA SED, Dresden IV B 2/5/401.

45. Harry Maier, *Innovation oder Stagnation: Bedingungen der Wirtschaftsreform in sozialistischen Ländern* (Cologne: Deutscher Instituts-Verlag, 1987), 89.

46. *Direktive des XI. Parteitages der SED zum Fünfjahresplan für die Entwicklung der Volkswirtschaft der DDR in den Jahren 1986–1990* (Berlin: Dietz, 1986), 13.

47. Günter Kusch et al., *Schlußbilanz—DDR: Fazit einer verfehlten Wirtschafts- und Sozialpolitik* (Berlin: Duncker & Humblot, 1991), 41.

48. Other scholars report that the 30 percent renewal goal not only included the products themselves but the processes by which the products were made. Also, products were to be considered new up to twenty-four months after manufacture. See Manfred Melzer and Authur A. Stahnke, "Product and Process Renewal in the GDR Economic Strategy: Goals, Problems and Prospects," in Ian Jeffries and Manfred Melzer, *The East German Economy* (London: Croom Helm, 1987), 135.

49. Maier, *Innovation oder Stagnation*, 90.

50. Ibid., 90. Maier goes on to use this fact to help solve a statistical mystery for the GDR. With the help of phony innovations and price increases based on a less than commensurate value increase, it was relatively easy for enterprises to show sinking material use per unit of manufacture and rising labor productivity. Any country could show growth in such a way if it did not correct its statistics for changes in price.

51. *Die Wirtschaft*, no. 9 (1974): 14.

52. Ibid., 9.

53. Ibid.

54. Schabowski, *Der Absturz*, p. 144.

55. Ibid.

56. BPA SED, Dresden 13199.

57. BAP SPK, E-1 56318.

58. Carl Heinz Janson, *Totengräber der DDR* (Düsseldorf: Econ Verlag, 1991), 83.

59. *DDR Journal: Zur Novemberrevolution*.

60. Jeffrey Kopstein and Karl Otto Richter, "Communist Social Structure and Post-Communist Elections: Voting for Unification in East Germany," *Studies in Comparative Communism* 25, no. 4 (1992): 363–80.

61. The statistics are drawn from two sources. The social indicators can be calculated based on the *Statistical Yearbook of the GDR (1989)* (Berlin: VEB Deutscher Zentral-verlag, 1989). The final voting results can be found in *Frankfurter Allgemeine Zeitung*, March 21, 1990, 2.

Conclusion

1. Hannah Arendt, *The Origins of Totalitarianism* (New York: Harcourt Brace Jovanovich, 1973); Corneilius Castoriadis, *Political and Social Writings* (Minneapolis: University of Minnesota Press, 1988); Kenneth Jowitt, *New World Disorder* (Berkeley: University of California Press, 1992); Siegrid Meuschel, "Überlegungen zu einer Herrschafts- und Gesellschaftsgeschichte der DDR," *Geschichte und Gesellschaft* 19, no. 1 (1993): 5–14.

2. Zbiegniew K. Brzezinski, *The Grand Failure: The Birth and Death of Communism in the Twentieth Century* (New York: Scribner, 1989); Ferenc Feher, Agnes Heller, and Gyorgy Markus, *Dictatorship over Needs* (Oxford: Blackwell, 1983).

3. Nicholas Xenos, *Scarcity and Modernity* (London: Routledge, 1989), 1–66.

4. Thorstein Veblen, *Theory of the Leisure Class* (Harmondsworth: Penguin Books, 1979).

5. Andrew C. Janos, *Politics and Paradigms* (Stanford, Calif.: Stanford University Press, 1986), chap. 4.

6. Ernest Gellner, *Nations and Nationalism* (Ithaca, N.Y.: Cornell University Press, 1983), 24.

7. As Janos, the author of this table, notes, these numbers relate to production and not consumption, "and if we had reliable sources to calculate the latter we would, in view of the high investment rates and military spending, likely find even greater economic disparities between the two halves of the Continent." Andrew Janos, "Continuity and Change in Eastern Europe: Strategies of Post-Communist Politics," *East European Politics and Societies* 8, no. 1 (1994): 4.

8. Martin Kohli, "Die DDR als Arbeitsgesellschaft? Arbeit, Lebenslauf und soziale Differenzierung," in Hartmut Kaelble, Jurgen Kocka, and Hartmut Zwahr, eds., *Sozialgeschichte der DDR* (Klett Cotta: Stuttgart, 1994), 32.

9. Hans-Peter Brunner, "German Blitz-Privatization: Lessons for Other Reforming Economies?" *Transition: The Newsletter about Reforming Economies* 6, no. 4 (1995): 13.

10. Jörg Roesler, "Privatisation in Eastern Germany—Experience with the Treuhand," *Europe-Asia Studies* 46, no. 3 (1994): 505–17.

11. As German public opinion expert Dieter Roth notes in a 1993 study of political attitudes since the 1990 Bundestag elections: "The basis for political stability in the Federal Republic was in the past its economic strength, and there are no indications that this will not be true in the future." Dieter K. Roth, "Wandel der Politischen Einstellungen seit der Bundestagswahl 1990," *German Studies Review* 16, no. 2 (1993): 265.

12. See the collection of articles on the German nation and Germany's international role in *Die Zeit* during 1993 and 1994, collected in *Zeit-Punkte*, no. 3 (1994).

13. See, for example, the responses to the lengthy article in *Der Spiegel*, "Wir, die Deutschen—Eine verkrampfte Nation [We, the Germans, an uptight nation]," a play on a speech by German president Roman Herzog, who called for a more relaxed (*unverkampft*) approach to the idea of the German nation, in *Der Spiegel*, nos. 24–25 (1994).

Germanness, 9; and virtues, 19. *See also* Culture; German identity

German question, 11, 48. *See also* Unification

Gorbachev, Mikhail, 52, 63; and intensification, 101

Grüneberg, Gerhard, 57

Hager, Kurt: attack on cybernetics, 76, 128; on intensification, 101, 223 (n. 82); as ideology czar, 125

Halbritter, Walter, 48, 49; demotion of, 124

Hallstein Doctrine, 42, 214 (n. 2)

Hennecke, Adolf: as labor hero, 32, 33

Hennecke movement, 32, 33

Herrnstadt, Rudolf, 37

Higher Party School: admission to, 56

Hoffman, Heinz, 91

Honecker, Erich, 2, 68, 77, 104, 111; criticism of Ulbricht, 11, 70; as SED leader, 12; resignation of, 13; support of Ulbricht, 37; as leader of conservatives, 59, 60; supported by Brezhnev, 70, 71; letter to Ulbricht, 71; and stability, 73; and national question, 73, 74, 92; and populism, 75; and recentralization, 75; and institutional standardization, 76; relations with USSR, 76, 86, 224 (nn. 89, 92); justification of nationalizations, 78, 79; relations with Schürer, 78, 89; ideas on social policy, 80–84, 86, 87; and call for intensification, 82; as head of FDJ, 83; and price increases, 86; accumulation of debt under, 86–88; and balance of trade crisis, 89, 90; plans to visit West Germany, 90; and trade relations with West, 90–95; and Solidarity, 91, 92; reaction to oil cut, 92, 93; relations with Gorbachev, 101; and cadres policy, 117; and orientation of party, 124–26; and planning process, 151; and wage structure, 158, 159; and housing problem, 174, 182; and final Politburo meeting, 192

Hough, Jerry: and prefect model, 7, 8, 127, 131, 132, 173; on personnel selection, 121, 123; on supplies procurement, 137, 138

Housing, 13; as field of local politics, 174, 181–86; shortages of, 174, 185; history of, 181–82; closing gap of with West Germany, 182; as ideological vehicle, 183; and the Zlobin method, 183–84; and power of local elites, 185

Hungary, 128

Ideology, 127; importance to structure of authority, 111, 126; importance to cadres policy, 117, 127; and party apparatus, 122–29; as power, 127

Industrial administration: compared to that in China, 155–58

Industrial production: growth of, 17; compared to West, 38. *See also* Consumer goods

Industrial relations, 2; Soviet-type in GDR, 18; structure of, 18; cost of stabilization of, 38; and reform, 61–64. *See also* Labor; SED: and labor relations; Working class

Institutional uniformity, 74–80

Intellectuals: role of in revolution, 13

Intensification campaigns. *See* Soviet production techniques

International political economy, 85; confining conditions of, 12

Jarowinsky, Werner, 103, 104

Kennedy, John F., 44

Khrushchev, Nikita, 11, 37, 72, 133; and establishment of communist discourse, 43; and reform, 47; and performance comparisons, 142

Kleiber, Günther, 124

KLs, 109; membership of, 125; role of, 132, 136; and supplies procurement, 137–38; and deployment of labor, 166; and housing, 174, 181–86; and con-

Scarcity, 65, 70, 203; relationship to freedom, 5; of consumer goods, 13, 35, 74, 192; of labor, 22, 34, 156; connection with profits, 63; and socialist competition, 89; of resources for production, 179; meaning of in industrial society, 195–97

Schaarschmidt, Wolfgang: and "A Man Came from the West to the East," 41–43

Schabowski, Günter: description of enterprise visit, 135–36; and planning process, 150–51; and supply of consumer goods, 190–91

Schalck-Golodkowski, Alexander, 88, 89, 94

Schattschneider, E. E., 152

Schenk, Fritz, 149

Schürer, Gerhard, 73; letter to Stoph, 56; addressing of economic problems, 78; attacked by Politburo, 82; concern with debt, 87, 88; meeting with Tikhonov, 90; meeting with Baibakov, 93; calling for cut in living standards, 102–3; and wage structure, 159

Schwedt initiative, 155, 168–72; worker response to, 170

Scott, James, 27

Secret police, 11; monitoring of work force, 97; as source of economic information, 133

SED, 1, 132, 166; role of in economy, 6–17, 78, 83, 84; and working-class relations, 11; and local politics, 13; and industrial production, 17, 29; and public opinion, 18; and labor relations, 18, 29, 35, 36, 155, 157; and Order 234, 25–29; and Soviet relations, 29, 102; implementing of Taylorism, 31, 38; and the Hennecke movement, 34; and social policy, 36, 81; and socialism, 76, 105; and combine formation, 95; ideological dependence of on USSR, 100, 101; choosing of leaders of, 114; commitment of to ideological education, 128, 129; and labor policy, 155–72; and socialist competitions, 161–65; performance of at local level, 174, 175, 177–94; concern with quality of life, 191–92. See also Party apparatus; SED elite

SED elite: recruitment of, 6; and working-class relations, 11, 12, 18, 197; autonomy of, 47; and Soviet relations, 47; and economic reform, 48, 65; and Ulbricht's fall, 71; and production enterprises, 77; and combine reform, 97, 100; and debt crisis, 104; and "really existing socialism," 109; retreat of into campaign economy, 174, 175. See also Honecker, Erich; SED; Ulbricht, Walter

Selbmann, Fritz, 32

Shchekino method, 168–69

Shortage economy, 29. See also Scarcity

Šik, Ota, 66, 68

SMAD, 10; and economy, 17, 22; and Order 234, 28; and Taylorism, 30, 32; encouraging of activist movement, 32–35; support for Ulbricht, 37

Social Democratic Party: Socialist economic campaigns, 126; in GDR 1990 elections, 194. See also Campaign economy; Socialist competition

Socialism, 1, 48, 64, 67, 131; consumer, 11; German worker commitment to, 19; SED plans for, 35, 37; values of, 47; Ackermann's ideas of, 66; German path to, 80; market, in Czechoslovakia, 66; Solidarity's effect on, 93; "really existing," 103, 109; and local politics, 175, 176; and retail system, 187; and lack of consumer goods, 192–93

Socialist competition, 12, 155, 171; working-class resistance to, 12; and Order 234, 23; problems with, 89; in the computer age, 161–64; forms of, 162; execution of, 162–65; appeal of, 164–65. See also Aktivist movement; Schwedt initiative

Socialist Unity Party of Germany. See SED

Social policy, 80–84; initiation of, 86

Sokolovski, Marshall, 28, 36

Solidarity: GDR's reaction to, 91; in Poland, 91; effect of on GDR trade, 92; Soviet reaction to, 92, 93

Soviet labor practices: in GDR, 19, 22, 24

Soviet Military Administration. *See* SMAD

Soviet Prefects. See Hough, Jerry

Soviet production techniques, 140–43. *See also* Materials economy

Soviet Union, 17, 91; retreat of into conservatism, 50, 51; shortage of consumer goods in, 51. *See also* Brezhnev, Leonid; Khrushchev, Nikita

Soviet Zone: integration of, 22; German participation in governing of, 23; productivity within, 29; wage policy within, 32; and regional identity, 175

SPK, 48, 49, 70, 109; and NES, 54, 58, 59, 61; and centralization, 65; paper of on welfare, 82; and debt crisis, 103; and labor deployment, 167; and local politics, 178, 179

Stalin, Josef, 6, 17, 19, 22; and integration of GDR into East bloc, 35, 208 (n. 1); death of, 36, 37; on party commitment to working class, 114–15; on federalism, 175

Stalinism: mobilization techniques of, 6

Stasi. *See* Secret police

State Planning Commission. *See* SPK

Stoph, Willi, 56, 57, 68, 91; as head of working groups, 48; resistance to NES, 54; support of Rumpf against Ulbricht, 60; and price reform, 61; criticism of Ulbricht, 70, 71; criticism of planners, 80; and debt, 88

Strauss, Franz Josef, 94

Strikes, 62; of June 1953, 35–40, 61, 62

Supplies procurement, 136–40

Taylorism, 11, 18, 160; corruption of, 29–32, 38; within socialism, 31

Technocracy, 7–10, 56, 111, 153; theory of, 6–9, 112; reform of, 11; limits to,

39; under Ulbricht, 46; worker resistance to, 49; officials' resistance to, 54; NES as example of, 55; problems with, 64; dismantling of, 75

Tikhonov, Nikolai, 68, 90–91

Tisch, Harry, 103, 124

Trade, 2; imbalance of with West Germany, 84; with USSR, 84; crisis of, 87–90, 92, 94; relations with West, 90–95, 99

Trade unions. *See* FDGB

Truman Doctrine, 22

Ulbricht, Walter, 2, 74, 75, 77, 83, 85, 87, 90, 96, 104, 111, 124; and reform, 11, 43–72, 78; removal of from office, 11, 70–72; and industrialization, 17; and industrial relations, 19, 36, 37; disagreement with Politburo, 37; relations with USSR, 37, 48, 205 (n. 6), 213 (n. 78), 218 (n. 90); view of on communism, 42–44; attacks on Behrens and Benary, 45, 46; and retreat from Stalinization, 47; plans for NES, 48–50, 53; secret meeting of with Brezhnev, 51; encouraging of VVB independence, 54, 55; and fall of Apel, 57, 60; and price reform, 62; bureaucratic opposition to, 64; and socialism, 64; oversights of, 65; desire of to overtake West, 65, 67–69, 72, 73; letter to Brezhnev, 67; on the German question, 67; criticism of USSR, 69; criticized by colleagues, 70; criticized by Brezhnev, 71; refusal of to leave politics, 72; reforms of dismantled, 76; and local politics, 176

Unification, 13, 68, 72, 200, 201; vote for, 193; and German identity, 200; problems as a result of, 201, 202. *See also* German question

Verba, Sydney: on political culture, 5

Verner, Paul, 69; opinion of on cybernetics, 76; criticism of SPK report, 82